Legislatures of Small

This book provides a comparative study of the legislatures of small nations, states and territories, to explore the extent to which size is a factor in how they function and fulfil the roles and responsibility of a legislature.

Though the physical nature and environment of states is a neglected subject in political science research, this book examines the impact of small state size on the structure and functions of legislatures and contributes to a better understanding of the interplay of physical and social factors. Focusing on legislatures in democratic nations or in territories that are parts of democratic units, the book features case studies on Malta, Bermuda, Jersey, Guernsey, Gibraltar, Hong Kong, Lesotho, Liechtenstein, the Isle of Man, the Commonwealth Caribbean, Nunavut (Canada), the Pacific islands, Swaziland and Scotland. Contributors employ an interdisciplinary approach to examine both the outcomes and the causes of different political mechanisms, and bring to the surface underlying correlation between small states through their analysis.

Legislatures of Small States will be of interest to students and scholars of international politics, comparative politics and legislative studies.

Nicholas D. J. Baldwin is Dean and Lecturer in government and politics at Wroxton College, UK, the British campus of Fairleigh Dickinson University, USA.

Library of Legislative Studies

Edited by Lord Philip Norton of Louth, University of Hull, UK.

Legislatures of Small States

A comparative study

Edited by Nicholas D. J. Baldwin

Routledge
Taylor & Francis Group

LONDON AND NEW YORK

First published 2013
by Routledge
2 Park Square, Milton Park, Abingdon, Oxfordshire OX14 4RN

Simultaneously published in the USA and Canada
by Routledge
711 Third Avenue, New York, NY 10017

First issued in paperback 2014

Routledge is an imprint of the Taylor & Francis Group, an informa business.

British Library Cataloguing in Publication Data
A catalogue record for this book is available from the British Library

Library of Congress Cataloging in Publication Data
Legislatures of small states : a comparative study / edited by Nicholas D.J. Baldwin.
    p. cm. – (Library of legislative studies)
    Summary: "This book provides a comparative study of the legislatures of small nations, states and territories, to explore the extent to which size is a factor in how they function and fulfil the roles and responsibility of a legislature" – Provided by publisher.
    Includes bibliographical references and index.
    1. Legislative bodies–Cross-cultural studies. 2. States, Small–Cross-cultural studies. I. Baldwin, Nicholas.
    JF511.L39 2012
    328 2 23   2012027346

ISBN 13: 978-0-415-53833-6 (hbk)
ISBN 13: 978-1-138-83030-1 (pbk)

Typeset in Times New Roman
by Swales & Willis Ltd, Exeter, Devon

Contents

Contributors

Editor

Nicholas D.J. Baldwin, Dean and Director of Operations, Wroxton College, Fairleigh Dickinson University, UK.

Foreword by

Peter Riddell, Director, Institute for Government, and former chair of the Hansard Society.

Contributors

Dag Anckar, Emeritus Professor of Political Science, Abo Akademi University, Finland.

Susan Booysen, Professor, Graduate School of Public and Development, Management, University of the Witwatersrand, South Africa.

Walton Brown Jr, Senator, Bermuda.

Haresh K. Budhrani, Speaker, Gibraltar Parliament.

Michael Frendo, Speaker, House of Representatives, Malta.

Marion Frick-Tabarelli, Director of Government Legal Services, Liechtenstein.

Hamid Ghany, Dean, Faculty of Social Science, the University of the West Indies, Trinidad, West Indies.

Michael de la Haye, Greffier of the States of Jersey, Jersey, Channel Islands.

Jonathan King, Deputy Clerk of Tynwald and Clerk of the Legislative Council, Isle of Man.

Richard McMahon QC, Deputy Bailiff of Guernsey and Deputy Presiding Officer, States of Deliberation, Guernsey, Channel Islands.

Wilfried Marxer, Associate, Department of Political Science, Liechenstein Institute, Liechenstein.

Michael Rush, Emeritus Professor, Department of Politics, University of Exeter, UK.

Mark Shephard, Department of Government, University of Strathclyde, UK.

Lam Wai-man, Assistant Professor and Program Director (Government and Laws), Department of Politics and Public Administration, the University of Hong Kong.

Graham White, Professor, Department of Political Science, University of Toronto at Mississauga, Canada.

Foreword

Rt Hon. Peter Riddell, Director, Institute for Government and former Chair, Hansard Society

The most studied legislatures are in the largest and longest-established democracies. But this collection of essays shows that much can be learnt from the legislatures of small states. There is no common pattern. They differ substantially in size and role, reflecting their very different historical backgrounds.

Revealingly, twenty-seven of the thirty-six legislatures covered in this book are based on islands or groups of islands – ten in the Commonwealth Caribbean and twelve in the Pacific – plus Bermuda, Malta, Guernsey and the Isle of Man. Moreover, as Michael Rush points out, four are virtual islands – Liechtenstein, Gibraltar, Lesotho and Swaziland. The sense of isolation has played a part in their development. All have distinctive histories and cultures which have often been more significant than their size. Predictably, former British colonies have almost all adopted, and retained, parliamentary systems, while some of the Pacific islands that came under American influence adopted presidential systems.

Leaving aside the individual characteristics of these legislatures – which, though fascinating, are not necessarily significant – the key question is: what difference does size make? Unlike larger legislatures, nine of the countries covered, notably those in the Pacific, either have no parties or are dominated by non-party individuals.

Another distinguishing feature is that the executive constitutes a much higher proportion of the legislative membership than in larger bodies – giving the executive more control. Size also affects the number of committees. Most small chambers operate fewer than ten permanent committees, though almost all have a public accounts committee or the equivalent.

So small is unquestionably different – and, refreshingly, with some exceptions in the Pacific, most smaller countries can still sustain vibrant democracies.

Peter Riddell, June 2012

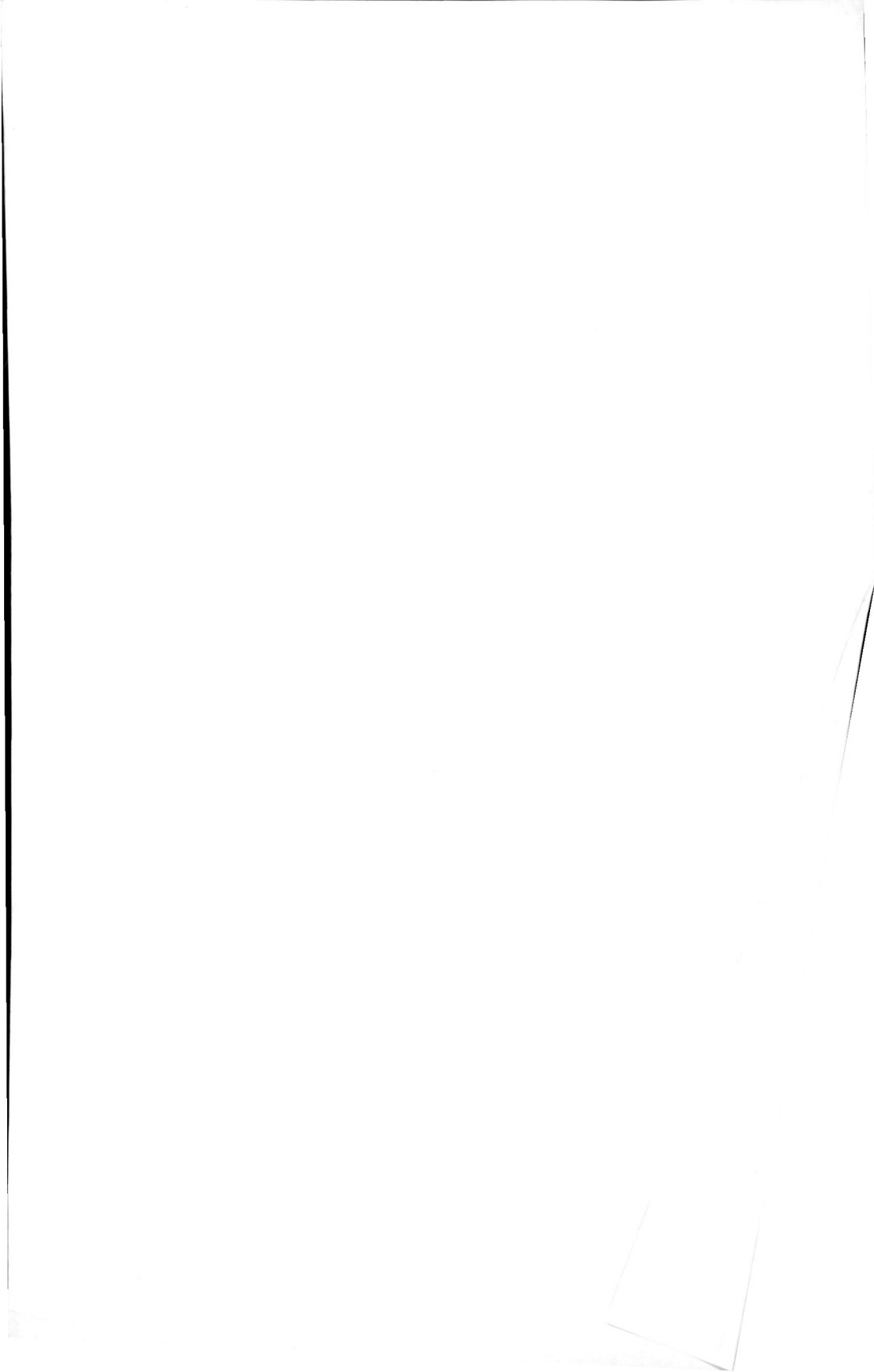

Foreword

Rt Hon. Peter Riddell, Director, Institute for Government and former Chair, Hansard Society

The most studied legislatures are in the largest and longest-established democracies. But this collection of essays shows that much can be learnt from the legislatures of small states. There is no common pattern. They differ substantially in size and role, reflecting their very different historical backgrounds.

Revealingly, twenty-seven of the thirty-six legislatures covered in this book are based on islands or groups of islands – ten in the Commonwealth Caribbean and twelve in the Pacific – plus Bermuda, Malta, Guernsey and the Isle of Man. Moreover, as Michael Rush points out, four are virtual islands – Liechtenstein, Gibraltar, Lesotho and Swaziland. The sense of isolation has played a part in their development. All have distinctive histories and cultures which have often been more significant than their size. Predictably, former British colonies have almost all adopted, and retained, parliamentary systems, while some of the Pacific islands that came under American influence adopted presidential systems.

Leaving aside the individual characteristics of these legislatures – which, though fascinating, are not necessarily significant – the key question is: what difference does size make? Unlike larger legislatures, nine of the countries covered, notably those in the Pacific, either have no parties or are dominated by non-party individuals.

Another distinguishing feature is that the executive constitutes a much higher proportion of the legislative membership than in larger bodies – giving the executive more control. Size also affects the number of committees. Most small chambers operate fewer than ten permanent committees, though almost all have a public accounts committee or the equivalent.

So small is unquestionably different – and, refreshingly, with some exceptions in the Pacific, most smaller countries can still sustain vibrant democracies.

Peter Riddell, June 2012

1 Introduction I

Legislatures

Nicholas D. J. Baldwin

Introduction

Legislatures have different names from one nation to another – 'Parliament' in the United Kingdom, 'States General' in the Netherlands, 'Cortes Generales' in Spain, 'Federal Assembly' in Russia, 'Diet' in Japan, 'Supreme Council' (or 'Verkhovna Rada') in Ukraine and 'Congress' in the United States, for example. They also vary in structure, form, shape, size, powers, functions, autonomy, procedures and traditions.[1] Some are unicameral (single-chamber) legislatures, such as in both Denmark (the Folketing) and New Zealand (the House of Representatives); others are bicameral (two-chamber) legislatures, such as in the United Kingdom (the House of Commons and the House of Lords), France (the National Assembly and the Senate), Russia (the State Duma and the Council of the Federation) and the United States (the House of Representatives and the Senate), for example. According to the Inter-Parliamentary Union there are currently 114 unicameral legislatures (59.07 per cent) and 79 bicameral legislatures (40.93 per cent) functioning in the world today.[2]

Whether or not a nation has a unicameral or a bicameral legislative structure does not depend on the size of its population. For example, the People's Republic of China with a population of more than 1.3 billion has a unicameral legislature with a statutory 3,000 members (though currently 2,978 members), while Antigua and Barbuda with a population of some 87,884 is bicameral, consisting of the House of Representatives (with 19 members) and the Senate (with 17 members). Similarly, some countries were bicameral but have moved to a unicameral structure – Denmark in 1953, Sweden in 1970 and Peru in 1993, for example. Yet others were unicameral and subsequently moved to a bicameral structure – Tunisia in 2005, for example (although both chambers ceased to function as a result of the political upheavals in early 2011). Some have even gone from one format to the other and back again: Turkey was unicameral from 1921, became bicameral in 1961 and reverted to unicameralism in 1982. When Czechoslovakia went through its velvet divorce, the Czech Republic adopted a bicameral legislative structure while the Slovak Republic adopted a unicameral one. In short, structure in this regard is the result of the political and constitutional history and development of each country.

In addition, there are the highly disciplined, tightly controlled legislatures of one-party authoritarian states such as the former Soviet Union, the German Democratic

Republic (East Germany) and other Soviet bloc countries, or those that can be seen today in the People's Republic of China (the National People's Congress) and the Islamic Republic of Iran (the Islamic Parliament of Iran, or Majles). On the other hand there are unruly, fragmented legislatures, the Knesset in Israel, for example, in which any idea of control often appears difficult if not impossible to establish. Similarly, in the United States, the working relationship between the House of Representatives and the Senate, particularly when one party has a majority in one chamber and a different party is in a majority position in the other (as in 2010–12 when the Republicans controlled the House and the Democrats controlled the Senate), can lead to an inability to get anything through the legislative process, producing 'legislative logjam'.

Nonetheless, almost all these legislative bodies have one thing in common, namely: 'They are constitutionally designated for giving assent to binding measures of public policy, that assent being given on behalf of a political community that extends beyond the government élite responsible for formulating those measures.'[3]

It is for this reason that legislatures are generally categorised according to their capacity to influence policy. Consequently, the following four types of legislatures can be identified:

- policy-making legislatures (sometimes termed 'active' legislatures);
- policy-influencing legislatures (sometimes termed 'reactive' legislatures);
- legislatures with minimal or marginal policy effect (sometimes termed 'marginal' legislatures);
- legislatures with no real policy effect (sometimes termed 'rubber-stamp' legislatures).

Policy-making legislatures enjoy significant autonomy: not only can they amend or reject measures brought forward by the executive but they can substitute their own policy. The US Congress is the prime example of such a legislature. Policy-influencing legislatures react to executive initiatives in that they can either amend or reject measures brought forward by the executive but cannot – either formally or in practice – substitute for these measures policy of their own. The British Parliament – both the House of Commons and the House of Lords – is an example of such a legislature. Legislatures with only minimal or marginal policy effect have very little ability in theory or in practice to amend or reject measures brought forward by the executive or to generate and substitute their own policies. Such legislatures are under executive domination and simply rubber-stamp executive decisions. Examples include the National People's Congress in the People's Republic of China and the Supreme People's Assembly in North Korea.

There are three questions that are particularly important in this regard when looking at legislatures:

1   Does a legislature have authority over the full array of public policy issues or only over certain aspects of public policy?
2   Does a legislature have not only the ways but the means to intervene in policy issues?

3 Does a legislature have the ability, not only in theory but in practice, to exercise independent analysis and formulate an independent judgement on public policy?

The functions of legislatures

There is however more to legislatures – much more – than either formulating policy or influencing the formulation of policy. Indeed, a wide range of functions – some intended and some unintended – can be identified. (See Table 1.1.)

From analysis it is apparent, firstly, that we cannot expect legislatures to operate and function in the same way in every country or political system. There may indeed be similarities, but they should not blind us to the differences that exist. Secondly, it is apparent that legislatures are very often subordinate institutions within the framework of the constitutional and political system within which they operate. Whatever theories of the constitutional responsibility of ministers and governments to the legislature in parliamentary systems may say, the reality of the position is that real power resides in the executive – the Prime Minister and Cabinet – and not in the legislature. Indeed, instances of policy-making legislatures are rare – with, as previously stated, the United States Congress being the most notable example. Thus, although the President of the United States can exercise executive power (by his position as commander-in-chief and through issuing executive orders), he

Table 1.1 Functions of a legislature

Representation, redress and express	On behalf of constituents. On behalf of interests. On behalf of causes. On behalf of a party.
Legitimisation	Latent – through meeting regularly and uninterruptedly. Manifest – the formal stamps of approval. 'Safety valve' – as an outlet for tensions and an arena for resolving disputes.
Recruitment, socialisation and training	Recruitment – of individuals into the political system. Socialisation – of individuals into the norms of political behaviour. Training – of individuals in political skills.
Education and informing	Educating – to teach the nation what it does not know. Informing – to bring matters to the forefront through discussion and deliberation.
Legislative	The scrutiny of legislation. The revision of legislation. The passage of legislation.
Scrutiny	Of the actions (and inactions) of the executive. Of the activity of the executive.

Sources: Derived from Bagehot (1867), Packenham (1970), Norton (1990) and Forman and Baldwin (1999).

cannot control the Congress in the same way as a British Prime Minister can normally control the House of Commons (though not necessarily the House of Lords). Indeed, the President's ability to lead or influence the Congress is lessened even more if his party does not control either or both of the houses, as President Obama found when the Democrats lost control of the House of Representatives in the mid-term elections of 2010.

Most legislatures can be identified as either policy-influencing legislatures or legislatures with only marginal policy effect. Against this backdrop it is interesting to note that one concept that appears to permeate the topic is the idea of 'the decline of legislatures'. Such a concept is not new. Viscount Bryce published his *Modern Democracies* in 1921,[4] in which, although stating that legislatures were an indispensable part of the machinery of government, he identified a number of what he described as 'chronic ailments' that had undermined such bodies. Ever since then the literature has been dominated by the thought that legislatures have been in decline, not least of all in comparison with – and as a direct result of – the increased power of executives. Within the literature a variety of specific causes for this decline have been identified, including:

- the emergence of organised, disciplined political parties;
- the growth in the activity and scope of government at both the national and the international level and the resulting increase in the size of governmental bureaucracies;
- the greater capacity of an executive to respond to developments in a timely fashion, formulating policy and providing leadership on the national stage and in the international arena;
- the rise of pressure group politics;
- the power of the media, the impact of 24-hour news coverage and the media's tendency to portray politics in terms of personalities.

Despite the increased institutional capacity of legislatures within the new democratic structures found among the nations of Eastern Europe, they have not been able to enhance their position. In fact the contrary has been the case because of changes in the context in which they operate, with increasingly assertive executives, centrally controlled state administration and better organised and disciplined political parties. Also important in this regard has been admittance into the European Union and the executive, administrative and legislative consequences flowing from this. These factors combined show that legislatures in the new democracies of Eastern Europe have begun to resemble their sister institutions in more established democracies, in terms both of internal organisation and procedures and of the external constraints that are normally placed upon such institutions in a modern democracy.

Japan provides another example following increased and strengthened executive leadership within the political system. Indeed, while the Japanese Prime Minister may still be weaker than many other chief executives, the position has been strengthened over the past 25 years and even more so in recent years, a direct result of changes in both party and electoral systems as well as administrative reforms.

Scandinavia similarly illustrates the increased importance of the Prime Minister as the chief political executive, despite the fact that, with the exception of Finland, this is not based upon an assessment of the formal powers of the office. Nonetheless, within Scandinavia elections have increasingly focused on rival prime ministerial 'candidates', media coverage has led to a personalisation of the office and – in the three Nordic countries that are members of the European Union – prime ministerial involvement in European Council meetings has allowed the incumbent to appear statesmanlike, if not 'presidential'. Having said this, however, it is nonetheless still evident that prime ministers who are no longer able to carry their parliamentary group fall.

Executive leadership in the legislative arena is a highly complex phenomenon. Take for example the case of the Federal Republic of Germany: despite the genuinely parliamentary character of the contemporary polity, analysis draws attention to the need for a broader perspective on the changing nature of executive leadership which reveals that the historically central role of the Bundestag as the foremost playing ground of governments has been challenged by significantly altered conditions of executive leadership. The empirical and theoretical implications of this transformation are highly contested issues and, although observers have identified a gradual 'de-parliamentarisation' of the public policy-making process in Germany, there has been a rather limited willingness to accept the vision of a 'post-parliamentary democracy' as a normative model.

On the other hand, some evidence points to an increased ability on the part of legislatures to hold executives to account. For example, in the case of the Republic of Ireland, there has been an overall increase in the level of parliamentary activity by the Taoiseach – head of government – over time, suggesting that there is today a greater degree of accountability in the Irish system than was previously the case. Similarly, in the United Kingdom, a comprehensive reform of the select committee structure was introduced in 1979 and, since that time, the influence and salience of these committees, whose task it is to scrutinise the activities of the executive in given policy areas, has increased. Indeed, research over the period 1997 to 2010 found that select committees produced almost 1,500 inquiry reports and almost 40,000 recommendations, of which 19,000 were aimed at central government. Around 40 per cent of these recommendations – around a third of recommendations calling for 'significant' policy changes – were accepted by government, and a similar proportion went on to be implemented.[5] In addition it has been noted that committees have a deterrent effect: that government insiders – ministers and civil servants – often ask themselves 'How would this look if examined by the select committee?' before taking decisions. This key form of influence – largely invisible and the least measurable – has been described as 'perhaps the most important of all'.[6]

In 2010, following a report by a new Select Committee on Reform of the House of Commons, chaired by the Labour MP Tony Wright, the independence of House of Commons select committees vis-à-vis the executive was strengthened by the introduction of a number of changes, including the election of select committee chairmen by secret ballot amongst the membership of the whole House and the election of committee members by secret ballot from within party groups. As a result, backbench members, not whips, determine who should represent their party on each committee, removing patronage powers from the party whips.[7]

The coming to power of the Coalition Government in 2010 saw an executive which was committed – as stipulated in its *Programme for Government* – to strengthen the powers of House of Commons select committees to scrutinise major public appointments.[8] To this end it granted the Treasury Select Committee a veto over the appointment and removal of the head of the new Office for Budget Responsibility, agreed in principle to give the Public Administration Committee a role in approving the creation of new quangos, and promised the Education Select Committee a role in approving key education appointments. Nonetheless, when in February 2012 MPs on the Business, Innovation and Skills Select Committee voted against accepting the nomination of Professor Les Ebdon as the new director of the Office for Fair Access (OFFA) and instead called for the recruitment process to begin again, the Business Secretary Vince Cable ignored this and confirmed the appointment.[9]

Also arising from recommendations of the Wright Committee has been the introduction of a new category of 'backbench business', for approximately one day per sitting week, to be scheduled by a new Backbench Business Committee.[10] This approach has also seen the incorporation of e-petitions from the general public into the parliamentary timetable.[11] The result of these initiatives has been to reduce the government's hold over the business agenda of the House of Commons.

Also important in this respect – again taking the case of the United Kingdom as an example – has been both the growth in backbench dissension in the House of Commons[12] and the increasing willingness amongst members of the House of Lords to challenge the executive, sometimes leading governments to modify policy.[13]

In addition the House of Commons has in effect secured a greater role with regard to going to war. This results from the fact that in March 2003 Prime Minister Tony Blair assured MPs that it was his intention to give MPs the opportunity to vote on a substantive motion in advance of hostilities commencing in Iraq. Such a vote took place on 18 March, the House of Commons voting by a majority of 179 in favour of military action.

Notwithstanding a House of Lords report on *Waging War: Parliament's Role and Responsibility*[14] concluding that 'the exercise of the Royal Prerogative by the Government to deploy armed forces is outdated and should not be allowed to continue as the basis for legitimate war-making in our 21st century democracy. Parliament's ability to challenge the executive must be protected and strengthened',[15] the Blair government rejected the idea of any formal change.[16]

Although on becoming Prime Minister in 2007 Gordon Brown said that he would surrender or limit the power to declare war without parliamentary approval,[17] no constitutional changes on war powers were made before his government lost office in 2010. Similarly, despite the fact that the Conservatives' 2010 manifesto included a pledge to make them 'subject to greater democratic control so that Parliament is properly involved in all big national decisions'[18] and the fact that the Liberal Democrats were in favour of such a reform, a pledge on war-making powers was not included in the coalition agreement. In March 2011 MPs approved UK participation in military action in Libya – although it should be pointed out that the vote took place a day after UK warplanes had carried out the first strikes against targets in Libya. During the debate the Foreign Secretary William Hague stated that: 'We will also enshrine in law for the future the necessity of consulting Parliament on military action.'[19] Subsequently, however, Political and Constitutional Reform Minister Mark Harper stated that, 'As the Government has already committed to observing the convention, the case for urgency has not been established, and I do not therefore believe it would be appropriate to set out a fixed timetable for progress on this matter.'[20]

Despite the fact that no formal change has – as yet – been made, the precedent set by there having been a vote in 2006, as well as the subsequent assurances given by government ministers, would make it politically very difficult indeed for a future government to go to war, except in circumstances where militarily for the security of the country it needed to act immediately, without holding a Commons vote.

The operation of legislatures

The extent to which a legislature is able to exercise power and exert influence is dependent upon a variety of variables, including:

- the institutional nature of the system within which it operates, for example either presidential or parliamentary, unitary or federal;
- electoral factors, for example the nature of the electoral system, the use of different systems for the choice of the head of the executive and for the legislature, and the staggering of executive and legislative elections;
- its position as outlined in the constitution and the extent of its constitutional authority;
- its working practices and the extent of its political independence from the executive;
- the extent to which it is affected by the nature of the party system;
- its standing in the eyes of the public;
- its organisational coherence, particularly the independence and strength of its committee system and the professionalism of its membership.

The experience of the United Kingdom Parliament reinforces such an analysis, pointing to the importance of such factors as:

- the party balance, particularly whether one party forms a majority government or whether coalition or minority governments are the norm;
- the size of the majority;
- the perceptions among MPs of the authority and popularity of the Prime Minister;
- the skills of the Prime Minister in managing Parliament;
- the skills and abilities of parliamentary business managers (such as the Chief Whip);
- the prevalence of 'divisive issues';

- the quality of the institutional structures by which Parliament can scrutinise the executive;
- the unity and quality of the opposition;
- national and international events.

It is only by taking into account such variables that one can assess the nature and status of the relationship between the legislature and the executive and determine whether it is the legislature or the executive that has the upper hand.

However, it is also necessary to recognise and to take account of the fact that influence can be exerted 'behind the scenes', something that makes analysis very difficult. For example, much executive leadership may not be directly observed or measured, as it is often exerted primarily in private meetings with other political actors, and, when the interests of the executive and the legislature align, it may be difficult to determine to what extent the executive is leading the legislature or responding to it.

However, an additional factor needs to be borne in mind, namely that, as the public or people have increasingly looked to executives (governments) to solve problems and governments have in turn found it difficult to meet such demands, this has tended to bring political institutions (and, of course, politicians) under greater criticism, weakening legislatures in the process.

As Forman and Baldwin have argued,[21] against the backdrop of the growing complexity of modern, global society, the policies and aspirations of even the most powerful political entities – be they legislatures or executives – are vulnerable to developments and decisions elsewhere over which they have little influence and even less control. This has been highlighted most recently by the credit crunch and banking crisis. The fact that the US banking sector had packaged sub-prime home loans into mortgage-backed securities which had been sold on to banks and other financial institutions around the word ensured that, when borrowers started to default on their loans, the value of these investments plummeted, resulting in huge losses for banks and financial institutions globally. Many banks around the world had invested large sums in these sub-prime-backed investments and had to write off billions of pounds in losses. They had been using the investment market to fund substantial parts of their mortgage business; this now dried up. In addition, investors became nervous about buying any investment linked to mortgages. Confidence is key; the lack of confidence spells disaster. As fear spread it became impossible to sell these investments, leaving a black hole in the finances of many banks and financial institutions. Governments intervened to rescue banks that were – allegedly – 'too big to fail', doing so at considerable cost to public finances. The result was that lending largely dried up – in short, a credit crunch. Mortgages, even viable ones, became more difficult to obtain as borrowing rates soared. Lenders became more selective about whom they lent money to by, for example, demanding bigger deposits. Stock markets dropped dramatically as turmoil in the mortgage market and the banking sector caused confidence to plunge. This had a significant, adverse knock-on effect on pensions and other savings. Whole countries, in essence, collapsed financially – Iceland, Ireland and Greece. The inability of politicians in these countries and elsewhere to control the situation became evident for all to see.

This fact, along with others, including the growing interaction between computer, phone and television technologies, and the tendency for hundreds of thousands of people to migrate across national borders in search of a better life, poses significant threats to the ambitions and jurisdictions of national political entities, be they legislatures or indeed executives. The dilemma for legislatures and executives is that, if they stubbornly persist in making claims to competence and control within their national jurisdictions, they are likely to discredit themselves in the eyes of their electorates because of their almost inevitable inability to deliver upon what they have promised. On the other hand, if they give up most of their traditional pretensions, more and more people in their electorates may begin to look elsewhere for satisfaction of their material needs and aspirations.

Conclusion

The reality of the position of a legislature in a political system – and indeed the relationship between the legislature and the executive in a political system – is dependent upon the history, traditions and special circumstances within an individual polity. Analysis illustrates the complexity of the position and not least of all in such a relationship. It is not simply the case of a legislature controlling an executive or of the executive controlling a legislature. Even in those instances where the balance of power undoubtedly favours an executive it is not to the point of total subordination, as there are examples, even in these instances, of the legislature being able to have an impact. In short, the executive–legislative relationship is relative, except in the most extreme cases of executive dominance.

In conclusion, when looking at legislatures, what can be identified is:

> a complex set of inter-relationships involving, in most cases, the capacity to influence, as opposed to determine; the ability to advise, rather than to command; the facility to criticise but not to obstruct; the competence to scrutinise rather than to initiate; and the desire to ensure that light is shed upon what is going on rather than to have things covered by a veil of secrecy. In short, the ability to hold the Executive to account and ensure that it is required to explain and justify its actions – and inactions – before the representatives of the people.[22]

As such, many modern legislatures are better equipped than previously to scrutinise and oversee the executive, and they possess a unique authority not only to force the executive to account for their actions but also to hold them responsible for those actions before a body which represents the people. Indeed, despite the fact that many legislatures may be weaker in their capacity to influence policy, they remain the linchpin joining the people to the political system of a nation, as intermediaries in the peaceful transfer of executive power, as raisers of grievances, as agencies of oversight and, above all, as forums for scrutiny of the executive.

But does size matter? Can a legislature in and of itself be either too big or too small to be effective? In a report by the Constitution Unit of University College London published in April 2011 and entitled *House Full*, referring to the British

House of Lords and the addition of 117 new members in less than a year, taking the membership to 792 (831 once those temporarily excluded from the chamber were included), it was noted that this 'has had negative effects on the functioning of the chamber', that any further increase in size risked rendering the House of Lords completely unable to do its job,[23] and that 'This rapid growth in membership has caused problems for the effective operation of the chamber. There is now a major concern that if appointments continue, the House of Lords will simply cease to be able to function.'[24]

The report went on to highlight three interconnected problems for the functioning of the House of Lords:[25]

1   There is an increasing pressure on – limited – resources whereby members are faced with working in overcrowded conditions with limited access to computers and telephones and with little or no space for staff.
2   The increasing number of members seeking to contribute to debates, ask questions and participate in committee work has created a more fractious atmosphere in the chamber and growing frustration amongst members who cannot contribute effectively.
3   The influx of a large number of new members has had a negative impact upon the culture of the House – in short it has resulted in changed behaviour.

But what of legislatures of small nations, states or territories? Does size matter in this regard? This question takes us to Introduction II.

Notes

1   For example, see George Thomas Kurian (ed.) (1998) *World Encyclopedia of Parliaments and Legislature*, Vols I and II (Washington, DC: Congressional Quarterly); Gerhard Loewenberg, Peverill Squire and D. Roderick Kiewiet (eds) (2002) *Legislatures* (Ann Arbor: University of Michigan Press); Michael Mezey (ed.) (1979) *Comparative Legislatures* (Durham, NC: Duke University Press); Philip Norton (ed.) (1990) *Legislatures* (Oxford: Oxford University Press); Nelson Polsby (1975) Legislatures, in F. I. Greenstein and N. W. Polsby, *Handbook of Political Science*, Vol. 5, pp. 277–96 (Reading, MA: Addison-Wesley).
2   Inter-Parliamentary Union Parline database on national parliaments. See http://www.ipu.org/parline-e/ParliamentsAtaGlance.asp.
3   Philip Norton (1990) General introduction, in Philip Norton (ed.), *Legislatures* (Oxford: Oxford University Press), p. 1.
4   See Viscount Bryce (1921) *Modern Democracies* (London: Macmillan).
5   See Meg Russell and Meghan Benton (2011) *Selective Influence: The Policy Impact of House of Commons Select Committees*, June (London: Constitution Unit, University College London).
6   Ibid., p. 8.
7   See House of Commons Reform Committee (2009) *Rebuilding the House*, HC1117, 24 November (London: Stationery Office); House of Commons Reform Committee (2010) *Rebuilding the House: Implementation*, HC372, 15 March (London: Stationery Office); also see Meg Russell (2011) 'Never allow a crisis go to waste': The Wright Committee reforms to strengthen the House of Commons, *Parliamentary Affairs*, 64 (4), pp. 612–33.

8 HM Government (2010) *The Coalition: Our Programme for Government*, 401238/0510, May (London: Cabinet Office), p. 21.

9 Department for Business, Innovation and Skills press release, 20 February 2012. See http://nds.coi.gov.uk/content/Detail.aspx?ReleaseID=423368&NewsAreaID=2.

10 See http://www.parliament.uk/business/committees/committees-a-z/commons-select/backbench-business committee/.

11 For the e-petition website see http://epetitions.direct.gov.uk. If an e-petition reaches 100,000 signatures, it will be sent to the Office of the Leader of the House of Commons, who will check it against the terms and conditions for e-petitions and the rules of the House. Successful e-petitions are communicated to the Backbench Business Committee, which decides if the issue will be debated in the House of Commons.

12 See Philip Cowley and Mark Stuart (2010) A coalition with wobbly wings: Backbench dissent since May 2010, November, http://www.Revolts.co.uk.

13 See Meg Russell (2010) A stronger second chamber? Assessing the impact of House of Lords reform in 1999 and the lessons for bicameralism, *Political Studies*, December, 58 (5), pp. 866–85.

14 House of Lords Select Committee on the Constitution (2006) *Waging War: Parliament's Role and Responsibility*, HL Paper 236-I and II, 27 July (London: Stationery Office).

15 Ibid., p. 41.

16 See *Government's Response to the House of Lords Constitution Committee's Report, Fifteenth Report of Session 2005–06 – Waging War: Parliament's Role and Responsibility*, Cm 6923, 7 November 2006 (London: Stationery Office).

17 See *The Governance of Britain*, Cm 7170, July 2007 (London: Stationery Office), p. 18, paras 25–30.

18 *Invitation to Join the Government of Britain: The Conservative Manifesto 2010*, 2010 (London: Conservative Party), p. 67.

19 The Rt. Hon. William Hague MP, House of Commons *Hansard*, 21 March 2011, Col 799.

20 Written response by Mark Harper MP, Minister for Political and Constitutional Reform, to the House of Commons Political and Constitutional Reform Committee's Ninth Report of Session 2010–12 entitled *Parliament's Role in Conflict Decisions: Government Response to the Committee's Eighth Report of Session 2010–12*, 6 December 2011. See http://www.publications.parliament.uk/pa/cm201012/cmselect/cmpolcon/1673/167304.htm.

21 See F. N. Forman and N. D. J. Baldwin (1999) *Mastering British Politics* (London: Macmillan), pp. 533–4.

22 See Nicholas D. J. Baldwin (2006) Concluding observations: legislative weakness, scrutinising strength?, in Nicholas D. J. Baldwin (ed.), *Executive Leadership and Legislative Assemblies* (London: Routledge), p. 302.

23 Meg Russell (2011) *House Full*, April (London: Constitution Unit, University College London), p. 3, para. 2.

24 Ibid., p. 5, para 2.

25 Ibid., p. 9.

References

Bagehot, Walter (1867) *The English Constitution* (Fontana/Collins, Glasgow, Scotland, 1975).

Forman, F.N. and Baldwin, N.D.J. (1999) *Mastering British Politics* (Fourth Edition) (Basingstoke: Palgrave Macmillan).

Norton, P. (Ed.) (1990) *Legislatures* (Oxford: Oxford University Press).

Packenham, R.A (1970) 'Legislatures and Political Development', in A. Kornberg and L.D. Musolf (eds), *Legislatures in Developmental Perspective* (Durham, NC: Duke University Press).

2 Introduction II

Legislatures in small polities

Dag Anckar

Introduction

Although not all institutions have goals in terms of which their existence may be explained or justified, most institutions do. This is certainly true of institutions that are formed by design, i.e. through legislation or constitutional convention (Nurmi 1991, 10–11). Legislatures are as a rule designed institutions, as the norms and rules that shape the legislatures and define as well as set bounds to their tasks and functions are laid down in constitutions or similar frameworks. The considerations that regulate in separate cases the extent and content of such norms and rules may of course stem from various sources, like the political culture and history of the country in question, its ethnic composition and heterogeneity, its colonial history or its international obligations. One set of causes that has been rather neglected in research hitherto is about the physical nature and environments of states, as captured in terms of categories like size, islandness, topography and others. Admittedly, this neglect is not a characteristic of research on institutions alone, but rather marks the empirical study of politics at large (e.g. Dahl and Tufte 1973, 1–3; Hadenius 1992, 122–7; C. Anckar 1998, 198–200).

Dealing with the impact of small state size on the structure and functions of legislatures, the subsequent chapters contribute to meeting the want for an understanding of the interplay of physical and social factors. Following an authoritative definition, the term 'legislature' is taken here to denote bodies that are constitutionally designated for giving assent to binding measures of public policy (Norton 1990, 1). Although the definition is broad, it does exclude some legislature-like institutions in small states, like, for instance, the appointed Legislative Council in Brunei, which has consultative functions only, the Majlis ash-Shura in Oman, which is an elected advisory council with consultative tasks only, and the corresponding Majlis ash-Shura in Qatar, which has appointed members with only consultative tasks. However, most small states have legislatures that satisfy the above definition, and the small states certainly for their part justify the popular sayings that legislatures 'span the globe' (Norton 1993, 4) and are 'resilient creatures' (Hague *et al.* 1998, 185). These institutions may have different names from one small context to another, being named, for example, Maneaba Ni Maungatabu (Kiribati), Olbiil era Kelulau (Belau), Landtag (Liechtenstein),

Libandla (Swaziland) or Kamra tad-Deputati (Malta). The legislatures are different in other respects as well, but they also display many similarities and parallelisms. While certainly giving due attention to relevant differences between legislatures, the following chapters still focus on the question to what extent the similarities may be looked upon as consequences of small state size.

Defining smallness

'Smallness' is an elusive and contested concept which has been defined in terms of, for instance, population, area, international power position, economic performance, and the extent of government involvement (Maass 2009). The last three of these are examples of ill-considered definitions that equate the consequences of smallness with smallness per se; the first two are the most common among the many definitions. They are similar in so far as they correlate strongly: small population usually combines with small area, and large population usually combines with large area. Also, to insert an important observation, small is usually about islandness. Indeed, islands and island groups make up the great majority of the world's small states (Lowenthal 1992, 18–19), and the same is true of the nations and territories, the legislatures of which are scrutinized in the following chapters. Not all nations and territories are islands, but most are.

The use of cut-off points between 'small' and 'not small' varies in accordance with different sets of criteria. Economists usually prefer somewhat more relaxed criteria than political scientists (Sutton and Payne 1993, 581), and political science studies of relations between states and thereby of the place of microstates in the international community are likely to employ higher cut-off points than political science studies of the relation between the state and the citizen. Studies in this last category often equate smallness with microstates, i.e. states with populations of less than one million. Clearly, then, the term 'small state' means different things to different people (Maass 2009, 68). However, most cut-off points are selected arbitrarily, and this appears to be true also of the microstate threshold. The finding that microstates are conducive to democracy is much endorsed, especially in regard to small island states, and one remark in the literature states that a significant feature about many small island jurisdictions is their ability to maintain democratic political systems (Srebrnik 2004, 338–9). However, as is evident from recent studies, a size threshold in regard to democracy operates even within the microstate universe. The critical cut-off point appears to be 500,000 individuals: when the population size surpasses this threshold, there are no longer any associations between size and democracy (C. Anckar 2008, 440–41); indeed, there is a difference in terms of democracy between being small and being diminutive (D. Anckar 2010, 4–7).

Imprecise definitions of the small state of course impair the possibility of comparing the results from multiple studies (Maass 2009, 66). However, this weakness is not characteristic of the chapters that follow, as they are predominantly about states and entities that are well within the range of the microstate conception and in fact are below even the before-mentioned threshold of 500,000 people. For instance, the Principality of Liechtenstein has a population of 35,000 and the Principality of Monaco has a population of 33,000, whereas Andorra has a population of 83,000 and Nunavut, a federal territory of Canada, has a population of 30,000. The population figures of the British overseas territories of Bermuda and Gibraltar respectively are 68,000 and 29,000, and the Isle of Man, which is a self-governing British Crown dependency, has a population of 80,000. Some cases are truly diminutive: for example, the Pacific island states of Nauru and Tuvalu have populations of 14,000 and 12,000 respectively. In contrast, a few cases represent somewhat larger varieties of smallness and thereby offer, albeit to a limited extent, some fuel for comparison between size levels. Lesotho has a population of 1,800,000, Hong Kong has a population of 7 million people, and the Pacific islands case of Papua New Guinea has a population of approximately the same size.

The impact of size

In itself, of course, small size does not mean much and does not explain much. Its impact is through a variety of mechanisms and channels that are sensitive to variations in size and transmit the effects of size to political style and political structure. As regards legislatures, two interconnected aspects may be expected to be influenced by such mechanisms and channels. Legislatures differ in terms of structure, and the differences may well be conceptualized as outcomes of differences in state size. For one thing, variations in state size may be expected to bring forth variations in legislature size: indeed, as a rule, small countries tend to have small parliaments, whereas large countries tend to have large parliaments (e.g. Helander 1991, 53; Taagepera and Recchia 2002). An early finding in research on this topic was that the size of parliaments increases with the population of a country, but at a lower rate (Dahl and Tufte 1973, 80–84). However, exceptions to this rule abound even in the universe of smallness. To give just one example: whereas there are 55 seats in the legislature of the small African island state São Tomé and Príncipe with a population of 163,000, there are 30 members of the House of Assembly of the small island state of Dominica with a population of 72,000, and only 21 members of the House of Assembly of the small island state of St Vincent and the Grenadines with a population of 120,000. Ethnic heterogeneity may be one of several factors that contribute to an increased legislature size in small states; however, an excessive heterogeneity may even contribute to a decreased legislature size. 'Problems of uniting people from different cultural and ethnic backgrounds quickly surfaced', it is said in one comment on early political life in the Federated States of Micronesia (Hanlon and Eperiam 1988, 92). It is easy to understand that such problems created a need for decentralization and autonomy measures, which involved the creation of state legislatures. The establishment of such institutions made it possible, in turn, for the country to manage with an undersized federal legislature with 14 members only.

Further hypotheses may be derived and tested concerning the impact of small size on structure. First, legislatures are unicameral or bicameral, and one would certainly be inclined to believe that unicameral assemblies are more streamlined and effective than bicameral ones in terms of responding to the needs of small and cohesive societies (Heywood 1997, 301). Second, while legislative chambers are as a rule too big to deal efficiently with matters of detail and therefore have committee systems (Laundy 1989, 97), and while there is much truth to the saying that 'committees have become the workhouses of effective legislatures' (Hague and Harrop 2004, 250), one would still expect that small legislatures, precisely because they are small, would refrain from developing full-fledged committee systems. Third, quite often legislatures are not elected in their totality by the people in their totality, as, for a variety of reasons, in several countries a certain number of parliamentary seats are reserved for designated groups, organizations or interests. The expectation would be that small territories, again precisely because they are small, are less than obvious candidates for the maintenance of such devices for the representation of particular interests. However, according to one count, surprisingly, no less than 40 per cent out of a total of 38 microstates with assemblies have this apportionment device (D. Anckar 2006, 197–8). One example is the small island state of Cape Verde, as diaspora residents in Africa, America and Europe send six deputies to the National Assembly, two from each region (Hawthorne 1999, 186).

In terms of whether legislatures formulate policy or influence the formulation of policy, one well-known distinction is between policy-making legislatures, policy-influencing legislatures, legislatures with minimal or marginal policy effect, and legislatures with no real policy effect (Mezey 1979). Since the capacities of legislatures are influenced by a variety of factors, it may be difficult in research to encircle and isolate the impact of size. Some small states may because of regime and political culture factors have rubber-stamp or close-to-rubber-stamp legislatures – this is true, for instance, of Swaziland, where the King must approve legislation passed by Parliament before it becomes law. At the same time, however, this reference to the case of non-democratic Swaziland is illustrative of a fact that much improves the prospects for managing in the following chapters the problem of extraneous variation. With a few exceptions only, like the Pacific island states of Fiji, the Solomon Islands and Tonga (e.g. Lawson 1996; Dinnen and Firth 2008), the chapters in this collection are about legislatures in democratic nations or in territories that are parts of democratic units. This means that many albeit not all variations in control variables are taken care of by means of case selection: studying democratic legislatures avoids the conclusions concerning marginal and no legislature effects that are more or less inherent in studies of legislative institutions in non-democratic contexts and nations.

What makes investigations of the importance of size a challenging task is that contradictory but still equally plausible hypotheses may be derived. For instance, as regards the well-known idea of the decline of legislatures, stated by James Bryce as far back as the early 1920s (1921), small size may be taken to promote as well as counteract the decline. On the one hand, the emergence of organized and disciplined political parties is generally regarded as one factor that strengthens executive leadership and thus expedites the decline of legislatures. Because of their homogeneity and a lesser overall need for formal and impersonal organizations, small territories, theory suggests, are associated with a lack of parties or with only a few parties (Dahl and Tufte 1973, 91–7); they are therefore less instrumental in promoting executive leadership. And indeed, as is evident from empirical investigation, in several instances small democracies manage without political parties at all (D. Anckar and Anckar 2000). On the other hand, however, smallness may be expected to advance a personalization of politics that promotes, in turn, the authority and popularity of leaders in small contexts and thus increases executive capability in managing Parliament. Examples of long-time leaders of democratic or semi-democratic small nations are Forbes Burnham, Premier of pre-independence Guyana in 1964–66, Prime Minister 1966–80, and executive President 1980–85 (Lewis 2001, 92–120); Vere Cornwall Bird, Prime Minister of Antigua and Barbuda 1981–94 (Sealy 1991, 35–47); and Mary Eugenia Charles, Prime Minister of Dominica 1980–95 (Liswood 1996). Small size, in other words, may work in the one direction or the other, and it remains a vital task for empirical research to find out the underlying patterns that are at work here.

The researcher faces similar challenges in the study of legislature functions, these being, according to one listing, about representation, deliberation, legislation, authorization of expenditure, the making of governments and the oversight of government activity (Hague and Harrop 2004, 253). Again, expectations may be contradictory, as is evident, for example, from efforts to conceptualize the impact of smallness as moderated by colonial history and metropolitan relations (D. Anckar 2007, 638). On the one hand, because the entities that are studied are small, they are also less resourceful and less resistant. In consequence, they are likely to show allegiance to metropolitan patterns and to resign themselves to the cultural constraint. A guiding hypothesis, then, would be that small countries are likely to resort to imitation and diffusion. On the other hand, however, the impact of smallness may be quite different. It is argued in the theoretical literature that small size carries a variety of consequences for political life and political rationalities (Dahl and Tufte 1973; D. Anckar and Anckar 1995, 220–22). To the extent that this is true, small states may be expected to entertain ways of thinking and frames of reference that are different from the perceptions and inducements characteristic of larger metropolitan states; the guiding hypothesis, now, would be that small countries are likely to pursue their own rationalities.

Also, findings may in separate cases be counter-intuitive. Concerning representation, it is a valid expectation that representative assemblies reflect social diversity, and, since this stands out as a less challenging task in small than in large units, one would assume that small units would make less use of particular devices in terms of electoral and institutional design for the promotion of representation. Exceptions abound, however. For instance, in diminutive Niue, which is a Pacific island nation in free association with New Zealand and with a population of 1,400, there are in addition to 14 members of the Niue Legislative Assembly, who are elected from the village communities, six common roll seats for a constituency that represents the entire country. The intention of this provision was and is that the total membership of the legislature should be more representative of the people as a whole and that the legislature would have more of a national outlook (Ghai 1988, 60–61).

Considerations on methodology

Explanatory studies may follow different paths. One is to select cases that represent variation in relevant independent variables and then look empirically for variations in relevant dependent variables; predominantly, such studies make use of a statistical mode of explanation (e.g. Lijphart 1971, 685–91). Another strategy implies selection on the dependent variable, this meaning that cases are picked out for scrutiny that represent similar outcomes, the task of the researcher being to find out to what extent this similarity is a product of similarities also in causation factors, i.e. the independent variables. Obviously, variations in the dependent variable being removed in this design from the research configuration, this strategy can do no more than accumulate knowledge of necessary conditions (Dion 1998, 127–8). Focusing on cases that are small in terms of state size and investigating impacts of smallness, the research that follows applies still another strategy, which selects on the independent variable. Obviously, this is not a good research design for testing claims that concern necessary conditions; however, if the task is one of testing sufficient conditions, there is more to say in favour of the design (Dion 1998, 133). The choice here of this particular design follows, however, from other and less demanding ambitions. Given the scarcity of research findings and theoretical frameworks in the field of study, rather than applying and modifying existing theories, the research that is reported here aims for no more than problem charting and erecting scaffoldings for future theory-building. From this follow two methodological considerations and implications.

First, the question whether size matters is approached in the following via a case study avenue. This is to some extent only natural and implies the following of a beaten track, as the case study, it has been said, remains by far the most common method of research in political science in general, and more particularly in comparative politics (Peters 1998, 137). As is well known, case studies have different functions, move on different levels of ambition, and make use of different methods and techniques. The common problem of this research field is how to fit separate single cases into a more general framework and how to develop methods for moving beyond individual cases and for making individual case studies more comparable. Following the terminology of a somewhat dated but still influential typology of case studies (Eckstein 1975), it is probably pertinent to characterize the case studies that follow as belonging to a 'plausibility probe' category, which covers attempts at testing proto-theories that the researcher wants to try out (Peters 1998, 150), the proto-theory presently at hand, then, being if size matters or not in investigations of legislatures.

Second, while there are evidently many ways to think about causation, the studies that follow subscribe to a minimal definition of causation, which states that causes may be said to refer to events or conditions that raise the probability of some outcome occurring (Gerring 2005, 169–70). This means, then, that any summation of the studies that follow must be occupied with the question of whether it is the case or not that a small state size factor raises the probability of outcomes that relate to legislature structure, legislature functions, or both, structures and functions being, of course, to some extent coupled together. With reference to the distinction between causal arguments that are correlational in nature and those that rely on the identification of causal mechanisms or processes (Gerring 2005, 191), one is probably justified in saying that the following chapters move in both directions. On the one hand, quite a few cases are dissected and discussed, which promotes the prospects for charting correlation patterns. On the other hand, the case study approach invites in itself an examination of mechanisms: as the studies are located in particular historical and cultural milieus, they can look at the sequence of events that produced an outcome rather than just at the outcome (Peters 1998, 141).

References

Anckar, C. (1998) *Storlek och partisystem: En studie av 77 stater* (Åbo: Åbo Akademi University Press).

Anckar, C. (2008) Size, islandness, and democracy: A global comparison, *International Political Science Review*, 29 (4), pp. 433–59.

Anckar, D. (2006) Assembly quotas in microstates, *Parliaments, Estates and Representation*, 26, pp. 197–210.

Anckar, D. (2007) Westminster Lilliputs? Parliaments in former small British colonies, *Parliamentary Affairs*, 60 (4), pp. 637–54.

Anckar, D. (2010) Small is democratic, but who is small?, *Arts and Social Sciences Journal*, 1 (1), pp. 1–10.

Anckar, D. and Anckar, C. (1995) Size, insularity and democracy, *Scandinavian Political Studies*, 18 (4), pp. 211–29.

Anckar, D. and Anckar, C. (2000) Democracies without parties, *Comparative Political Studies*, 33 (2), pp. 225–47.

Bryce, J. (1921) *Modern Democracies* (London: Macmillan).

Dahl, R. A. and Tufte, E. (1973) *Size and Democracy* (Stanford, CA: Stanford University Press).

Dinnen, S. and Firth, S. (eds) (2008) *Politics and State Building in Solomon Islands* (Canberra: ANU E Press).

Dion, D. (1998) Evidence and inference in the comparative case study, *Comparative Politics*, 30 (2), pp. 127–45.

Eckstein, H. (1975) Case study and theory in political science, in F. I. Greenstein and N. W. Polsby (eds), *Handbook of Political Science*, Vol. 7, pp. 94–137 (Reading, MA: Addison-Wesley).

Gerring, J. (2005) Causation: A unified framework for the social sciences, *Journal of Theoretical Politics*, 17 (2), pp. 163–98.

Ghai, Y. (1988) Systems of government – I, in Y. Ghai (ed.), *Law, Politics and Government in the Pacific Island States*, pp. 54–75 (Suva, Fiji: Institute of Pacific Studies, University of the South Pacific).

Hadenius, A. (1992) *Democracy and Development* (Cambridge: Cambridge University Press).

Hague, R. and Harrop, M. (2004) *Comparative Government and Politics: An Introduction* (New York: Palgrave Macmillan).

Hague, R., Harrop, M. and Breslin, S. (1998) *Comparative Government and Politics: An Introduction* (London: Macmillan).

Hanlon, D. and Eperiam, W. (1988) The evolution and development of the Federated States of Micronesia, in R. Crocombe and A. Ali (eds), *Micronesian Politics*, pp. 85–106 (Suva, Fiji: Institute of Pacific Studies, University of the South Pacific).

Hawthorne, W. (1999) Republic of Cape Verde, in D. A. Kaple (ed.), *World Encyclopedia of Political Systems and Parties*, 3rd edn, pp. 186–7 (New York: Facts on File).

Helander, V. (1991) *Euroopan poliittiset järjestelmät* (Helsinki: Valtionhallinnon kehittämiskeskus).

Heywood, A. (1997) *Politics* (London: Macmillan).

Laundy, P. (1989) *Parliaments in the Modern World* (Aldershot: Dartmouth).

Lawson, S. (1996) *Tradition versus Democracy in the South Pacific: Fiji, Tonga and Western Samoa* (Cambridge: Cambridge University Press).

Lewis, L. (2001) Linden Forbes Burnham (1923–85): Unravelling the paradox of post-colonial leadership in Guyana, in A. Allahar (ed.), *Caribbean Charisma*, pp. 92–120 (Kingston, Jamaica: Ian Randle Publishers).

Lijphart, A. (1971) Comparative politics and the comparative method, *American Political Science Review*, 65 (2), pp. 682–93.

Liswood, L. A. (1996) *Women World Leaders: Fifteen Great Politicians Tell Their Stories* (New York: New York University Press).

Lowenthal, D. (1992) Small tropical islands: A general overview, in H. M. Hintjens and M. D. D. Newitt (eds), *The Political Economy of Small Tropical Islands*, pp. 19–29 (Exeter: University of Exeter Press).

Maass, M. (2009) The elusive definition of the small state, *International Politics*, 46 (1), pp. 65–83.

Mezey, M. (1979) *Comparative Legislatures* (Durham, NC: Duke University Press).

Norton, P. (ed.) (1990) *Legislatures* (Oxford: Oxford University Press).

Norton, P. (1993) *Does Parliament Matter?* (Hemel Hempstead: Harvester Wheatsheaf).

Nurmi, H. (1991) Understanding institutions through theoretical models, in M. Wiberg (ed.), *The Political Life of Institutions*, pp. 10–32 (Helsinki: Finnish Political Science Association).

Peters, B. G. (1998) *Comparative Politics: Theory and Methods* (London: Macmillan Press).

Sealy, T. (1991) *Sealy's Caribbean Leaders* (Kingston, Jamaica: Kingston Publishers).

Srebrnik, H. (2004) Small island nations and democratic values, *World Development*, 32 (4), pp. 329–41.

Sutton, P. and Payne, A. (1993) Lilliput under threat: The security problems of small island and enclave developing states, *Political Studies*, 41 (4), pp. 579–93.

Taagepera, R. and Recchia, S. (2002) The size of second chambers and European assemblies, *European Journal of Political Research*, 41 (2), pp. 165–85.

Part I
Sovereign entities

3 The Commonwealth Caribbean

Legislatures and democracy

Hamid Ghany

Introduction

The Commonwealth Caribbean consists of Antigua and Barbuda, the Bahamas, Barbados, Belize, Dominica, Grenada, Guyana, Jamaica, St Kitts–Nevis, St Lucia, St Vincent and the Grenadines, and Trinidad and Tobago. In the intervening years between 1962, when Jamaica and Trinidad and Tobago attained their independence, and 1983, when St Kitts–Nevis attained its independence, it is to be noted that all the constitutions of these countries resembled each other.

This similarity between countries and the similarity of constitutional design has been referred to as the Westminster model in the Commonwealth Caribbean. According to S. A. de Smith:

> the Westminster model can be said to mean a constitutional system in which the head of state is not the effective head of government; in which the effective head of government is a Prime Minister presiding over a Cabinet composed of Ministers over whose appointment and removal he has at least a substantial measure of control; in which the effective executive branch of government is parliamentary inasmuch as Ministers must be members of the legislature; and in which Ministers are collectively and individually responsible to a freely elected and representative legislature.[1]

This definition properly captures the kind of constitutional arrangements that were instituted in Commonwealth countries when they got their independence. The timeline of independence in the Commonwealth Caribbean is as follows : Jamaica (1962), Trinidad and Tobago (1962), Guyana (1966), Barbados (1966), the Bahamas (1973), Grenada (1974), Dominica (1978), St Lucia (1979), St Vincent and the Grenadines (1979), Belize (1981), Antigua and Barbuda (1981), and St Kitts–Nevis (1983).

The deviation in the constitutional design between these countries was minimal, with the most significant deviation being between those with bicameral as opposed to unicameral legislatures. There are eight bicameral legislatures – Antigua and Barbuda, the Bahamas, Barbados, Belize, Grenada, Jamaica, St Lucia, and Trinidad and Tobago – and four unicameral legislatures – Dominica, Guyana, St Kitts–Nevis, and St Vincent and the Grenadines.

Apart from this structural difference, the constitutions of all of these countries at independence would have been described as being of Westminster stock. The definition applied by de Smith and the export of that model as discussed by Alan Burns[2] would have suited the 1960s and 1970s. This was an era when many new states gained their independence from Great Britain and the composition of the Commonwealth assumed a greater developing-world representation.

At that time, it would have been too early to assess the impact and the significance of the constitutions that had been established in many of these newly independent states. However, by the late 1970s doubts about the Westminster model and its export were being expressed.

A. F. Madden[3] rejected, in a general sense, the idea that the Westminster model could be exported and established overseas. Indeed, he argued that it was never the intention of British colonial administrators to export the model in its purest form. According to him, 'the only true Westminster model remained inevitably at home in Westminster: it was not intended for export, but was strictly "to be consumed only on the premises"'.[4]

This argument, therefore, begs the question that, if the Westminster model was not exported, then what was? Madden never answered this question, but offers an opinion which can be challenged. According to him:

> The new generation of constitution makers in the 1950s and 1960s were not concerned with creating a permanent instrument for government so much as a device for securing independence which could be altered subsequently at will. Something akin to the British model might serve its temporary purpose in allaying fears in Britain about transferring power. But it remains to be proved that it is appropriate for the tasks of self-government anywhere else than in Britain.[5]

In 2012, both Jamaica and Trinidad and Tobago celebrated their 50th anniversaries of independence, and the other countries of the region will follow in the years to come. At the time of writing, only two countries (Guyana and Trinidad and Tobago) have undertaken any significant changes to their original independence constitution. The alterations were cosmetic for Guyana in 1970 and Trinidad and Tobago in 1976, as the fundamental parliamentary structure was retained. However, Guyana undertook significant reform in 1980 when a presidential model was introduced, and this was buttressed by further reforms of this nature in 2001.

The constitutions of these countries in the Commonwealth Caribbean have been able to survive attempts to alter them 'subsequently at will' to the extent that the only other major attempt at reform failed at the referendum stage in St Vincent and the Grenadines in 2009.

The reality is that the Commonwealth Caribbean countries do not have the Westminster model. Leslie Wolf-Phillips[6] used the term 'Whitehall model' to describe these constitutions. It would, perhaps, be more comfortable to describe these constitutions in the Commonwealth Caribbean countries (with the exception of Guyana) today as belonging to the Westminster–Whitehall model.

Unlike the United Kingdom, which has a partly unwritten, partly written but uncodified constitution, all of the countries of the Commonwealth Caribbean have formal, written, codified constitutions. The main features of the Westminster–Whitehall model are: (1) a unique bicameral system; (2) a bill of rights in the constitution; (3) the codification of Westminster constitutional conventions; (4) a recently developed equivalence in the separation of powers; and (5) the entrenchment of constitutional articles.

The unique bicameral system

Of the 54 members of the Commonwealth, there are 18 bicameral national parliaments. Eight of those are to be found in the Commonwealth Caribbean. The members of the senates in the Commonwealth Caribbean do not enjoy security of tenure like their senatorial colleagues in Canada or their noble colleagues in the House of Lords. Their appointments are made by the head of state on political advice or in the discretion of the head of state as the case may be. Those appointments can be revoked at any time, and all senatorial positions become vacant at the next dissolution of parliament. There is no guarantee of continuation of service beyond a dissolution unless there is an invitation on the basis of fresh political advice or favourable discretion from the head of state to continue.

The same political reality applies to those unicameral parliaments in the Commonwealth Caribbean that have nominated senators, who sit side by side with elected MPs in Dominica, St Kitts–Nevis, and St Vincent and the Grenadines.

In the case of Guyana, there is a National Assembly that is elected on the basis of the party list system of proportional representation. Accordingly, their arrangements are defined for them on the basis of the will of the electorate and the decisions of political parties in the extraction of names from those lists to determine who sits in the National Assembly.

There is no similarity with the Westminster model in the United Kingdom.

A bill of rights in the constitution

All of the constitutions of the Commonwealth Caribbean countries have a bill of rights in them, which is a chapter that recognizes, declares and protects fundamental human rights and freedoms. In 11 countries, the bill of rights has been influenced by the European Convention on Human Rights 1950, while Trinidad and Tobago has been influenced by the Canadian Bill of Rights 1960. The constitutional effect of this is to permit the individual to challenge the State on the ground of human rights violations being a constitutional infringement. The courts are used as the vehicle of challenge, and the judiciary has the constitutional power to overturn executive or judicial action and parliamentary will in order to redress such infringements.

Such powers are not exercised in the Westminster model in the United Kingdom, as the doctrine of the supremacy of parliament operates in an environment in which there is no formal, written, codified constitution. The Commonwealth Caribbean is very different where these arrangements are concerned when compared to the United Kingdom.

The codification of Westminster constitutional conventions

Constitutional conventions largely provide the rules by which the affairs of state are conducted in the United Kingdom. Their transference to the constitutions of Commonwealth Caribbean countries at independence represents a desire to maintain, as far as possible, a reproduction of the Westminster model in the region. Such a desire was unambiguously expressed by Dr Eric Williams immediately prior to his becoming the Chief Minister of Trinidad and Tobago in 1956.

According to Williams:

> The Colonial Office does not need to examine its second hand colonial constitutions. It has a constitution at hand which it can apply immediately to Trinidad and Tobago. That is the British Constitution. Ladies and Gentlemen, I suggest to you that the time has come when the British Constitution, suitably modified, can be applied to Trinidad and Tobago. After all, if the British Constitution is good enough for Great Britain, it should be good enough for Trinidad and Tobago.[7]

This type of approach was copied in other Commonwealth Caribbean countries when they attained their independence. The best expression of this can be gleaned from the codification of Westminster constitutional conventions in the constitutions of these countries at the time of their independence. The only deviation that has occurred from this of any substance was the introduction of the Constitution of the Co-operative Republic of Guyana Act 1980,[8] which completely altered the foundation of the Guyanese constitution away from its previous Westminster–Whitehall base towards a presidential model.

Despite its reform in 1976, the Trinidad and Tobago republican constitution[9] that replaced its independence constitution[10] retained most of its Westminster–Whitehall traditions and its parliamentary character.

No other country in the Commonwealth Caribbean besides Guyana and Trinidad and Tobago has undertaken any similar systematic overhaul of its constitutional arrangements, and so the Westminster conventions as codified remain as the basis for the operation of their political and constitutional systems.

Recently developed equivalence in the separation of powers

The establishment of the United Kingdom Supreme Court on 1 October 2009 created an equivalence between the separation of powers in Commonwealth Caribbean countries and the new Westminster model in the United Kingdom. No longer was the upper house of the British parliament to serve as both a legislative and a judicial body. This brought a measure of similarity between the House of

Lords in its current form and the senates in West Indian legislatures and brought them into harmony as legislative bodies exclusively.

The revisions to the office of Lord Chancellor in the United Kingdom through the establishment of the offices of Lord Speaker and the Secretary of State for Justice together with the establishment of the role of the Lord Chief Justice in the United Kingdom Supreme Court have created a separation of powers that mirrors what exists in West Indian polities.

There was never any equivalent office for the Lord Chancellor in West Indian jurisdictions, and that set the region apart from the Westminster model. Such a marked distinction was part of an analytical framework that would have been called the Westminster–Whitehall model or Whitehall model.[11]

The entrenchment of constitutional articles

The concept of entrenchment is one that regulates the way in which parliament exercises its legislative authority in respect of the amendment of the constitution that guarantees its existence. There are three major types of entrenchment methods that are used in Commonwealth Caribbean legislatures. They are: (1) special majorities for bills seeking to amend the constitution; (2) time delay mechanisms between first and second readings of bills that seek to amend the constitution; and (3) the use of post-parliamentary referenda to validate or reject amendments approved by parliament.

The constitutions of Barbados, Belize, and Trinidad and Tobago make no provision for a post-parliamentary referendum in the amendment of their constitutions. In relation to the use of time delay measures between the first and second readings of bills seeking to amend the constitution, only the constitutions of the Bahamas, Barbados, Guyana, and Trinidad and Tobago make no provision in this regard.

Needless to say, there is no comparison with the Westminster model in the United Kingdom on this subject, as there is no formal, written, codified British constitution with articles in need of protection by entrenchment.

The pendulum of power between government and opposition

The Commonwealth Caribbean countries have largely chosen to have Westminster-style constitutions that are based on a majoritarian principle as opposed to the principle of consensus. Under such constitutional arrangements, the government and the opposition are expected to hold political power on an alternating basis, because the premise of that system of government is that electorates will change their minds in significant enough numbers to permit such a pendulum swing. The core of the argument is that political power is a zero sum entity that must be transferred in its entirety from one side to the other, as there is no room for partial transfers of power.

In other systems of government, political change is less of an expectation, as opposed to political consensus, which must always be guaranteed. In such systems power is shared by virtue of institutional arrangements that permit this on a consistent basis so that changes in the control of the executive branch of government are not a zero sum calculation that must also include the legislature.

The model of consociationalism as espoused by Arend Lijphart[12] embraces the notion of accommodative behaviour among competing leaders in the political process. This model is designed to work in both majoritarian and consensual models, but the key to its success lies in the domain of the recognition of diversity and the development of political techniques to manage that diversity in order to maintain political stability.

Waves of democratization

Samuel Huntington[13] has argued that democracy can be measured globally in terms of waves. He demarcates these waves of democratization as follows:

1828–1926	First long wave of democratization
1922–42	First reverse wave
1943–62	Second, short wave of democratization
1958–75	Second reverse wave
1974–	Third wave of democratization

Huntington places Jamaica and Trinidad and Tobago in the period starting in the second wave, owing to their attainment of independence in 1962. He places Guyana in the second wave and also the second reverse wave, which he reserves for those countries that enter non-democratic phases after initially being democratic.

However, the applicability of Huntington's theory about waves of democratization excludes many countries in the Commonwealth Caribbean. He recognizes the 'decolonization pattern' as a central piece of his theory, but he uses the argument of size to eliminate many island nations from his analysis. According to him:

> A democratic country imposes democratic institutions on its colonies. The colony becomes independent and, unlike most former colonies, successfully maintains its democratic institutions. Papua New Guinea was one third wave case. As Myron Weiner has pointed out, this pattern pertains primarily to former British colonies, most of which became independent in the second wave. Those left to become independent and democratic in the third wave were mostly small and mostly insular. They included Antigua and Barbuda, Belize, Dominica, Kiribati, Saint Christopher – Nevis, Saint Lucia, Saint Vincent and the Grenadines, Solomon Islands, Tuvalu, and Vanuatu. With the possible exception of a very few remaining colonies (e.g. Hong Kong [as was so at the time this was written], Gibraltar, the Falklands), these countries are the last legacy of the British Empire to democratization. Because of their small size they are, unless stated to the contrary, excluded from analyses of third wave countries in this study.[14]

This approach by Huntington represents a major deficiency in his methodology, as his findings about the third wave of democracy, as he calls it, would have been considerably strengthened if he had not engaged in such a deliberate omission. By eliminating Antigua and Barbuda, Belize, Dominica, St Kitts–Nevis, St Lucia, and St Vincent and the Grenadines, he has left a void in the analysis of democracy (separate and apart from his own findings) in the Commonwealth Caribbean that must now be challenged.

Additionally, it should be noted that Huntington treats Grenada as if it were a country that had a communist regime in power all along and that it experienced democratization during the third wave of democracy that he identifies as having started in 1974. Furthermore, his theory about Grenada is that it only experienced democracy as a result of violent external intervention during the third wave. According to him, 'Violent external intervention produced democracy in several cases in the second wave and in Grenada and Panama in the third wave.'[15]

In addressing the need to challenge Huntington's theory in relation to the Commonwealth Caribbean, it is important to recognize the distinction between those states that were granted associated statehood in 1967 and subsequently determined their own termination of association with Great Britain as opposed to those states that negotiated their independence with Great Britain.

There is a qualitative difference between the associated statehood that was granted to Grenada, St Vincent and the Grenadines, St Lucia, Dominica, Antigua and Barbuda, and the then St Kitts–Nevis–Anguilla in 1967 when compared to the manner in which Jamaica, Trinidad and Tobago, Guyana, Barbados, the Bahamas and Belize attained their independence.

The fundamental difference can be measured by the way in which the Colonial Laws Validity Act 1865[16] was applied in the final stage before independence. Associated statehood saw the removal of the Colonial Laws Validity Act 1865 from applicability to the parliaments of those states that had this new status conferred upon them. With it went the doctrine of repugnancy, and these legislatures enjoyed a facility that other legislatures did not enjoy at a similar stage in their advance to full independence, that is, the right to enact legislation that could be repugnant to British law.

Huntington's failure to include the large majority of Commonwealth Caribbean states in his analysis about waves of democratization in the world does not mean that his theory is not applicable to the region. He also established criteria by which the consolidation of democracy in any country can be measured, and for that he offers a particular test.

The Commonwealth Caribbean has represented a virtual oasis of political stability when compared to other emerging democracies in Africa, Asia and Central and South America. Apart from political abuses in Guyana under the Forbes Burnham regime (1964–83) and the overthrow of constitutional government in Grenada by Maurice Bishop (1979), there have not been any other serious challenges to the political order in the region and, indeed, the region has largely fitted into the waves of democratization that Huntington discussed in his 1991 book.

However, the need to adjust his lack of theoretical application to the majority of Commonwealth Caribbean countries does not diminish the value of his theory as much as it represents an affront to the issue of small size as being valuable or relevant to political analysis.

In spite of this, his development of a test to measure the consolidation of democracy by means of what he calls 'the two-turnover test' is a useful yardstick by which to test Commonwealth Caribbean democracies.

The two-turnover test

According to Huntington:

> By this test, a democracy may be viewed as consolidated if the party or group that takes power in the initial election at the time of transition loses a subsequent election and turns over power to those election winners, and if those election winners then peacefully turn over power to the winners of a later election. Selecting rulers through elections is the heart of democracy, and democracy is real only if rulers are willing to give up power as a result of elections.[17]

The clear implication of Huntington's theory is that one party that has power must be able to regain it peacefully after losing it peacefully for democracy to be consolidated.

He goes on further to say:

> A second turnover shows two things. First, two major groups of political leaders in the society are sufficiently committed to democracy to surrender office and power after losing an election. Second, both elites and publics are operating within the democratic system; when things go wrong, you change the rulers, not the regime. Two turnovers is a tough test of democracy. The United States did not clearly meet it until the Jacksonian Democrats surrendered office to the Whigs in 1840.[18]

In the post-independence era in the Commonwealth Caribbean, almost all of the independent states have experienced two turnovers of government based on different political majorities up to the end of 2010.

However, two countries in the Commonwealth Caribbean have yet to experience the two-turnover test as of 2010, namely Antigua and Barbuda and the Co-operative Republic of Guyana. In both cases there has been political change from one party to another since independence, but there has been no political change-back or even change to another political force.

Given the analysis that was offered earlier about the stages of advance to full independence, a debate might arise about the timing of the starting point to be used in this two-turnover test analysis in the Commonwealth Caribbean. Should the analysis begin with the first general election after the attainment of independence? Or should the analysis begin with the last general election before the attainment of independence?

Given the psychology of the independence movement in the countries of the Commonwealth Caribbean, the last election before the attainment of independence was of tremendous significance owing to the fact that the winner was expected to become the first ruling political directorate when the transition from colonial or semi-colonial status to independence took place. There was not going to be any other means by which to test the validity or legitimacy of a political party that formed the government at the time of independence.

The democratization process existed before independence in all of the Commonwealth Caribbean countries by virtue of the fact that they all evolved as part of a wider trend of British colonial constitutional graduation that resulted in full independence on negotiated or self-determined agendas. What would have discounted the value of this democratization process was the fact that the levels of representation and responsibility accorded to these former colonies would have varied over time.

In essence, the Commonwealth Caribbean had its own waves of democratization in the twentieth century in the form of its evolution to fully responsible status at independence. Perhaps it is significant that the measurement of that process by Huntington tends to coincide with the waves outlined by him in terms of when independence came to the region.

What was not measured by him was the very evolution to independence itself and the stages of democracy that emerged during the last century. That kind of approach represents a different form of measurement along a path from Crown colony status to fully responsible status. Along the way, these colonies developed representative and responsible government on a pathway to independence.

The Commonwealth Caribbean and the two-turnover test

For purposes of applying the two-turnover test to the Commonwealth Caribbean up to the end of 2010, the last general election before the attainment of independence would mark the starting point for this analysis as follows:

- Antigua and Barbuda – yet to achieve the two-turnover test.
- The Bahamas – two-turnover test achieved in 2002 with the return to power of the PLP.
- Barbados – two-turnover test achieved in 1986 with the return to power of the DLP.
- Belize – two-turnover test achieved in 1998 with the return to power of the PUP.
- Dominica – two-turnover test achieved in 1995 when the UWP came to power.
- Grenada – two-turnover test achieved in 1990 when the NDC attained power. However, if the measurement is commenced after the resumption of constitutional government in 1984 following the interruption of constitutional government during the period 1979–83, then it may be argued that the two-turnover test was achieved when the NNP returned to power in 1995.
- Guyana – yet to achieve the two-turnover test.

- Jamaica – two-turnover test achieved in 1980 with the return of the JLP to power.
- St Kitts–Nevis – two-turnover test achieved in 1995 with the return of the SKLP to power.
- St Lucia – two-turnover test achieved in 1982 with the return of the UWP to power.
- St Vincent and the Grenadines – two-turnover test achieved in 2001 when the ULP captured power.
- Trinidad and Tobago – two-turnover test achieved in 1995 when the UNC/NAR coalition came to power.

Constitutional reform

Across the region, there are two undercurrents that resonate among governments in the public domain – one is a desire for regional unity and the other is a desire for an examination of the constitutional arrangements that govern these societies.

They are intertwined in many respects. Accomplishing true regional integration will require constitutional amendments that must be driven by compromise and consensus. The Commonwealth Caribbean systems of government are designed to operate on an adversarial basis of division, that is, a government and an opposition.

This is the fundamental premise of the Westminster–Whitehall tradition. It has operated in the United Kingdom with great success because of the fact that it evolved together with British society so that no formal, written, codified constitution is required for its general working on a day-to-day basis.

The Opposition in the British political system is considered to be the alternative government, and there is common allegiance to the Crown so that Her Majesty's Government and Her Majesty's Loyal Opposition function on the basis of the potential for the reversal of roles. The Leader of the Opposition is made a member of Her Majesty's Privy Council and is allowed briefings on privy councillor terms in certain situations together with ministers of the Crown.

In Commonwealth Caribbean systems of government, the opposition is usually regarded as the outcast of the system, and there is little inclusion, so that when oppositions do become governments they tend to offer payback to their previous opponents by denying that which they too were denied.

If the Commonwealth Caribbean is to make any fundamental advance on the issue of regional unity, it will have to embrace constitutional reform. In order to overcome the hurdles of entrenched provisions in its written constitutions, there will have to be consensus and compromise.

Consensus will be required for the attainment of special majorities for bills seeking to amend these constitutions in the legislatures as well as in the referenda that some countries will require. Compromise is the tool that will bring this consensus.

Governments in the region cannot afford to underestimate their systems of government. The winner-take-all approach may be fine on the local front, but it provides too many contradictions on the regional front. The Commonwealth Caribbean does not have political systems that encourage reaching across the aisles for consensus. Additionally, that approach is not ingrained in the political culture of the region.

Regional unity is not going to get the political support that it requires if opposition parties (and by extension their supporters) are excluded from the national and Caribbean Community (CARICOM) stages. They are going to try to bring down their governments in the hope that they can return to power and the vicious cycle will continue, because that is what the system allows them now and nothing else.

The best example of this was the defeat of the Constitution Bill 2009 in St Vincent and the Grenadines on 25 November 2009 at the constitutionally required referendum. The requirement of a two-thirds majority among the electorate is likely to be a steep hurdle that will deny Vincentians the opportunity to change their constitution for generations to come. The adversarial government–opposition dichotomy will be the key suppressant to the achievement of such a high level of consensus among the population.

Concomitantly, one must also consider the views of the famous St Lucian Nobel laureate Sir Arthur Lewis in his work *Politics in West Africa*: 'to exclude the losing groups from participation in decision-making clearly violates the primary meaning of democracy'.[19]

There is much to agree with in this statement. Lewis may have been writing about West Africa, but as a theorist of democracy he was an advocate of the consensual rather than the majoritarian model.

Compromise and consensus will then become a reality. That is a missing ingredient from the movement for regional unity and constitutional reform. Perhaps the political changes that have to be made may help to unite the people of the region by building consensus internally. That may only come if the Commonwealth Caribbean political leaders on all sides adopt the spirit of Lewis's meaning of democracy.

The issue of small size may have diminished the value of measuring the overall contribution of the Commonwealth Caribbean to the movement for democracy on a global scale. However, as a collection of islands and territories, the Commonwealth Caribbean represents an oasis of democracy that stands out if it were to be counted.

Huntington has made a case for diminution and may have erroneously categorized the region as being of little importance to the measurement of democracy. Perhaps the evolution of Westminster-style democracy has contributed to this oasis effect, yet it must be noted that there is an emerging movement to engage in processes of reform which will represent the next stage in the evolution of democracy in this region.

Notes

1 S. A. de Smith (1964) *The Commonwealth and Its Constitutions*, pp. 77–8 (London: Stevens and Sons).

2   A. Burns (1966) *Parliament as an Export* (London: George Allen & Unwin).

3   A. F. Madden (1979) 'Not for export': The Westminster model of government and British colonial practice, *Journal of Imperial and Commonwealth History*, 8 (1), pp. 10–29.

4   Ibid., p. 24.

5   Ibid., p. 24.

6   L. Wolf-Phillips (1984) A long look at the British constitution, *Parliamentary Affairs*, 37 (4), pp. 385–402.

7   E. Williams (1955) *Constitution Reform in Trinidad and Tobago*, Public Affairs Pamphlet No. 2, p. 23 (Port-of-Spain, Trinidad: Teachers' Educational and Cultural Association).

8   Guyana, Act No. 2/1980.

9   Laws of Trinidad and Tobago, c. 1:01, Schedule.

10   SI 1962/No. 1875, Schedule.

11   Hamid Ghany (1994) The creation of legislative institutions in the Commonwealth Caribbean: The myth of the transfer of the Westminster model, *Congressional Studies Journal*, January, 2 (1), pp. 34–49.

12   A. Lijphart (1999) *Patterns of Democracy* (New Haven, CT and London: Yale University Press).

13   S. Huntington (1991) *The Third Wave: Democratization in the Late Twentieth Century* (Norman and London: University of Oklahoma Press).

14   Ibid., p. 43.

15   Ibid., p. 207.

16   UK Laws, 28 & 29 Vict., c. 63.

17   Huntington (1991), pp. 266–7.

18   Ibid., p. 267.

19   A. Lewis (1965) *Politics in West Africa*, pp. 64–5 (London: George Allen & Unwin).

4 Pacific islands

Legislatures in the Pacific islands

Dag Anckar

Introduction

Throughout the Pacific Ocean are widely scattered a number of small states and territories. They are usually divided into three cultural and geographical categories, namely Melanesia, Micronesia and Polynesia, which represent somewhat differing social structures, societal ideologies and ethnic homogeneities (e.g. Ghai 1988a, 2–3; Henningham 1995, 1–15). Most states in these categories are reviewed in this study: of the 16 present members of the Pacific Islands Forum, which is an intergovernmental organization to promote cooperation between the countries of the Pacific Ocean and represent their interests, no fewer than 12 are included. Outside remain Australia, Papua New Guinea and New Zealand, which are oversized in terms of the purpose of the study. The associate members since 2006 of New Caledonia and French Polynesia are likewise excluded. Also excluded is Fiji. The membership of Fiji in the Pacific Islands Forum has been suspended since 2009, owing to the inability of the country to provide for free and fair elections and for human rights and democracy. Ethnic rivalry triggering a military coup in 1987, the repute of the country was to some extent restored by the introduction in 1997 of a democratic constitution. However, violent coups again took place in 2000 and in 2006 which deposed the democratically elected government and installed a military-appointed administration (e.g. Lal 2007), and in 2009 the Fiji constitution was suspended. Included, then, in this study are the following Pacific microstates and territories: the Cook Islands, Kiribati, the Marshall Islands, the Federated States of Micronesia (Micronesia), Nauru, Niue, Palau, Samoa, the Solomon Islands, Tonga, Tuvalu and Vanuatu.

Table 4.1 reports for each of the countries that are studied some relevant background data; these data are about the present population size, the independence year, the colonial history and the political regime of the countries. The table also assigns each case a percentage value which is called 'democracy rating'. This percentage is a measure of the frequency by which the state in question has been rated by the Freedom House organization as democratic in the monitoring of the progress and decline of political rights and civil liberties in the nations of the world and in related territories (Freedom in the world: Comparative and historical data). The observation period covers the time span from independence up to 2007; because of the lack of availability of data, however, events before 1972 have not been recorded. Following the authoritative view that the 'Free' rating in the Freedom House survey is the best available empirical indicator of liberal democracy (Diamond 1996, 24), cases rated by Freedom House as 'Free' are classified here to be democratic. To give an example: a state which is independent in, say, 1975, has been ranked by Freedom House each year in the time span 1976–2007, which adds up to 32 classifications. If they have all been in the 'Free' category, the democracy rating of this state is 100. If the state has not once during the 32 years of classification been ranked in the 'Free' category, the democracy rating is of course 0. And if the state is ranked in the 'Free' category, say, 14 times out of 32, the resulting percentage calculation gives this state a democracy rating of 44.

The compilations in Table 4.1 invite some comments on frequencies and preponderances. First, almost all of the 12 cases are independent states. The two exceptions are the Cook Islands and Niue, which are not in a formal sense fully independent, both having internal self-government in free association and common citizenship with New Zealand. They are, however, free to conduct a policy of their own and have their own democratic institutions. Second, all cases are below the microstate threshold of 1 million people, and all with the exception of the Solomon Islands are below the 500,000 ceiling; furthermore, five of the cases have populations of 20,000 people or fewer. This chapter, then, is indeed about small members of the international community. This, by the way, as small units are often left outside data banks and similar research undertakings (Anckar 1998, 282–3), somewhat hampers efforts at reporting and cultivating analytical materials. For instance, covering 158 countries and reporting for each country a most interesting legislative powers survey, a recent and authoritative handbook of national legislatures deals with every country in the world that had a population of a half-million or more as of 2000 (Fish and Kroenig 2009, 4). This means that almost all cases

Table 4.1 The small Pacific island states: selected background data

Country	Population ('000)	Independence	Colonial power	Democracy rating	Regime
Cook Islands	11	No	New Zealand	100	PD
Kiribati	100	1979	Britain	100	PD
Marshall Islands	67	1991	United States	100	PD
Micronesia	106	1991	United States	100	PRD
Nauru	9	1968	Britain	100	PD
Niue	1	No	New Zealand	100	PD
Palau	20	1994	United States	100	PRD
Samoa	193	1962	Britain	54	PD
Solomon Islands	571	1978	Britain	73	PD
Tonga	105	1875	None	0	M
Tuvalu	10	1978	Britain	100	PD
Vanuatu	224	1980	Condominium	74	PD

Key: Regime – PD = parliamentary democracy; PRD = presidential democracy; M = monarchy.

in this study remain outside the scope of the handbook. Third, with the exception of the Kingdom of Tonga, which was never fully colonized (Campbell 1992, 112–13), all cases have a colonial history, which is in most cases about British rule. The Marshall Islands, Micronesia and Palau are independent from US rule, and the Cook Islands and Niue, as already mentioned, are somewhat special cases, being tied themselves to a former British colony. Vanuatu is likewise a special case, freed from a condominium status as a joint British–French colony (Trease 1995).

As is evident from the democracy ratings, two-thirds of the cases are always classified by Freedom House to be 'Free' nations; they are therefore in a category of full-fledged democracies. However, of these cases, because of economic decline, Nauru has lately acquired most of the characteristics of a failed state (Connell 2006). Concerning the Solomon Islands, violent anarchy and subsequent military intervention in recent times (Dinnen and Firth 2008) have affected negatively the democracy rankings since 2000. The country was classified by Freedom House as a democracy during the years 1978–2000 and has thereafter been regarded as a non-democracy. The odd one out in this regard is the Kingdom of Tonga, which is one of a handful of microstates in the world that are non-democracies of long standing (Anckar 2010).

Finally, in terms of political regime, no fewer than 9 out of the 12 cases represent a parliamentary form of government. The former US territories of Micronesia and Palau have provided for a system of government which is close to the US presidential model, and Tonga represents monarchy rule. In sum, then, this chapter is in the main about legislatures in a handful of small and very small parliamentary democracies, independent from British or semi-British rule, with immaculate or very good democracy records.

Featuring Pacific legislatures

Table 4.2 summarizes some central features that relate to the composition and structure of the Pacific legislatures. Given that similarities open the door for at least tentative conclusions that pertain to an impact of small size, the ideal finding would be one that pictures a similarity pattern. In fact, the real finding comes rather close to such an ideal configuration. While there are obvious variations between the countries in terms of the length of the legislative mandate, the remaining features display similarities and therefore stand out as springboards for interpretations that picture the significance of the size factor. Four specific comments are called for:

1   A striking similarity appears when looking at the election systems by means of which legislatures are composed. Reflecting colonial heritages, the overwhelming majority of the cases have adopted straightforward or modified versions of plurality voting, several operating pure first-past-the-post systems, and Kiribati operating a two-round system (Fraenkel 2008, 47). By way of contrast Nauru has adopted a system of preferential voting and has, in consequence, put in place a quite unique electoral system (Reilly and

Table 4.2 Legislatures in the small Pacific island states: selected characteristics

Country	Plural electoral system?	Term	Seats	Unicameralism?	Special representation?
Cook Islands	Yes	5 years	24+14	Modified	No
Kiribati	Modified	4 years	46	Yes	Yes
Marshall Islands	Yes	4 years	33+12	Modified	No
Micronesia	Yes	2–4 years	14	Yes	No
Nauru	No	3 years	18	Yes	No
Niue	Yes	3 years	20	Yes	Yes
Palau	Yes	4 years	16+13	No	No
Samoa	Yes	5 years	49	Yes	Yes
Solomon Islands	Yes	4 years	50	Yes	No
Tonga	Yes	4 years	28	Yes	Yes
Tuvalu	Yes	4 years	15	Yes	No
Vanuatu	No	4 years	54+	Modified	No

Gratschew 2001, 699), while Vanuatu incorporates an element of proportional representation, introduced to ensure fair representation of different groups and opinions (Morgan 2008, 132) and perhaps mainly to protect minority francophone interests (Trease 2005). The case of Tonga is unique, as the legislature includes hereditary members, nominated members and elected members, the aristocracy of nobles nominating members, government members being members of parliament ex officio, and the people electing representatives under a plurality system which is applied in constituencies of different size (Campbell 2001, 810–15).

2   In regard to legislature structure, unicameralism is the rule, whereas bicameralism is the exception. In fact, federal Palau is the only case that maintains bicameralism proper. The Federated States of Micronesia have established a quite specific unicameral variety: to the unicameral federal legislature are elected two types of senators, namely senators-at-large, elected one for each of the four states for a term of four years, and regular senators, elected for a term of two years in constituencies of approximately equal population size (Somoza 2001, 634). The differing principles of representation reflecting also in the parliamentary voting procedure, it is a valid comment that Micronesia has perhaps 'managed to avoid bicameralism only at the expense of other rigidities and complexities' (Ghai 1988b, 63). In still some other places, mirroring the role traditional leadership still plays in Pacific communities, rudimentary forms of bicameralism may be found. The Parliament of the Marshall Islands has an upper house, the Council of Iroij, which is composed of 12 traditional leaders and has the power to request consideration of any bill that affects traditional practices or land rights (Carucci 1997, 199). A somewhat similar arrangement may be found in the Cook Islands, where there is a House of Ariki, composed of hereditary chiefs, which has a purely advisory role (Hassall 2001, 622), and in Vanuatu, where the government is advised on

matters of culture and language by a National Council of Chiefs (Lindstrom 1997, 214–17).

3   There are very few instances of special representation. As noted in Introduction II, diminutive Niue has in addition to the 14 members of the Niue Legislative Assembly, who are elected from village communities, six common roll seats for a constituency that represents the entire country. The other cases of special representation are all somewhat unusual and perhaps not very significant. In Samoa, two out of 49 members of the legislature are chosen by non-Samoans on separate electoral rolls (So'o 2001, 782–3), and in Kiribati there is one appointed member from the Banaban community on Rabi Island in Fiji. Before the independence of Kiribati in 1979 the entire population of Banaba was resettled to Fiji to make way for mining operations. Although now citizens of Fiji, the Banabans retained through their ownership of Banaban land an interest in the state of Kiribati, which is duly recognized in the Kiribati electoral order (Brechtefeld 1993, 43). The quite specific arrangement in Tonga, providing for representation in Parliament of the government and the nobles, has already been mentioned. Apropos of special representation, the Pacific has the doubtful reputation of being the region in the world with the lowest number of women in Parliament. As of 2010, of the 10 independent Pacific island countries that are reviewed here, five had no women in the national parliament, whereas there was one woman parliamentarian in each of two parliaments, two women in each of another two parliaments, and four women in Fono, the legislative assembly of Samoa (Women in parliaments: World classification). This less than satisfying gender balance is, however, not to be conceptualized as a consequence of small size. It is rather a matter of a range of cultural barriers to women's participation in higher levels of decision-making, with only a few women being nominated for positions and only a few of the nominated being elected. Several measures have been discussed in the region to introduce a better balance, the measures pertaining to electoral reform and even to developing legislation to provide seats in national parliaments that are reserved for women.

4   In regard to legislature size, the idea that small states are alike does not seem to get much support, as some small states have much smaller legislatures than other small states. Whereas, for instance, Tuvalu and Nauru have legislature memberships of 15 and 18 seats respectively, the corresponding figures for the Solomon Islands and Vanuatu are 50 and 54 respectively. When, however, the idea of size thresholds within smallness is introduced and controlled for, the picture changes significantly, and size appears, after all, to make a difference. The rank correlation between population size and legislature size is in fact as high as 0.84, which means that very small states tend to have very small legislatures while somewhat larger units tend to have somewhat larger legislatures. In conclusion, then, size appears to make a difference, albeit that this difference is not between small and not-small, but between diminutive and small.

Legislative frameworks

A concluding statement from a roundtable meeting in 2002 of heads of government of Pacific island countries, organized to ward off challenges to democracy and governance in the region, emphasized, among other things, that measures ought to be enacted to enhance the stability of governments (Commonwealth Secretariat). In itself, this concern does not correspond well to theory. The impact of size variation on stability is namely through fragmentation, and it certainly makes sense to believe that the relation is in the direction of fragmentation following from larger size. This is because the threshold to dissent and thus to underpin and contribute to instability may be expected to be lower in larger polities (Dahl and Tufte 1973, 90–91). When and if this is true, the expectation is that small size links to a low degree of fragmentation and thereby to stability, whereas larger size links to a higher degree of fragmentation and thereby to instability.

And indeed, while common and current, the concern about Pacific instability is perhaps to some extent an exaggeration. In fact, it would appear from cursory examinations of governmental practice that several Pacific cases like the Cook Islands, Kiribati, the Marshall Islands, Niue and Samoa stand out as reasonably stable units. On the other hand, however, it cannot be denied that other Pacific entities stand out as prominent instability cases which challenge the view that small leads to stability and legislative efficiency. For instance, it has been said about the Solomon Islands that, 'With fluid party affiliations and a significant number of independent MPs, no-confidence motions have become a potent weapon in the continuous struggle for power' (Steeves 2001, 795). This concern for a lack of political efficiency is echoed by another observer, emphasizing that frequent floor-crossings illustrate 'the porous nature of the boundary between the Opposition and Government, and the fact that Solomon Island politicians, generally, have weak loyalties to parties' (Kabutaulaka 2008, 104). Consequently, according to the same source, 'political allegiances change regularly and political instability is endemic' (Kabutaulaka 2008, 104). Nauru certainly is in the same camp. According to one count, between 1968 and 2000 there were no fewer than 16 changes of government in Nauru; most of these changes took place on the floor of Parliament as a result of successful no-confidence motions. The figures certainly bear witness to an apparent and chronic instability of Nauruan parliamentary life (Reilly and Gratschew 2001, 697–8). Furthermore, Vanuatu is an evident case of political instability to the extent that in the late 1990s it 'appeared to be on the brink of a serious breakdown of law and order' (Morgan 2008, 129). Indeed, observers find it likely that Vanuatu will undergo further political instability, as 'the formulation of policy will be subjected to further strains as the political manoeuvring in Parliament is intensified by the reliance on numerous parties to form government' (Morgan 2008, 139).

The thought is near at hand that an overall reduction of Pacific political instability requires the sustenance of larger and stronger political parties. Differences between countries and cultures in the region notwithstanding, party politics still remains in several places undeveloped and fragmentary, and the scholarly literature on Pacific politics is abundant with observations that emphasize that parties are shifting parliamentary factions rather than objects of voter choice, that people vote for candidates on the basis of performance rather than party politics, and that politics are based on personalities and island affiliations rather than ideologies (e.g. Anckar and Anckar 2000; Larmour 2005; Rich 2008). In theory at least, this is devastating for government stability, which requires a solid and dependable party system to organize and structure the interplay between government and opposition, and to subdue and discipline more occasional cleavages as well as solidarities. Still, there is much to the general observation that Third World party competition may fail to advance scrutiny of the executive (Pinkney 2004, 451–2), and evidence also from the Pacific suggests that the sheer existence of a working party system is in itself no guarantee for the origin of stability and legislature dominance. Following the rise of parties and groups in Samoa since the 1979 elections and aiming at consolidating the party system, an electoral amendment in 1995 introduced party identification of candidates, and today most constituencies vote along party lines in parliamentary elections (So'o 2001, 782). However, although the party system is becoming entrenched, according to findings, it still remains a problem in the legislative politics of the country that the parliament feels powerless to control the executive (So'o 2008, 204).

Summary

All small Pacific island states are not freed from British rule, but most of them are, directly or indirectly, and they testify to the prevalence of Westminster-style systems in former British colonies. Admittedly, the Westminster adherence is less than perfect. Research on the compliance of former small British colonies with Westminster criteria in fact suggests that Caribbean nations are somewhat closer to Westminster standards than are non-Caribbean nations (Anckar 2007, 649–50), and separate cases like Kiribati, the Solomon Islands and Vanuatu deviate in important aspects from Westminster rule proper. In short, therefore, more is in the Pacific picture than straightforward diffusion only. Still, a general summing-up observation is that a Westminster-styled metropolitan conception of the legislature has been introduced and maintained in the region. Revolving around varieties of plural voting, the method for legislature recruitment clearly satisfies a Westminster criterion; parliamentary democracy is the dominating regime form; while uni-cameralism is the norm, institutional albeit weak manifestations of traditional leadership bear some resemblance to the aristocratic-styled bicameralism that characterizes the British House of Lords. Furthermore, the states adhere closely to the Westminster yardstick of parliamentary sovereignty, meaning that power is concentrated in parliament, the democratic form dissociating from devices like the referendum, popular initiative and recall. True, several Pacific states have introduced the constitutional referendum, but this particular use of a direct democracy is a poor test case, as the device is in wide use among nations with written constitutions and rather belongs in a compartment of routine and constitutional convention. As a rule, the small countries of the world are as disinterested as large countries, or even more so, in more differentiated instruments of direct democracy (Anckar 2004, 387–8); this disinterest is evident in the Pacific context as well. One observation in the literature is that the prevalence of Westminster-style systems in former British colonies is a product of forced diffusion (Peters 1998, 4); while the extent to which the diffusion has really been forced in the Pacific still needs to be clarified in research, the prevalence in itself is certainly there.

References

Anckar, D. (1998) Mikrostater som företeelser och forskningsobjekt, *Politiikka*, 40 (4), pp. 273–85.

Anckar, D. (2004) Direct democracy in microstates and small island states, *World Development*, 32 (2), pp. 379–90.

Anckar, D. (2007) Westminster Lilliputs? Parliaments in former small British colonies, *Parliamentary Affairs*, 60 (4), pp. 637–54.

Anckar, D. (2010) Undemocratic miniatures: Cases and patterns, *International Journal of Politics and Good Governance*, 1 (1.2), pp. 1–22.

Anckar, D. and Anckar, C. (2000) Democracies without parties, *Comparative Political Studies*, 33 (2), pp. 225–47.

Brechtefeld, N. (1993) The electoral system, in H. van Trease (ed.), *Atoll Politics: The Republic of Kiribati*, pp. 42–7 (Christchurch, New Zealand: Macmillan Brown Centre for Pacific Studies, University of Canterbury).

Campbell, I. C. (1992) *Island Kingdom: Tonga Ancient and Modern* (Christchurch, New Zealand: Canterbury University Press).

Campbell, I. C. (2001) Tonga, in D. Nohlen, F. Grotz and C. Hartmann (eds), *Elections in Asia and the Pacific: A Data Handbook*, pp. 809–22 (Oxford: Oxford University Press).

Carucci, L. M. (1997) Irooj Ro Ad: Measures of chiefly ideology and practice in the Marshall Islands, in G. M. White and L. Lindstrom (eds), *Chiefs Today: Traditional Pacific Leadership and the Postcolonial State*, pp. 197–210 (Stanford, CA: Stanford University Press).

Commonwealth Secretariat, Roundtable of heads of government of Commonwealth Pacific island countries, accessed 10 July 2010, http://www.thecommonwealth.org/press/31555/34582/34969/roundtable_of_heads_of_government.

Connell, J. (2006) Nauru: The first failed Pacific state?, *The Round Table*, 383, pp. 47–63.

Dahl, R. A. and Tufte, E. (1973) *Size and Democracy* (Stanford, CA: Stanford University Press).

Diamond, L. (1996) Is the third wave over?, *Journal of Democracy*, 7 (3), pp. 20–37.

Dinnen, S. and Firth, S. (eds) (2008) *Politics and State Building in Solomon Islands* (Canberra: ANU E Press).

Fish, M. S. and Kroenig, M. (2009) *The Handbook of National Legislatures: A Global Survey* (Cambridge: Cambridge University Press).

Fraenkel, J. (2008) Political consequences of Pacific island electoral laws, in R. Rich, L. Hambly and M. G. Morgan (eds), *Political Parties in the Pacific Islands*, pp. 43–67 (Canberra: ANU E Press).

Freedom in the world: Comparative and historical data, accessed 10 July 2010, http://www.freedomhouse.org/template.cfm?page=1.

Ghai, Y. (1988a) Constitution making and decolonisation, in Y. Ghai (ed.), *Law, Politics and Government in the Pacific Island States*, pp. 1–53 (Suva, Fiji: Institute of Pacific Studies, University of the South Pacific).

Ghai, Y. (1988b) Systems of government – I, in Y. Ghai (ed.), *Law, Politics and Government in the Pacific Island States*, pp. 54–75 (Suva, Fiji: Institute of Pacific Studies, University of the South Pacific).

Hassall, G. (2001) Cook Islands, in D. Nohlen, F. Grotz and C. Hartmann (eds), *Elections in Asia and the Pacific: A Data Handbook*, pp. 621–32 (Oxford: Oxford University Press).

Henningham, S. (1995) *The Pacific Island States* (New York: St Martin's Press).

Kabutaulaka, T. T. (2008) Parties, constitutional engineering and governance in the Solomon Islands, in R. Rich, L. Hambly and M. G. Morgan (eds), *Political Parties in the Pacific Islands*, pp. 103–16 (Canberra: ANU E Press).

Lal, B. V. (2007) 'Anxiety, uncertainty, and fear in our land': Fiji's road to military coup, 2006, *The Round Table*, 389, pp. 135–53.

Larmour, P. (2005) *Foreign Flowers* (Honolulu: University of Hawai'i Press).

Lindstrom, L. (1997) Chiefs in Vanuatu today, in G. M. White and L. Lindstrom (eds), *Chiefs Today: Traditional Pacific Leadership and the Postcolonial State*, pp. 211–28 (Stanford, CA: Stanford University Press).

Morgan, M. G. (2008) The origins and effects on party fragmentation in Vanuatu, in R. Rich, L. Hambly and M. G. Morgan (eds), *Political Parties in the Pacific Islands*, pp. 117–42 (Canberra: ANU E Press).

Peters, B. G. (1998) *Comparative Politics: Theory and Methods* (London: Macmillan).

Pinkney, R. (2004) Selling democracy abroad or rescuing it at home? The hazards of democracy promotion, *The Round Table*, 375, pp. 437–55.

Reilly, B. and Gratschew, M. (2001) Nauru, in D. Nohlen, F. Grotz and C. Hartmann (eds), *Elections in Asia and the Pacific: A Data Handbook*, pp. 697–704 (Oxford: Oxford University Press).

Rich, R. (2008) Analysing and categorizing political parties in the Pacific islands, in R. Rich, L. Hambly and M. G. Morgan (eds), *Political Parties in the Pacific Islands*, pp. 1–26 (Canberra: ANU E Press).

Somoza, A. (2001) Federated States of Micronesia, in D. Nohlen, F. Grotz and C. Hartmann (eds), *Elections in Asia and the Pacific: A Data Handbook*, pp. 633–42 (Oxford: Oxford University Press).

So'o, A. (2001) Samoa, in D. Nohlen, F. Grotz and C. Hartmann (eds), *Elections in Asia and the Pacific: A Data Handbook*, pp. 779–94 (Oxford: Oxford University Press).

So'o, A. (2008) The establishment and operation of Sämoa's political party system, in R. Rich, L. Hambly and M. G. Morgan (eds), *Political Parties in the Pacific Islands*, pp. 185–206 (Canberra: ANU E Press).

Steeves, J. S. (2001) Solomon Islands, in D. Nohlen, F. Grotz and C. Hartmann (eds), *Elections in Asia and the Pacific: A Data Handbook*, pp. 795–808 (Oxford: Oxford University Press).

Trease, H. van (1995) The colonial origins of Vanuatu politics, in H. van Trease (ed.), *Melanesian Politics: Stael Blong Vanuatu*, pp. 3–58 (Christchurch, New Zealand: Macmillan Brown Centre for Pacific Studies, University of Canterbury).

Trease, H. van (2005) The operation of the single non-transferable vote in Vanuatu, *Commonwealth and Comparative Politics*, 43 (3), pp. 296–332.

Women in parliaments: World classification, accessed 10 August 2010, http://www.ipu.org/wmn-e/classif.htm.

5   Lesotho

The legislature of Lesotho –
diminished in the context of
dependence

Susan Booysen

Introduction

The legislature of Lesotho has battled for political predominance in encounters that
have been distant from the conventional notions of 'asserting policy influence
over the executive' or 'holding the executive to account'. Its struggles for policy
influence have frequently been overshadowed by the efforts simply to gain
predominance over the military and assert itself alongside the monarchy. At their
fiercest, military interventions in civilian politics had led to the total suspension of
parliament and party politics. In other contests intra- and inter-party fissures have
frequently detracted from the effectiveness of the legislature.

In the years since the turning-point election of 1998 and subsequent electoral
reform that reshaped and repositioned the National Assembly, Lesotho can be
seen as being on a road to tentatively consolidating elective multipartyism. In this
context, the role of the legislature has been growing. However, the executive
remains by far the most dominant force in matters of policy and legislation.

Beyond the issues of standing and functions of the legislature and other
institutions of government, the role of the legislature is also largely determined by
the economic standing of the country.[1]

Lesotho is an extremely poor and indebted country, dependent on aid and the
good will of international donor organisations. Beyond the programmes that are
funded by, for example, the International Monetary Fund (IMF), World Bank (WB),
or United States and British government-related non-governmental organisations,
little policy occurs. Governance and financial management provisos have
accompanied international assistance operations. The interventions tend to empha-
sise soundness of state administration and policy-programme implementation,
rather than policy roles that the national legislature might fulfil.[2]

This chapter argues the case of a severely circumscribed and subject legislature,
operating in an impoverished, landlocked and mountainous country. The analysis
takes stock of the context of party political and legislative politics, as conditioned
by military and monarchical cross-permutations. The legislative-executive and
state-government configurations of the political institutions of the state in Lesotho
are profiled. The analysis follows through with trends in the National Assembly
elections and vacillating party political fortunes, all of which have a direct impact

on the Lesotho legislature and its role in politics and policy. As part of the explanation of the limited standing and impact of the legislature the argument positions Lesotho economically, in Southern African, international finance institution (IFI) and other international contexts.

Institutional configuration of the government of Lesotho

Lesotho is designated a 'constitutional hereditary monarchy' (Constitution of Lesotho 1993, articles 1, 2). The government of Lesotho is conventionally structured in its configuration of the relationship between the legislative and the executive. In the period since the eclipse of military domination of politics (see Kabemba 2003), traditional-monarchical and modern institutional arrangements have co-existed. The legislature comprises the National Assembly of 120 elected members, on the mixed member proportional (MMP) system, and the Senate (upper house) of 33 members, of which 22 are the 'principal chiefs'. This arrangement incorporates Lesotho's continuously strong system of traditional leadership into legislative operations (Tsikoane *et al.* 2007, pp. 21–2).

Executive power in Lesotho is three-pronged, with the King as constitutional monarch and head of state. The King is designated by the College of Chiefs, in accordance with the customary law of Lesotho (Constitution of Lesotho 1993, articles 44, 45, 91). Such designations take place upon the death of a predecessor or in the event of a vacancy in that office (Tsikoane *et al.* 2007, p. 39). The 15-member Council of State assists the King in his national duties. The council consists primarily of key members of state structures, such as the Prime Minister, the Speaker of the National Assembly, two judges appointed on the advice of the Chief Justice, an attorney-general, a commander of the armed forces, a principal chief nominated by the College of Chiefs, the leaders of the two largest opposition parties, and three experts appointed on the advice of the Prime Minister and a lawyer appointed by the Law Society (Constitution of Lesotho 1993, article 95(2)).

The King at the advice of the Council of State appoints the Prime Minister – a member of parliament who is the leader of the majority party in the National Assembly, or the leader of a coalition of parties that constitutes the majority and commands the requisite support of the house. The King appoints the Cabinet ministers, on advice from the Prime Minister, from the ranks of the National Assembly or the Senate. The Cabinet also advises the King.

Evolution of legislative and policy-making institutions

Lesotho's chequered history through colonial government, into times of political independence, saw continuous alterations in the composition of and participation in the national 'legislatures' or their approximate antecedents. A brief review of main trends illuminates the contemporary standing of the legislature.

Basotholand (Lesotho's preceding designation) was annexed by the British in 1868, but never became a protectorate. Simultaneously, its political evolution remained intermingled with that of South Africa. At one time the British incorporated it into the Cape Colony (one of the four areas that would later constitute the Union of South Africa, thereafter the Republic of South Africa). The British-determined legislative institutions were anchored in traditional-monarchical arrangements. The British ruled through the paramount chief (the King) and the chiefs. The monarchy gradually declined in influence (but still retains a central position). The Basotholand Council, predecessor to the current National Assembly, evolved in composition through the late nineteenth century until 1949, when Basotholand was divided into nine administrative districts that came with their associated chiefs as representatives.

The executive institutions in general prevailed, across historical periods. Colonial powers leant on the Basotholand traditional and monarchical powers, and the declining monarchical powers in turn leant on the military and select political powers to constitute the executives that overpowered the legislative institutions. Their activities were also articulated in party politics, for example in the formation of the Marematlou Party in 1957, when royalists left the Basotholand Congress Party (BCP; it later became the Marematlou Freedom Party – MFP). In 1958, the Basotholand National Party (BNP) was formed by chiefs and teachers, with Chief Leabua Jonathan, a member of the National Council, also acting as regent to the King (see Lodge *et al.* 2002).

This system was partially modernised in 1959/60 in the form of the Basotholand National Council, which differed from the preceding Basotholand Council, but which saw the continuation of British executive power.[3] Its 80 members formed the legislature. Its membership was constituted though a combination of nomination and indirect election (the latter through electoral colleges formed in terms of district councils). The BCP was by far dominant, followed by the MFP, BNP and independents. The BCP's role was one of 'official opposition', and there was agitation for independence. Independence talks started in 1962. By 1965 there was a new constitution that included self-government, a Westminster-style party political system and a bicameral legislature. Independence followed in 1966.

The 60 members of the National Assembly were to be elected in single-member constituencies. The Prime Minister was the new executive leader of government. King Moshoeshoe II became the non-executive head of state of the Kingdom of Lesotho, signalling the subjugation of monarchical to civilian politics, yet not taking account of the rise of the military. The Prime Minister was Leabua Jonathan, who had the power to sign legislation should the King refuse to do so. The King's executive powers were dramatically restrained when in 1966 he was placed under house arrest in order to prevent his interference in politics (Tsikoane *et al.* 2007, 92).

Party politics and the surge for legislative representation and predominance

Lesotho's set of post-colonial executive-legislative institutions remains relatively unconsolidated. Monarchical infusions were continuous, albeit with a general decline being manifested. The military presences in the post-colonial time were more tangible, especially in the military's alignments with political parties and imposition of one-party rule. In a complex series of alliances and counter-alliances, the military, monarchy, governing party and opposition parties aligned to constitute multiple alternations in who was in power and who out. It amounted to a prolonged struggle for predominance of electoral and multiparty democracy and, in effect, of the legislature. The legislature could only emerge in the wake of party political victory over military predominance and the isolation of the monarchy from manipulation by the military and an institutionalised (and self-preserving through access to military and state power) governing party.

In the period since independence, five main phases can be differentiated in Lesotho politics (Matlosa 2006a). Each of these has had a particular bearing on the standing and operation of the country's legislature. The following sections selectively deal with these phases, which occurred as the 'embryonic democracy' of 1966–70, de facto one-party rule of 1970–86, military rule of 1986–93, fragile democracy of 1993–2002, and a relatively stable democracy since 2002.

Independence, military intervention, one-party rule

A period of 23 years of variations of one-partyism and military rule followed from 1970 to 1993 (from the 1970s to 1998, Lesotho suffered seven military coups). The period epitomised the legislature's struggle for predominance in Lesotho politics. In the 1970 events the electorate punished the BNP and gave the BCP a 13-seat majority. Instead of conceding defeat, the BNP declared a state of emergency. It suspended the Westminster constitution (Matlosa 1998). The King was forced into exile.

Prime Minister Leabua Jonathan established a unicameral legislature (1973), which included chiefs who had served in the former Senate. The opposition BCP rejected the arrangement. Its leader also fled into exile to lead an external BCP faction. In the mid-1980s Jonathan created a de facto single-party system. Opposition parties refused to nominate candidates for multiparty legislative elections, given their lack of access to essentials like a voters' roll. The Lesotho army took over government, and the King was made head of state, holding legislative and executive powers (Lodge *et al*. 2002, 93). The leader of the military government, General Metsing Lekhanya, advised the King. Parliament was dissolved and party politics restricted. In 1990 the military took over the King's legislative and executive functions, followed by the deposition of King Moshoeshoe II. His eldest son, Letsie III, became the (uninaugurated) head of state. He subsequently chose exile.

Return to civilian politics, dominated by wars of the political parties

Lekhanya announced a gradual return to civilian politics later in 1990, followed by his own deposition by junior officers a year later. The military government lifted restrictions on political parties, and a new constitution was accepted in 1993, modelled on the suspended 1966 constitution. Besides the National Assembly and

Senate there would be a Council of State (see above) to advise the King and help avoid a repetition of the constitution being suspended.

The first elections in 23 years took place in March 1993. The formerly marginalised BCP won power, but at the cost of upsetting the military and the BNP-aligned civil society. A new period of turbulence in the life of the legislature was precipitated, this time around aided by the incompetence of the BCP in power. A section of the army attacked the Deputy Prime Minister and other Cabinet members in 1994, and this was followed a few months later by the King dissolving the parliament, dismissing the Prime Minister, and appointing his own hand-picked government. National and international protests led to a reversal. BCP Prime Minister Mokhehle was party to the agreement. Mokhehle meanwhile fell out with the BCP and formed the Lesotho Congress for Democracy (LCD). The LCD, in which Pakalitha Mosisili succeeded Mokhehle in February 1998, was elected to power in the 1998 election (see Matlosa 1997, 148).

Electoral politics – the base for ascending into National Assembly politics – still did not stabilise. A tumultuous period of electoral contestation followed. Instability was linked to the dominance of one party, despite the multipartyism that existed formally. This was largely a function of the first-past-the-post electoral system. The opposition parties alleged fraud in the 1998 election, and their supporters disrupted the capital, Maseru. An army mutiny added to the turmoil. It precipitated the SADC military intervention of September 1998 to restore calm (see Parliamentary Monitoring Group 1998; Neethling 1999).

In early October 1998 the political parties agreed to form an interim governance structure. Internecine party clashes delayed the process, but a revised electoral system emerged and was adopted in 2002 – the MMP system (see Matlosa 2006a). It entailed the addition of 40 proportional representation seats, allocated on a compensatory basis, as well as the 80 pre-existing single-member constituency seats. This satisfied the opposition parties' quest for legislative representation (Makoa 2005). An apparent consolidation of perceivably fair (and peaceful) multiparty elections followed.

Leadership struggles in the run-up to the May 2002 elections, however, had had disruptive and party-splitting impacts, which again detracted from more concentrated policy foci. In the LCD Mosisili came up against Mokhehle, and the LPC was formed in 2001 when Mokhehle lost. The BNP struggles were settled without a split. In the BCP the struggles led to the formation of the split-off Basutoland African Congress (BAC). The LCD would split still further in 2006, with the formation of the All Basotho Convention (ABC).

The post-2002 election contests for legislative presence

Much of the electoral instability in Lesotho over time had thus been linked to the electoral system. It had commenced in the first democratic election of 1965, when the electoral system delivered a minority government – with the opposition parties jointly accounting for approximately 58 per cent of the vote. Significant parties felt cheated and excluded. The volatility continued into the 1970 election, which triggered the Prime Minister's annulment of the electoral process, suspension of the constitution and judiciary, and prohibition of party politics. Lesotho would not have another democratic election until 1993. The 1993 and 1998 elections brought the issue to a head, the MMP system was adopted, and the 2003 and 2007 elections followed (this chapter was finalised shortly before the May 2012 elections). Opposition parties gained more substantial representation than in previous elections.

The details in Table 5.1 demonstrate the extent of party political change and alteration in the periods that were relatively free from military or one-party dominance. Party political alternation indicated the clamour of political parties and their associated elites for representation in the legislature. It is also an indication of the frustration to get things done in a system where policy debates and alternatives are limited and party contests substitute for policy action. It also indicates elite rivalry for access to state power and resources 'in the context of poor resource endowment and declining economic conditions' (Santho 1998).

Over time, party political power in the legislature moved from the BNP, to the BCP, the LCD and in early 2012 the Democratic Congress (DC, constituted through an intra-legislature split of the LCD). This suggests vibrant contestation, at least on the level of inter- and intra-party contests for legislative control. In early 2012 then Prime Minister Pakalitha Mosisili carried out an intra-legislature 'coup' when he abandoned his LCD ticket (where others were plotting against his leadership), formed the DC, was followed by 45 MPs (to make the DC the largest party in the legislature, albeit without an outright majority) and was declared Prime Minister – with the DC the governing party – by a Speaker who was associated with the group of 45. Opposition parties decried this as unconstitutional on the grounds that only the King, acting on advice of the Council of State, could declare a government formed. They took the case to the High Court. Floor-crossing is permitted in the Lesotho legislature, but the Speaker also ruled that it was not necessary to follow those procedures (see *Lesotho Times*, 2012). Within weeks the King dissolved parliament to prepare for the parliamentary elections of 26 May 2012.

In many respects, however, legislature politics remained a sideshow. The issues, especially in the eras of BNP and BCP dominance, were largely those of obtaining first civilian rule and then fair representation of political parties that would in essential respects reflect the scope of electoral support. There continued to be little policy differentiation between the parties, and the executive remained predominant. Recurrent issues were the lack of service delivery, corruption in government and the Lesotho Highlands Development Authority, abuse of state resources, and Lesotho's continuous state of poverty and under-development.

Policy influence of the legislature

The role of the Lesotho legislature in policy and politics is shadowed by colourful electoral politics and the predominance of the executive. The constitution of Lesotho (adopted 2 April 1993; amended 1996, 1997, 1998, 2001 and 2004) specifies the functions of the legislature as to pass laws, approve the national budget, scrutinise expenditure of allocated funds, exercise oversight on the executive, and debate

Table 5.1 Party representation in the Lesotho legislature across six elections

Main parties	Election					
	Election 1965 60 seats	Election 1970 60 seats	Election 1993 65 seats	Election 1998 79 seats*	Election 2002 120 seats	Election 2007*** 120 seats
Lesotho Congress for Democracy (LCD)	–	–	–	78 98.73% 60.7%	79 (79+0) 65.8% 54.8%	62 (62+0) 51.7%
Basotho National Party (BNP)	31 51.7% 41.6%	23 38.3% 42.2%	0 0% 22.6%	1 1.3% 24.5%	21 (0+21) 22.4% 17.5%	–
Basotho Congress Party (BCP)	25 41.7% 39.7%	36 60% 49.8%	65 100% 74.7%	0 0% 10.5%	–	–
Marema-Tlou Freedom Party (MFP)	4 6.7% 1.5%	1 1.7% 7.3%	0 0% 1.4%	0 0% 1.3%	–	–
Lesotho People's Congress (LPC)	–	–	–	–	5 (1+4) 4.2% 5.8%	–
National Independent Party (NIP)	–	–	–	–	5 (0+5) 4.2% 5.5%	21 (0+21) 17.5%

All Basotho Convention (ABC)	—	—	—	—	17 (17+0) 14.2%
Lesotho Workers' Party (LWP)	—	—	—	—	10 8.3%
Other	—	—	—	Six other parties: 10-seat total	Eight other parties: 10-seat total
Total number of votes**	259,825	285,257	532,978	584,740	554,386	442,963

Sources: Lodge *et al.* (2002); Matashane-Marite *et al.* (2007); EISA (2008); Musanho (2010).

Notes:
The columns show, in this order: number of seats; percentage of seats; percentage of votes – in each election only the four top party political results are listed.
* By-elections are excluded from the results, accounting for 'missing' seats (79 instead of 80).
** The total number of votes includes the votes cast for a range of small parties, in each of the elections.
*** Because of some of the bigger parties' manipulation of the MMP electoral system in 2007, this column does not include the proportion of the vote for the parties. The ruling LCD formed an alliance with the NIP, and the ABC teamed up with the LWP. Both the LCD and the ABC chose to contest only the first-past-the-post seats on their own respective party tickets, while teaming up with the two smaller parties for the PR seats.

major issues that concern the nation (Lesotho Government 2003). As in the case, in effect, of many legislatures around the world, policy-making and power over the executive are not assured. In the case of Lesotho the legislature is clearly second not just to the executive but also to global-international partners that assist Lesotho as an impoverished, poorly resourced and donor-neighbour-dependent country.

This de facto situation is not clearly reflected in constitutional specifications. The constitution of Lesotho posits that legislative powers reside in the National Assembly. Main functional capacities, however, are focused on the technical-procedural matters on which legislatures have relatively guaranteed roles. Hence, the power of parliament is specified as being exercised through making laws via bills passed by both houses of parliament and assented to by the King. Observers have commented on the MPs often not doing justice to their formal roles. The 'Scrutator', parliamentary observer and political columnist of the *Lesotho Times*, has referred to the MPs as 'rent-seeking . . . passengers whose core business is to fight for self-interests' (Scrutator 2012). Regular party alliances and formation of new parties add to the image (see Table 4.1, and details above concerning the DC).

Formal versus de facto positions

The legislature has limited autonomy over Cabinet decisions, aided by the fact that Cabinet comprises ruling party members. Since Cabinet members are drawn from the ruling party, and given that the ruling party had a two-thirds majority on the basis of the 2007 result in the National Assembly, almost all decisions made by the executive are accepted without question by the majority of the legislature – a situation that also prevails in many legislatures around the world.

Formally, the executive has the prerogative to determine policies, and parliament the mandate to revise such policies and hold ministers accountable by asking questions relating to the performance of the ministries. There are divergent perceptions as to the level of effective scrutiny exercised by the Lesotho legislature. In a survey conducted by EISA (Matashane-Marite *et al*. 2007) some MPs reported that the legislature had enough powers to oversee the executive. Others insisted that parliamentarians may have the right to examine the budget, but do not have the power to change much of what is proposed. The National Assembly's Public Accounts Committee (PAC) has been active in its scrutiny of bills, in particular of the analysis of public expenditure and proposed budgets. The PAC, however, is regarded as relatively ineffective as a result of it being prohibited from *demanding* that ministers account for the expenditure of public funds (Matashane-Marite *et al*. 2007, 26).

Legislature operating in conditions of policy dependence

Legislatures that operate in conditions of proscribed policy options and oppor-tunities for advocacy may carry substantial paper and constitutional-intent power, yet have little to contribute or contest. This applies to the case of Lesotho. A scrutiny of both new policy initiatives and policy initiatives in the past decade reveals that there were limited proposals and few profound debates (see Lesotho Government 2010).

In many instances the initiatives originated from the United Nations (UN, including UNICEF), the WB and the IMF. The WB, for example, financed projects in education, roads, agriculture, industry, water-supply, urban development, health, privatisation and community development. The IMF and WB supported on-going programmes in trade, state enterprise reform, telecommunications, water, power, agriculture and the social sectors. These programmes speak to 'policies' that commonly fall into the genre of development assistance and poverty relief. Details are often beyond contestation, and the Lesotho government, including the legislature, has a limited say on the details. Some of the IMF assistance was under the auspices of the Poverty Reduction and Growth Facility Arrangement of 2002. IMF assistance to Lesotho was also in the form of maintenance of fiscal discipline.

The restricted national policy autonomy is further exacerbated by Lesotho's economic dependence on South Africa (see Matlosa 2006b). Lesotho does not have an industrial base of note, and serves as a labour reserve for South Africa. A large proportion of its food and manufactured goods are imported, and it has had limited success in the development of, for example, a textile industry. The global recession of 2006–10 had a harsh impact on Lesotho. Unemployment escalated. A range of South African policy issues are mirrored in Lesotho, including unemployment and the spread of HIV-AIDS. As a resource-restricted country Lesotho has little option but to accept whatever international assistance may be forthcoming. There is limited scope for bargaining on accompanying policy frameworks.

The governance focus in the Lesotho policy landscape was therefore far more frequently on compliance with the programme prerogatives of the IFIs and on ensuring capacity and integrity in the state bureaucratic apparatuses. The legislature and profound policy deliberations were largely left out of the equation.

Conclusion

The Lesotho legislature is thus one of high elite and electoral focus, yet it has a low policy and governance presence. The Lesotho legislature suffers many of the conventional problems related to legislative subservience to the executive, exacerbated by the fact that the political principals in the executive hold direct political sway over their same-party, more junior colleagues. The Lesotho legislature additionally suffers disempowering processes that are linked to operating in a country that is impoverished, poorly resourced and under-developed. Policy autonomy is affected, and the legislature has a constrained role. The legislature's policy action is further undermined by the country's IFI and donor dependencies. Policy issues frequently feature in the context of IFI- and donor-derivative programmes that had imposed policies without preceding processing through the hands of the legislative institutions of the country. The legislature thus has negligible policy effect. It rubber-stamps executive action. The executive, in turn, endorses internationally determined policy directions.

Notes

1 The World Bank estimates of the demographic and economic Lesotho specifics are: population: 2.066 million; GDP per capita: $851; GDP growth: 2.1%; life expectancy: 45; income level: lower middle; poverty ratio: 56.3%; see http://web.worldbank.org/WBSITE/EXTERNAL/COUNTRIES/AFRICAEXT/LESOTHOEXTN/0,,menuPK:356035~pagePK:141159~piPK:141110~theSitePK:356029,00.html (accessed 20 December 2010).
2 The review of the African Peer Review Mechanism (APRM), a South Africa-driven Africa initiative, sheds light on the limited role of the legislature (see Matlosa 2006a).
3 Lodge *et al.* (2002, pp. 87–96) provide a more detailed historical overview.

References

Constitution of Lesotho 1993, as amended in 1996, 1997, 1998, 2001 and 2004, Government of Lesotho, Maseru.

EISA (2008) *Election Observer Mission Report: Lesotho*, Report No. 26, 17 February 2007, www.eisa.org.za (accessed 5 June 2010).

Kabemba, C. (ed.) (2003) *From Military Rule to Multiparty Democracy: Political Reforms and Challenges in Lesotho*, EISA Research Report No. 2., www.eisa.org.za (accessed 5 June 2010).

Lesotho Government (2003) http://www.lesotho.gov.ls/parliament/mission.htm (accessed 10 December 2010).

Lesotho Government (2010) http://www.lesotho.gov.ls/ministries (accessed 8 December 2010).

Lesotho Times (2012) 'Deputy Speaker says DC government is illegal', *Lesotho Times*, 15 March, http://www.lestimes.com/?p=8660 (accessed 2 May 2012).

Lodge, T., Kadima, D. and Pottie, D. (eds) (2002) *Compendium of Elections in Southern Africa* (Johannesburg: EISA).

Makoa, F. K. (2005) Strengthening parliamentary democracy in Southern Africa – Country studies: Lesotho, *South African Journal of International Affairs*, 12 (1), pp. 61–76.

Matashane-Marite, K., Mapetla, M. M. and Monyake, M. (2007) *EISA Election Update 2007: Lesotho*, 1, 31 January, http://www.eisa.org.za/WEP/lesoverview8.htm (accessed 5 June 2010).

Matlosa, K. (1997) The 1993 elections in Lesotho and the nature of the BCP victory, *African Journal of Political Science*, 2 (1), pp. 140–51.

Matlosa, K. (1998) Democracy and conflict in post-apartheid Southern Africa: Dilemmas of social change in small states, *International Affairs*, 74 (2), pp. 319–37, http://www.jstor.org/stable/2623904 (accessed 4 June 2010).

Matlosa, K. (2006a) Democracy and political governance in Lesotho: Key issues and challenges, Background paper prepared on behalf of the APRM Secretariat, Midrand, Johannesburg, 7 August, http://www.eisa.org.za/aprm/pdf/Resources_Bibliography_Matlosa1.pdf (accessed 6 July 2010).

Matlosa, K. (2006b) Electoral system design and conflict mitigation: The case of Lesotho, in *Democracy, Conflict and Human Security: Further Readings*, International IDEA Handbook Series, www.idea.int/publications/dchs/upload/dchs_vol2_sec3_3.pdf (accessed 5 June 2010).

Musanho, B. (2010) Lesotho, in D. Kadima and S. Booysen (eds), *Compendium of Elections in Southern Africa: 20 Years of Multiparty Democracy*, pp. 146–85 (Johannesburg: EISA).

Neethling, T. (1999) Military in Lesotho: Perspectives on Operation Boleas and beyond, *OJPCR: The Online Journal of Peace and Conflict Resolution*, May, 2.2, http://www.trinstitute.org/ojpcr/p2_2neethling.htm (accessed 6 June 2010).

Parliamentary Monitoring Group (1998) *Report on Situation in Lesotho*, Joint meeting of the Joint Standing Committee on Defence, Foreign Affairs Portfolio Committee, and Security and Justice Select Committee, 2 November, http://www.pmg.org.za/minutes/19981101-report-situation-lesotho-0 (accessed 2 June 2010).

Santho, S. (1998) Lesotho: Lessons and challenges after a SADC intervention, 1998, in D. Philander (ed.), *Franco-South African Dialogue: Sustainable Security in Africa*, Institute for Security Studies (ISS) Monograph No. 50 (Pretoria: ISS).

Scrutator (2012) Self-serving MPs, *Lesotho Times*, 23 February, http://lestimes.com/?p=8455 (accessed 2 May 2012).

Tsikoane, T., Mothibe, T. H., Mamoeketsi, E. N., Ntho, M. E. N. and Maleleka, N. D. (2007) *Consolidating Democratic Governance in Southern Africa: Lesotho*, EISA Research Report No. 32 (Johannesburg: EISA).

6 Liechtenstein I

The Parliament of the Principality of Liechtenstein

Marion Frick-Tabarelli

Political system of the Principality of Liechtenstein

The Principality of Liechtenstein is a constitutional, hereditary monarchy on a democratic and parliamentary basis. The power of the state is inherent in and issues from the Reigning Prince and the people. In contrast to an absolute monarchy where only the monarch represents the state, a constitutional monarchy possesses a democratic element, namely the legislature (in the Principality of Liechtenstein, called 'Landtag' or 'Parliament').[1] In the dualistic conception of the system of state, the legislature exercises the important function of the lawful representation of the entirety of Liechtenstein citizens and, as such, has the duty of safeguarding and vindicating the rights and interests of the people. Owing to its relation to another, primary body – the people – the legislature may be considered a directly constitutional, secondary body.[2]

Parliamentary elections

Parliament is elected directly by the people. According to the Constitution, the term of office is four years. Regular parliamentary elections take place in February or March of the fourth year. The 25 Members of Parliament (MPs) are elected from two election districts; 15 MPs are elected from the 'Upper Country' election district, 10 MPs from the 'Lower Country' election district. The election procedure is universal, secret, equal and direct. All citizens 18 years of age or older who live in the country are eligible to vote. MPs are elected according to the system of proportional representation: seats are first allocated to parties in proportion to the total number of votes attained by each party (or by their candidates) in an election district. Within each party, those candidates are considered elected who have attained the highest number of votes. Only those parties that have attained at least 8 per cent of the votes cast in the entire country are assigned seats. During the legislative period 2009–13, Parliament consisted of three parties: the Patriotic Union (Vaterländische Union, VU) with 13 seats, the Progressive Citizens' Party (Fortschrittliche Bürgerpartei, FBP) with 11 seats, and the Free List (Freie Liste, FL) with one seat. The Patriotic Union and the Progressive Citizens' Party competed for the majority of parliamentary seats for decades. The stronger of the two parties is entitled to appoint the Prime Minister and holds the majority in the Government. The weaker party is represented as the junior partner in the Government.[3]

Because the Liechtenstein Parliament is a part-time legislature, all MPs perform their mandate in parallel with their professional involvement. MPs cannot be held legally responsible for any utterances or comments made during parliamentary sessions. They enjoy immunity inasmuch as they can only be arrested with the assent of Parliament during the official parliamentary period (unless apprehended red-handed). The election of Alternate Members of Parliament (AMPs) is a feature particular to Liechtenstein: for every three seats a political party obtains in an election district, the party is entitled to one AMP. Each party represented in Parliament is entitled to at least one AMP, however, so that small parties are not excluded from the rule pertaining to AMPs.

Organisation of Parliament

The Liechtenstein Parliament is based on a unicameral system. The term of office is structured into sessions lasting from the opening of Parliament (February or March) until the closing (December). In the opening session, the President of Parliament and his deputy are elected. The President calls the plenary sessions during the year; he chairs the meetings and represents Parliament externally. Parliament holds about 8 to 10 plenary sessions per year, each usually lasting one to three days. As a rule, sessions are open sittings. However, there are also closed sessions when the Government presents confidential information, or when Parliament discusses internal parliamentary business or personnel issues.[4] At least the Government minister responsible for the particular issue participates in the session. For a decision by Parliament to be valid, at least two-thirds of the MPs must be present. For amendments to the Constitution, unanimity or a three-quarters majority in two successive sessions is required. All other parliamentary decisions require a simple majority of those present. The instruments of Parliament are comparable with those of other parliaments. MPs may initiate constitutional and legislative initiatives, motions, postulates and interpellations as well as small enquiries.[5] Parliamentary groups form the bridge between the parties and the MPs: before an issue is dealt with in Parliament, the MPs come together for internal party group meetings, in order to be able to form a joint opinion on outstanding matters. A minimum of three MPs is needed to form a parliamentary group. The National Committee protects the rights of the entire Parliament when it is not convened and as a consequence cannot exercise its functions (i.e. from the closing at the end of the year until it is again opened at the beginning of the following year) or if Parliament is adjourned or dissolved. The National Committee comprises the President and four additional MPs, to be elected by the Parliament, considering both election districts equally.[6]

Parliament usually exercises its rights in the plenary sessions. Compared with other parliaments, few tasks are delegated to parliamentary committees.[7] When committees are formed, they essentially prepare bills for the plenary sessions and formulate pertinent motions. Committees do not act in their own name. As supporting bodies, committees reduce the burden on the plenary and create a basis for decision-making. Nevertheless, they do not relieve the plenary of its responsibility. Generally, committees cannot take binding decisions for the plenary or the Government.[8] Committees usually consist of three or five members.[9] Each party that forms a parliamentary group is entitled to be represented in committees. The party that holds the majority in Parliament also holds the majority in the committees. Sessions of the committees are closed. However, committees are entitled to include Government ministers in their meetings; Government ministers may be accompanied by experts.

At the suggestion of the parliamentary groups, Parliament elects standing committees, special committees and investigating committees. Standing committees are entrusted with preparing and dealing with affairs related to their responsibility as well as preparing and filing applications to Parliament. They are elected for one legislative term. All standing committees comprise five MPs. During the opening session, Parliament elects three standing committees: the Finance Committee, the Oversight Committee and the Foreign Affairs Committee.[10] The Finance Committee examines the preliminary budget estimate of the state and public institutions and surveys the involvement of the state in loans, guarantees, bonds, real estate and exceptional financial assistance. Depending on the price and the purpose of use, the Finance Committee has regulatory approval over Government proposals to purchase or sell real estate. The approval of Parliament sitting in plenary is required if the purchase or sale of real estate assets of administrative property exceeds the limit for a financial referendum. Further, Parliament has the right and the duty to scrutinise the entire state administration, including the administration of justice. Parliament exercises this right of control in particular through the Oversight Committee. Mostly, parliamentary control of the Government is exercised in this committee and not in the plenary.[11] The control exercised by the Oversight Committee includes general oversight and financial supervision. The Oversight Committee continually reports the results of the executed controls to Parliament, especially at the session dealing with the state accounts. In collaboration with the Government, the Foreign Affairs Committee represents Liechtenstein's interests with regard to foreign affairs. The Foreign Affairs Committee examines international treaties that require Parliament's approval. The Government periodically informs the Foreign Affairs Committee about recent developments in foreign policy as well as negotiations with international organisations or foreign states. In accordance with its rules of procedure, Parliament is also authorised to appoint special committees. The task of special committees is to undertake preparatory work concerning bills or other affairs and to present proposals to the plenary sitting of Parliament. For example, one of the special committees is the European Economic Area (EEA) Committee, which examines impending EEA legislation regarding the necessity of approval by Parliament. Parliament may establish investigating committees in order to ascertain facts and to clarify liabilities. Investigating committees are organised to protect the rights of parliamentary minorities: upon request of just seven members, Parliament is obliged to appoint an investigating committee. Investigating committees may question informants, interrogate witnesses and request the release of files. Further, investigating committees have the right to consult experts and carry out inspections. Investigating committees, formed in accordance with actual needs, represent an efficient tool of scrutiny. The last time an investigating committee was established was in 1999. The period of engagement of special committees and investigating committees terminates with the conclusion of the matter being dealt with, at the latest at the end of the legislative term. At the beginning of a legislative term, Parliament also elects delegations for the international parliamentary bodies in which it participates. There are two delegates and two deputies for the Parliamentary Assembly of the Council of Europe, the EFTA/EEA Parliamentary Committee and the OSCE Parliamentary Assembly, as well as four delegates for the Inter-Parliamentary Union (IPU) and three delegates for the Lake Constance Parliamentary Committee. These delegations are elected for the entire legislative term.

Functions of Parliament

The Constitution and Parliament's rules of procedure define the functions of Parliament. The principal task of Parliament relates to legislation. Without Parliament no law can be enacted or amended. Parliament, in addition to the Reigning Prince and the people, has the right of constitutional and legislative initiatives. By means of a motion, the Government can be instructed to draft a bill (or other parliamentary resolution) and to present Parliament with a relevant proposal. In practice, however, most legislative bills are prepared by the Government and its experts. The Government usually passes bills as reports and proposals to Parliament. Every bill is initially subjected to preliminary debate, which is followed by two readings and a final vote.[12] In the preliminary debate, Parliament decides whether it will deal with a bill at all. At the first reading, proposals can be made, which the Government examines in detail prior to the second reading. Each single article is voted on in the second reading. The definitive wording of each article is determined step by step. Subsequent to the second reading, final voting takes place, passing the bill in its entirety.[13] Parliament may reject governmental bills or form its own committees to revise them. If a bill is passed, Parliament may initiate a referendum (mandatory referendum). These three scenarios occur only rarely – a bill was last rejected in 2007, the last committee was formed in 2001, and Parliament has not initiated a referendum since 2002. In addition to the consent of Parliament, the validity of a law requires the sanction of the Reigning Prince, the countersignature of the Prime Minister, and publication in the *Liechtenstein Legal Gazette*. Every law passed by Parliament not declared to be urgent, as well as every international treaty adopted by Parliament, is subject to an optional referendum.[14] For an overview of the above-mentioned legislative process, see Figure 6.1.

In addition to Parliament's role in the legislative process, the authority of Parliament includes various electoral matters. One of the core tasks of Parliament is the formation of the Government. At the start of its four-year mandate, Parliament appoints the members of the Government. Formally, this election is only a

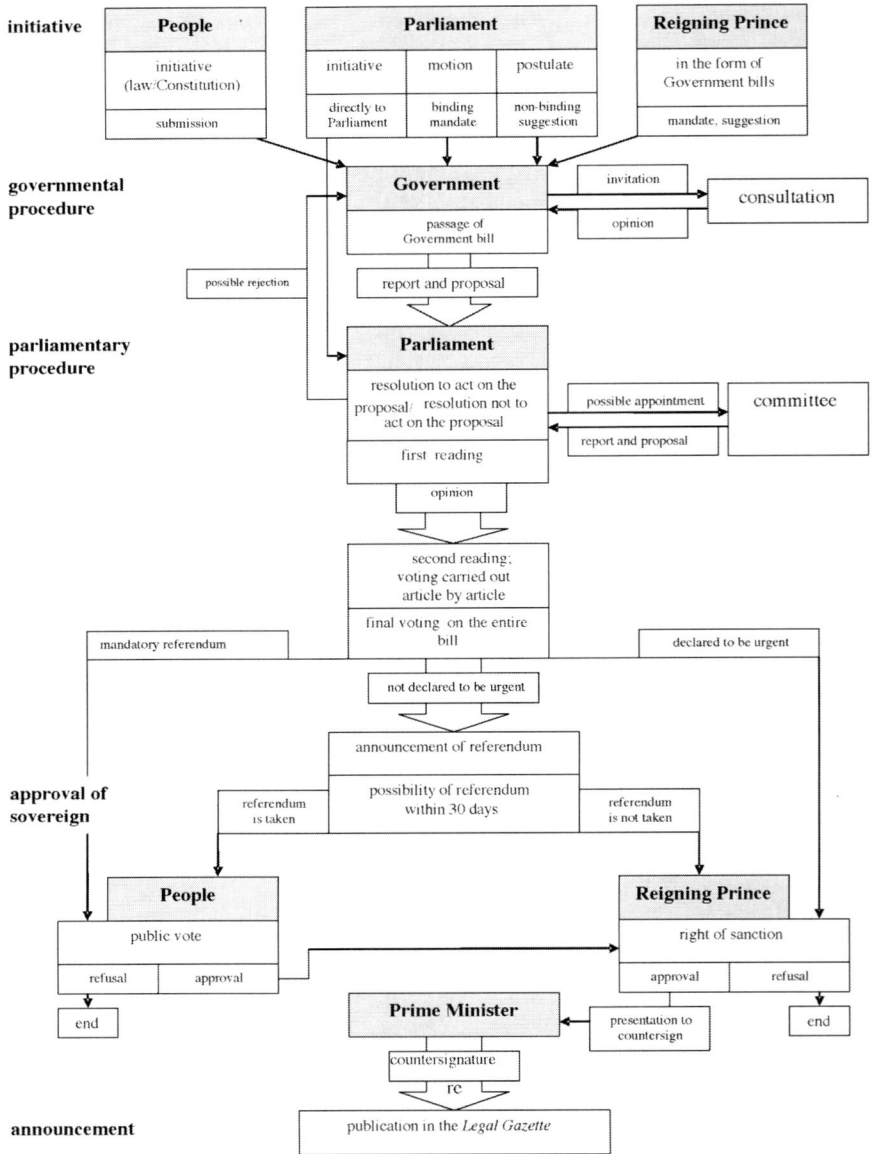

initiative

People	Parliament			Reigning Prince
initiative (law/Constitution)	initiative	motion	postulate	in the form of Government bills
submission	directly to Parliament	binding mandate	non-binding suggestion	mandate, suggestion

governmental procedure

Government		invitation	consultation
passage of Government bill		opinion	

possible rejection

report and proposal

parliamentary procedure

Parliament	possible appointment	committee
resolution to act on the proposal/ resolution not to act on the proposal	report and proposal	
first reading		

opinion

second reading;
voting carried out
article by article

final voting on the entire
bill

mandatory referendum   declared to be urgent

not declared to be urgent

announcement of referendum

referendum is taken	possibility of referendum within 30 days	referendum is not taken

approval of sovereign

People		Reigning Prince
public vote		right of sanction
refusal	approval	approval	refusal

end

Prime Minister

presentation to countersign

end

countersignature

re

announcement

publication in the *Legal Gazette*

Figure 6.1 The legislative process

Source: IPU Parline Database (n = 264).

nomination proposal to the Prince. The latter does not enjoy the right to make individual nominations, as he is bound by those proposed by Parliament. Further, the exercise of financial sovereignty is of particular importance. The state budget is prepared by the Government and passed by Parliament, which has the right to amend any item. Parliament resolves the budget of the following year in the yearly debate on the state budget, which takes place each autumn. Budgeted funds that are not expended expire. If the Government requires extra funds for new tasks during the course of a year or if it exceeds budget items, a supplementary credit must be applied for through Parliament. In the event of funds being required for plans stretching over several years (e.g. for large building projects), the Government must apply to Parliament to pledge a credit guarantee. As above described, Parliament has the right and the duty to scrutinise the entire state administration, including the administration of justice. Parliament entrusts this task on the one hand to the Oversight Committee, and on the other hand Parliament deals with it directly when discussing the annual statement of account of the authorities and the state accounts.[15] Furthermore, MPs can present oral or written enquiries to Government regarding any branch of the state administration. As an ultimate form of control, Parliament may dissolve the collective Government or – in consultation with the Reigning Prince – dismiss individual Government ministers. International treaties are negotiated by the Government and the responsible administrative bodies respectively. Treaties which involve sovereign rights, cause new burdens or encroach on the rights of the citizens are subject to Parliament's approval. A treaty signed by the Government cannot be amended by Parliament, but can only be accepted or rejected as a whole.

Power-limiting elements

As previously mentioned, Parliament shares its competences with other bodies. A first power-limiting element is the Reigning Prince. The Reigning Prince has the right to convene Parliament at the beginning of the year and to close it at the end. Traditionally, the Reigning Prince opens Parliament with a ceremonial speech from the throne. This opening of Parliament at the beginning of the year is essential for Parliament to have the right of assembly. During the course of the year, the Reigning Prince can – on grounds of considerable importance – adjourn Parliament for a maximum of three months or dissolve it entirely. Every law and every financial resolution must be sanctioned by the Reigning Prince. If no sanction is granted within six months, it must be considered refused. Further, Parliament's competences in electoral issues are limited by the Reigning Prince. With regard to the appointment of the Government, the agreement of Parliament and the Reigning Prince is required. Parliament proposes the Government ministers, and the Reigning Prince appoints them. The Government requires the confidence of the Reigning Prince and Parliament throughout its term of office; otherwise it can be dissolved by the one or the other. Conversely, the dismissal of an individual minister requires an understanding between Parliament and the Reigning Prince. For proposing judges to serve on civil and criminal courts, the Reigning Prince and Parliament rely on a joint body established for that purpose. If Parliament elects the recommended candidate, the Reigning Prince appoints the candidate as a judge. If Parliament rejects the candidate recommended by the body and no agreement can be reached within four weeks on a new candidate, Parliament recommends an opposing candidate and orders a popular vote. If there is a popular vote, eligible voters have the right to nominate candidates under the same conditions as for an initiative.[16] Furthermore, the Constitution grants significant rights to the Reigning Prince with respect to emergency decrees. By means of emergency decrees, the Reigning Prince can take urgent measures to ensure the security and welfare of the state without the involvement of Parliament, but with the countersignature of the Prime Minister. After six months at most, emergency decrees become inoperative.[17]

A second power-limiting element is the people. Owing to direct-democratic rights modelled on the Swiss system and implemented in the Constitution, the people not only have the right to elect Parliament; by means of an initiative, the people can also force Parliament to convene or force a referendum to be held regarding its dissolution. As yet, however, this theoretical right has never been exercised. Citizens can bring a parliamentary resolution to public vote by means of a referendum. In the case of legal and financial resolutions, 1,000 citizens entitled to vote must sign the demand for a referendum; in the case of constitutional amendments and international treaties, 1,500 signatures are required. However, Parliament can declare amendments to laws and the Constitution as well as financial resolutions as urgent and hence exclude them from referenda. Despite the rather restrained use of direct-democratic instruments (about one popular vote per year), they affect the legislation and the practice of Parliament. Most resolutions of Parliament are subject to referendum. Therefore, organisations and interested actors are already involved in a consultation process while drafting a bill. In this manner, referenda can be avoided. Civil society thus has a certain impact on Parliament through its direct-democratic rights.[18]

Close cooperation exists between Parliament and the Government. Government ministers participate with an advisory vote in the sessions of Parliament. They also have the right to take part and to be heard in the committees. As the Government plays an important role in legislation, it is another power-limiting element. Through its right of initiative, the Government may bring bills to Parliament. Parliament mostly responds to proposals of the Government and rarely becomes active by itself. Owing to its monopoly of information, expertise, full-time staff and infrastructure, the Government guides the legislative process of Parliament.[19] Accordingly, the Government is the body that dominates policy-making. As in other countries, there is a functional dominance of the executive, although Parliament retains the right to substitute its own policy for that of the Government. The Constitutional Court exercises its oversight of Parliament through the consideration of voting complaints and the review of the constitutionality of laws. The Constitutional Court has the competence to annul unconstitutional laws adopted by the people and sanctioned by the Reigning Prince. The Constitutional Court may review a law as applied if requested to do so by the Government, a municipality or a court, as well as if a constitutional question arises in a case encountered by the Constitutional Court itself ('abstract judicial review'). The annulment of a law becomes effective with its announcement, unless the Constitutional Court specifies a different period, which may amount to one year at the most. Finally, political parties also affect the practice of Parliament. Parties nominate candidates and instruct their MPs. Important political decisions are usually made in the political parties' bodies.[20] The theoretically free vote of the MPs is subject to an informal whip. Party groups often hold closed votes. Further, Liechtenstein's print media are dominated by two newspapers that also serve as the organs of the political parties represented in the Government.[21] Therefore, the impact of the parties on Parliament is substantial.

Conclusion

Parliament is embedded in a complex political system that limits its power. The rights of the Reigning Prince, the direct-democratic rights of the people, and the Constitutional Court limit the power of Parliament explicitly. Further, Parliament is subject to informal restrictions: the influence of the Government, civil society and the political parties.

Notes

1 T. Allgäuer (1989) *Die parlamentarische Kontrolle über die Regierung im Fürstentum Liechtenstein* (Vaduz: Verlag der Liechtensteinischen Akademischen Gesellschaft), p. 39.
2 G. Steger (1950) *Fürst und Landtag nach liechtensteinischem Recht* (Vaduz: Buch- und Verlagsdruckerei), p. 101.
3 W. Marxer (2009) Der liechtensteinische Parlamentarismus heute, in G. Kohl (ed.), *Parliamentarism in Small States: Parliamentarism and Monarchy*, pp. 43–57 (Pozna_: Wydawnictwo Pozna_skie), p. 45.
4 Allgäuer (1989), pp. 48f.
5 Liechtenstein Landtag Secretariat, J. Hilti (2009) *Landtag of the Principality of Liechtenstein* (Vaduz: Landtagssekretariat), p. 25.
6 P. Vogt (1987) *125 Jahre Landtag* (Schaan: Gutenberg), p. 39.
7 Therefore the Liechtenstein Parliament is characterised neither as a distinct working parliament nor as a mere debating parliament. Since it usually exercises its rights in the plenary sessions, where even detailed deliberations on bills take place and only a few tasks are delegated to committees, it is however closer to a debating parliament (Allgäuer 1989, p. 5).
8 Ibid., p. 303. Only the Finance Committee has the competence to make decisions; it is able to decide on certain financial business, i.e. primarily purchase of land.
9 The Oversight Committee may be increased up to seven members.
10 www.landtag.li/Committees.
11 Allgäuer (1989), p. 303.
12 www.liechtenstein.li.
13 H. Hoch (1994) Verfassungs- und Gesetzgebung, in G. Batliner (ed.), *Die liechtensteinische Verfassung 1921*, pp. 203–29 (Vaduz: Verlag der Liechtensteinischen Akademischen Gesellschaft), pp. 219–29.
14 Vogt (1987), p. 43.
15 www.landtag.li/About the parliament.
16 www.liechtenstein.li/State/Parliament/Duties.

17 www.liechtenstein.li/State/Reigning Prince.
18 Marxer (2009), p. 54.
19 Allgäuer (1989), p. 69.
20 Ibid., p. 70.
21 Marxer (2009), p. 55.

References

Allgäuer, T. (1989) *Die parlamentarische Kontrolle über die Regierung im Fürstentum Liechtenstein* (Vaduz: Verlag der Liechtensteinischen Akademischen Gesellschaft).

Constitution (English edition), www.llv.li/verfassung-e-01-11-09.doc-3.pdf.

Hoch, H. (1994) Verfassungs- und Gesetzgebung, in G. Batliner (ed.), *Die liechtensteinische Verfassung 1921*, pp. 203–29 (Vaduz: Verlag der Liechtensteinischen Akademischen Gesellschaft).

Liechtenstein Landtag Secretariat, Hilti, J. (2009) *Landtag of the Principality of Liechtenstein* (Vaduz: Landtagssekretariat).

Marxer, W. (2009) Der liechtensteinische Parlamentarismus heute, in G. Kohl (ed.), *Parliamentarism in Small States: Parliamentarism and Monarchy*, pp. 43–57 (Pozna_: Wydawnictwo Pozna_skie).

Steger, G. (1950) *Fürst und Landtag nach liechtensteinischem Recht* (Vaduz: Buch- und Verlagsdruckerei).

Vogt, P. (1987) *125 Jahre Landtag* (Schaan: Gutenberg).

7 Liechtenstein II

Parliamentarianism in a complex political system

Wilfried Marxer

Liechtenstein is a very small state in the middle of Europe with only 36,000 inhabitants. It is a German-speaking country situated in the heart of the Alps, surrounded by neighbouring Switzerland and Austria.

Traditionally, there is a very tight political and economic relationship to these neighbouring states. The political system of Liechtenstein, with state power divided between the power of the prince and the power of the people, is somewhat bizarre. The monarchic roots go back to the Holy Roman Empire, whereas distinct democratic rights were introduced rather late, in 1921. The prince continues to play an important role in Liechtenstein politics to this day. Experts speak of a dualistic regime (Riklin 1987), in which the prince (*Fürst*) and the people – the latter mainly represented by the parliament (*Landtag*) and the government (*Regierung*) – have to cope with each other. In fact, the prince's power is not simply theoretical: far from it. He can dismiss parliament, he formally appoints the government (on the recommendation of parliament), he can dismiss the government at any time and for any reason (as last occurred in 1993), he dominates the procedure for electing new judges (as he leads the board that nominates judges and he can veto their proposals) and, last but not least, he has the right to sanction any new law (Waschkuhn 1994; Marxer and Pállinger 2009). The veto right applies for parliamentary decisions as well as for popular votes, although it is not used very often. There was a single veto against a popular vote which occurred in 1961, and the last one against a parliamentary decision happened in 1998.

On the other hand, no new law can enter into force if it has not been approved by parliament, which is a unicameral parliament. It comprises 25 members, elected in two constituencies with 15 and 10 members respectively. In the day-to-day work of legislation, new legal provisions are normally drafted by the government and proposed to the parliament. Parliament can reject or accept the proposals, and also amend them in any way it chooses. In addition, parliament has the right to nominate the members of the government, whereas the prince formally appoints the government according to the parliamentary proposal. The Liechtenstein political system is thus basically of the parliamentarian type with respect to the relationship between government and parliament. Parliament, moreover, has the right to dismiss the government – something it did in 1993 for example, just as the prince may do. From a formal point of view, therefore, government is subordinated to the parliament.

The constitution does not allow a representative to hold a mandate in parliament and in government at the same time. If a member of parliament is appointed to the government, his or her parliamentary mandate is forfeited and his or her place is taken by a successor from the same party. On the other hand, it is not mandatory for members of the government to have been previously elected to parliament. In practice, it rarely happens that members of parliament switch to the government.

Formal and informal aspects of power sharing

The distinct rights of the parliament and the prince, relative to the government, give a false impression that the government is rather weak, since it is accountable to, and needs the support of, both the parliament and the prince. When we consider the political routine, however, this impression alters significantly. Although the government is formally accountable to the prince and to the parliament – if not directly to the people – in everyday politics the government is the main player. This is due to the fact that the government heads the whole administration and organises international relationships. The shaping of policy is, in fact, predominantly carried out by the government. It is unlikely that parliament will not cooperate with the government and support it, since the composition of the government reflects the party distribution in parliament. There has only been one case – in 1993 – of a dismissal of the government by parliamentary initiative. The reason for the dismissal had to do with the mode of government at the time rather than with any specific controversial political issues.

If, at this stage, one can observe a dominance of the executive, it is clearly not for formal reasons. Government has the right neither to dismiss parliament nor to veto parliamentary decisions. Only the prince or the people itself is allowed to dismiss parliament. The prince can only do so if there are serious grounds which justify the dismissal. In the past, this happened mostly when parliament had become unable to take decisions after a large political fraction had left parliament during a session. An attendance quorum of two-thirds of the members is necessary for parliamentary decisions. If the quorum is not met, parliament becomes incapable of acting; the prince then dismisses parliament and mandates the government to organise new elections. The voters also have the right to dismiss parliament by means of a popular recall, but so far this has never happened. The people's right of recall was introduced with the new constitution in 1921. Thus one can assume a very high level of legitimacy for the parliament, since not only is it elected by the people in free, fair and open elections, but it can also be dismissed by a popular vote if it loses public support.

The direct-democratic rights of the electorate go far beyond a recall, though. They include the rights of initiative and referendum, similar to the direct-democratic tools in Switzerland (Marxer and Pállinger 2007). They too were introduced with the constitution of 1921. By means of the collection of a certain minimum number of signatures, proposals on new ordinary law (1,000 signatures of an electorate of about 16,000 men and women) or the constitution (1,500 signatures), or on altering or abolishing these, can be put to a popular vote. This is called a popular initiative.

The popular referendum, on the other hand, includes popular votes aimed at rejecting parliamentary decisions on ordinary law, on constitutional amendments, on financial expenditures or on international treaties. Direct democracy limits the legal power of the parliament substantially, in addition to the limits already set by the strong position of the prince.

Finally, the constitutional court (*Staatsgerichtshof*) must also be mentioned. Following the principle of the rule of law, the court, in the event of complaint or appeal, can strike down any law or legal provision (Hoefling 1994; Wille 2001, pp. 36ff.). This restricts the legislative power of parliament once again, since these considerations significantly influence the legislative activities of the parliament. If parliament pays scant attention to the constitution its decisions might be subsequently overruled by the constitutional court. Therefore, it does not make much sense to legislate without due regard to and an understanding of the constitution.

Besides this domestic restricting factor, there are also international treaties and resulting legal requirements that influence parliament's activities substantially. Liechtenstein, like most other countries, is a member of many international organisations and has signed many international treaties. They have high relevance to the parliament, since the scope of decision-making is clearly limited by them. To mention only the two main such elements, one can refer to the cooperation with Switzerland (mainly through a customs treaty since 1923 and the use of the Swiss franc) and the Agreement on the European Economic Area since 1995. Both of these have the potential to set law, mainly in the field of the economy, trade, customs and currency, without any, or with only a weak, influence from Liechtenstein stakeholders, the parliament included (Frommelt 2010a, 2010b). This aspect once again weakens the power of the parliament. If such regulations are binding, they are also protected from popular initiatives and referendums (Wille 2005).

The dominance of the executive within the system is informal. The relative powers of parliament and government can be illustrated by their unequal strength in terms of financial resources and levels of support staffing. A comparison of trends over a period of less than two decades is striking. In 1994, parliamentary expenditure amounted to 1.4 million Swiss francs, compared to 3.2 million Swiss francs of government expenditure (Frommelt 2010a, p. 34). In relation to government, the figure includes only salaries for the members of the government and its staff, and expenditure on public relations and representation. It does not include the vast public administration. Expenditure by parliament mainly derives from attendance fees for the members of parliament, salaries for the parliamentary service, and contributions to political parties. Fifteen years later, in 2009, expenditure for the parliament had risen to 3.6 million Swiss francs, while government expenditure had risen exponentially, to 17 million Swiss francs. Thus, between 1994 and 2009, while parliamentary expenditure increased by 157 per cent, that of the government rose by 431 per cent. At present, government expenditure on administration is almost five times as high as parliamentary expenditure. The public administration at the national level was done by 769 employees in 2009 (459 in 1994). Among those, the governmental staff increased from 21 to 64 employees (ministers not included), whereas the parliamentary staff only increased from 3.5 to 8 full-time jobs during this period of time.[1]

Accountability and scrutiny

Nonetheless, the government is basically dependent upon the parliament. This is demonstrated ultimately by the right of the parliament to dismiss the government. Furthermore, parliament is the main body for deciding on new laws, for altering laws and for constitutional amendments. The principle of the rule of law demands legal provisions that are in accordance with the constitution and international treaties. It also implies that by-laws, decided upon by government, have to be in accordance with the constitution and ordinary laws. In general, the government is only allowed to enact by-laws if this competence has been expressly delegated by parliament. Thus the legislative process is widely under the control of the parliament – subject to the consent of the prince (through his right to sanction new laws) and of the people (through the right of initiative and referendum, should the situation arise). The direct-democratic rights are also valid for international treaties and financial expenditure. Certainly, the government negotiates international treaties, and it makes proposals for expenditure, be it by the annual budget or by single proposals concerning new buildings or other expenses. But in the end its proposals have to be supported and decided upon by parliament. The government always needs the support of parliament in these cases.

Additional tools of control on government and the administration are permanent parliamentary committees, parliamentary interpellations and parliamentary investigation commissions:

- Permanent parliamentary committees on finances, foreign affairs, and super-vision of the public administration serve as a close link between government and parliament, but also as an instrument for monitoring and controlling governmental activities.
- Parliamentary interpellations are critical questions raised in parliament and forwarded to the government by majority decision. They concern issues of public administration and are directed to the government, which has to answer such questions in a timely manner. Parliamentary interpellations are used frequently.
- Parliamentary investigation commissions, on the other hand, are rather rare, although there is no significant barrier to installing one: the votes of a quarter of all members of parliament suffice in order to activate a parliamentary investigation commission. Thus even a minority in parliament can use this instrument of scrutiny.

The regulations on the functioning of parliament include further elements relating particularly to the protection of political minorities. The right of a one-quarter minority in parliament to install a parliamentary investigation commission has already been mentioned. In addition, there is a minimum attendance quorum of two-thirds of members of parliament before any decision can be taken. The two main parties have continuously satisfied this quorum during recent decades, with the result that both have been able to block parliamentary proceedings and provoke new elections as a consequence. This holds also for the representatives of the two constituencies. Since they occupy 10 and 15 seats respectively, either of them can block parliamentary decision-making by leaving the floor. Finally, a qualified majority of three-quarters of valid votes in parliament is mandatory for any constitutional amendment. This again enables strong parties or representatives of the two constituencies to operate a veto.

Restrictions on parliament

Despite the formal importance of the parliament (shared with the prince and the electorate), there are several elements that limit its power. The relative strength of the government, compared to the parliament, in terms of financial and personnel resources has already been mentioned. There is also an unequal relationship between professionals, on the one hand, and amateurs on the other. All five members of the government, and of course the whole administration, are professionals. Members of parliament, by contrast, are part-time and voluntary. Besides their mandate, parliamentarians perform their individual jobs, whether employed or self-employed. To be a member of parliament is far from being a full-time job. Roughly speaking, there are about eight parliamentary sessions every year, lasting from one to three days each.

There are both potential advantages and disadvantages to having a parliament consisting of volunteers. On the one hand, practical skills and experience from different professional points of view feed into parliamentary work. Moreover, it is hardly possible for a 'political class' to emerge. On the other hand, the independence of members of parliament can be jeopardised. It is obvious that a member of parliament who works for a bank, an industrial enterprise or the public administration, for instance, may bring his or her professional background into his or her parliamentary work. Nevertheless, members of parliament receive their legitimacy through free and fair elections, and the professional background of the candidates is known to the electorate: it may even have been a reason for voting for that particular person. From a democratic point of view, therefore, the professional background is neither a clear danger for democracy, nor is it the opposite.

Besides the personal and professional interests and backgrounds of the individual members of parliament, there exists a wide range of additional influences upon parliamentary work in Liechtenstein. There are demands from other elements of the political system, such as the prince, the people, the government, the municipalities or the courts. Secondly, there are demands from civil actors and stakeholders, such as interest groups, organisations and unions. And, last but not least, there are requests, constraints and impulses from foreign institutions, international organisations and foreign states, with the European Union and the neighbouring countries of Switzerland and Austria in first place.

All of these significantly influence the day-to-day work of the Liechtenstein parliament. Regarding internal key players of the political system, we have already briefly highlighted the relationship between parliament and government, the prince and the electorate from a formal point of view. There is, on the other hand, also an informal relationship. These influences can hardly be examined in detail from the outside. They begin with informal consultations between members of the government and party fractions of the parliament, and continue with direct contacts to the parties, with talks and – maybe – negotiations with the prince and so on. All of these influences happen away from the public perception. The content and results of such talks are only known in detail to those who have taken part, since these contacts are not public and nor are documents or minutes publicly available.

Public awareness and political communication

It can be said, however, that informal contacts play an important role in the Liechtenstein political system. This is due to the fact that, being such a small state with a mere 36,000 inhabitants, Liechtenstein society is closely knit. Political representatives can be easily contacted by any stakeholder and even by individual voters, not only by lobby groups. And there are other ways to gain public attention, mainly by letters to the editor published in the two daily newspapers. These newspapers remain party newspapers, each affiliated with one of the two main parties (Marxer 2004). Reporting on domestic politics is strongly biased by this background. But a majority of the voters read both newspapers, a fact that reduces the manipulative power of the two newspapers to some degree. Letters to the editor can strongly contrast with the interests of the parties. Despite this, the newspapers do not dare to ignore readers' letters. They publish them in full – even the letters and statements of the non-affiliated parties and interest groups – as long as they are no more than 2,500 characters in length.

It is not difficult at all for voters to be able to watch political debates in parliament and to be well informed about politics; and this does not apply only to insiders. Usually, there are articles in the newspapers on important political issues before parliamentary debates, referring to the reports and drafts that, in most cases, stem from government. There may also be articles by journalists and letters to the editor. Parliamentary debates are then broadcast live on the state video channel, which is received in almost every household. Of course, it is also possible for members of the public to watch debates in the parliament building itself – with the exception of non-public debates. Non-public debates do not occur very often. They are reserved for issues with aspects of state security, the protection of personal data, commercial secrets and the like. Again, there are reports on parliamentary debates in the newspapers and on Liechtenstein radio. Since there is no dedicated Liechtenstein TV station, political and public communication occurs mainly via the newspapers, which reach about 80 per cent of the voters daily (Marxer 2004, p. 178).

Parties and parliament

Parties play an important role in democratic political systems. Their influence is normally greater in the case of a proportional electoral system, since this strengthens the power of parties to some degree. Majoritarian systems, in contrast, give more weight to the candidates' personality. The Liechtenstein electoral system is a proportional one and, therefore, one would expect the parties to have a rather strong impact on candidate selection and on the probability of candidates who are preferred by the party being elected. But this is not really the case, mainly for two reasons. First, parties face certain difficulties in recruiting candidates for both parliamentary and municipal elections. Clearly, it is not particularly attractive to obtain a parliamentary mandate under the circumstances of a voluntary, non-professional status. The parties, therefore, are forced to find and recruit candidates actively instead of being able to select candidates rigorously from a list in the run-up to parliamentary elections. Second, the electoral system allows voters to favour individual candidates or to cross them off the list, irrespective of the parties' wishes.

Thus in practice the parties do not have the power to determine which candidate will be at the top of the list after the ballot and which one will be at the bottom. So, for parliamentary elections, parties recruit candidates, hoping that the party will gain as many seats as possible. But there is no guarantee for any single candidate that he or she will make the list. For these reasons, the parties are not in a privileged position to discipline their candidates and their parliamentary members, or to reward them with a guaranteed mandate. Rather they have to support their own, elected party representatives, and the parties are very much dependent on what party representatives in government, in parliament and in the municipalities require and demand, rather than the other way round.

The parties may have strategic visions, but in the end it is very much up to the party representatives in parliament and government to take decisions, with very little remote control by the party leadership. Moreover, the formal independence of representatives is supported by the constitution. Parliamentarians are not accountable to their supporting party, but to their oath and their own convictions. They swear to observe the constitution and existing laws, and to promote the welfare of the country, without any ulterior motives, to the best of their ability and conscience (article 54 of the constitution). They also enjoy special protection: they cannot be arrested while the diet is in session, and they are responsible for their votes in parliament to the diet alone.

At the present moment, there are only three parties in parliament, and in fact there have never been more than three parties represented in parliament. The political parties were founded relatively recently, in 1918. For many decades after this, there were only two parties in parliament. But from 1938 until 1997, the parties formed ruling coalitions, followed by two majority periods with only the majority party in a single-party government. Since 2005 there has again been a grand coalition. Both parties can be characterised as Christian-democratic parties, without significant ideological differences. They are the Patriotic Union (*Vaterländische Union*) and the Progressive Citizens' Party (*Fortschrittliche Bürgerpartei*). It was not until 1993 that a third party, the Free List (*Freie Liste*), won parliamentary representation. At present, the Patriotic Union holds 13 of the 25 seats, the Progressive Citizens' Party 11, and the Free List one. Six representatives are female. In the government, two of its five members are women.

Policy-making legislature

Although it was previously said that the government launches most of the initiatives to make new laws, amend laws, accede to international treaties and the like, it is necessary to add that parliament itself is also allowed to initiate legislation. This does not happen very often, though, since in most cases a great deal of expertise is necessary in order to draft a legislative proposal. Nevertheless, there are occasional but repeated initiatives in parliament. Such parliamentary initiatives do not have to be first passed to the government; they can be debated directly in the parliament if a majority decides on it. During the last 10 years, there were up to five parliamentary initiatives each year. They covered issues like health insurance, people's rights, support for families, medical practitioners, civil union, mobile communications and subsidised building, just to mention a few. This is not much when compared to the total of new provisions every year. The numbered collection of laws, by-laws, financial decisions, international treaties and similar provisions totalled 393 issues in 2009, for instance. Thus parliamentary initiatives account for only a very small proportion of all the provisions.

The last example demonstrates once again that the Liechtenstein parliament is a policy-making legislature, at least in formal terms. As shown in this chapter, it has to share this competence with the electorate in the case of an initiative or a referendum and, not least, with the prince through his right to sanction new law. In reality, the main policy shaper is the government, although it is accountable to both the parliament and the prince at the same time. All in all, the political system is a highly complex one, with several formal and informal players. Parliament is one of them, though not the strongest.

Note

1   Staff appointment scheme, Reports of Liechtenstein government no. 68/1994 and no. 98/2009.

References

Frommelt, C. (2010a) *Die Europäisierung der Landtagsarbeit*, Arbeitspapiere Liechtenstein-Institut No. 29 (Bendern: Liechtenstein-Institut).

Frommelt, C. (2010b) *Die Europäisierung der liechtensteinischen Rechtsordnung*, Arbeitspapiere Liechtenstein-Institut No. 28 (Bendern: Liechtenstein-Institut).

Hoefling, W. (1994) *Die liechtensteinische Grundrechtsordnung* (Vaduz: Verlag LAG).

Marxer, W. (2004) *Medien in Liechtenstein* (Schaan: Verlag LAG).

Marxer, W. (2009) Der liechtensteinische Parlamentarismus heute, *Czasopismo Prawno-Historyczne*, 61 (2), pp. 43–56.

Marxer, W. and Pállinger, Z. T. (2007) System contexts and system effects of direct democracy: Direct democracy in Liechtenstein and Switzerland compared, in Z. T. Pállinger, B. Kaufmann, W. Marxer and T. Schiller (eds), *Direct Democracy in Europe*, pp. 12–29 (Wiesbaden: VS Verlag für Sozialwissenschaften).

Marxer, W. and Pállinger, Z. T. (2009) Die politischen Systeme Andorras, Liechtensteins, Monacos, San Marinos und des Vatikan, in W. Ismayr (ed.), *Die politischen Systeme Westeuropas*, pp. 901–55 (Wiesbaden: VS Verlag für Sozialwissenschaften).

Riklin, A. (1987) *Liechtensteins politische Ordnung als Mischverfassung* (Vaduz: Verlag LAG).

Vogt, P. (1987) *125 Jahre Landtag* (Vaduz: Selbstverlag des Landtages des Fürstentums Liechtenstein).

Waschkuhn, A. (1994) *Politisches System Liechtensteins* (Vaduz: Verlag LAG).

Wille, H. (2001) Verfassungsgerichtsbarkeit im Fürstentum Liechtenstein: Entstehung, Ausgestaltung, Bedeutung und Grenzen, in H. Wille (ed.), *Verfassungsgerichtsbarkeit im Fürstentum Liechtenstein*, pp. 9–64 (Vaduz: Verlag LAG).

Wille, H. (2005) Das Abkommen über den Europaeischen Wirtschaftsraum und seine Auswirkungen auf das liechtensteinische Verfassungs- und Verwaltungsrecht, in T. Bruha, Z. T. Pállinger and R. Quaderer (eds), *Liechtenstein: 10 Jahre im EWR* (Schaan: Verlag LAG).

8 Malta

The Parliament of Malta

Michael Frendo

Introduction

Ninety years ago, on 1 November 1921, the Prince of Wales of the United Kingdom opened the Malta Parliament after the promulgation of a new Constitution which provided the Maltese people with self-government within the framework of the British Empire. The Parliament at that time was bicameral, with a Malta Legislative Assembly and a Senate as part of the constitutional set-up. It was an experience never to be repeated, and all subsequent parliaments in that century, including the Parliament of the independent and sovereign State of Malta after 21 September 1964, were always unicameral, a model that survives today.

While it reflects its historical development drawing from the traditions of the British House of Commons and parliaments of the Commonwealth, the Parliament of Malta is specifically regulated by the Constitution of Malta and by the Standing Orders of the House and today also responds to the enhanced role of national parliaments within the institutional architecture of the European Union, as laid down in the Treaty of Lisbon.

Today, the Parliament of Malta is a small unicameral parliament in which the Members of Parliament are part-time and are expected to carry on with their professions and employment while serving as MPs. The pressures of parliamentary work and parliamentary time have markedly increased over the years, in particular since Malta became a member of the European Union in 2004. It is a Parliament which meets in the evening from 6 p.m. till 9.30 p.m., although there are occasional times when the committees meet at different times of the day.

The Constitution of Malta

Today the Constitution of Malta (as amended), including as amended in 1974 when Malta became a republic but remained a member of the Commonwealth, places Parliament in prime position. After its initial four chapters dealing with the symbols of sovereign statehood and a declaration of principles, citizenship and fundamental rights and freedoms of the individual, the Constitution proceeds to set out the structure of governance of the State. Chapter V deals with the office of the President, the head of state. Immediately after that it is the turn of Parliament to feature in the basic law of the land.

Parliament is the institution to which the Constitution dedicates most clauses, dividing the chapter into three parts, Part 1 covering the composition of Parliament, Part 2 powers and procedures of Parliament and Part 3 the summoning, prorogation and dissolution of Parliament. In all, 27 clauses cover various aspects of Parliament and its organisation and powers. Seventeen clauses are dedicated to the executive, and eight clauses to the judiciary.

Parliament is described as consisting of the President and a House of Representatives. The House of Representatives consists of an odd number of members divisible by the number of electoral divisions that Parliament determines by law from time to time. The constitutional rules governing the method of election of members to Parliament ensures that a political party enjoys a majority of members elected to Parliament if, in a general election in which only two parties elect members to Parliament, that party obtains at least a relative majority of the first-count votes.[1] This means that a compensatory adjustment is carried out by adding extra seats to a party in the case where a party which obtains a relative or absolute majority of first-count votes would have elected a number of Members of Parliament which is less than the majority in the House. Consequently, for example, after the 2008 elections, the majority party obtained a relative majority but had to be allocated an extra four seats in order to obtain a one-seat majority in Parliament, increasing the normal 65-member Parliament to a Parliament of 69 members.

These complex rules, which developed over time, particularly after a 'perverse' result in the 1981 election (where the party obtaining the absolute majority of votes in an election in which only two parties elected members to the House had obtained a minority of seats), and are well described within the Constitution itself, are the consequence of political consensus which resulted in Constitution changes to the chapter relating to Parliament.

A Member of Parliament can be validly elected to the Maltese Parliament only if such a person is himself or herself eligible to vote in the election and does not fall under a disqualification, such as being a citizen of another country (in a citizenship voluntarily acquired) or having made a declaration of allegiance to another country.

As already indicated, the Constitution regulates in detail various issues and processes relating to the method of elections in a general election, in particular the voting age of 18 years and that elections should be carried out in accordance with the principle of proportional representation by means of the single transferable vote in a number of electoral divisions in the country, which must not be fewer than 9 or more than 15.[2]

The House of Representatives elects a person to be the Speaker of the House and a person to be Deputy Speaker. The Constitution does not require the person to be elected as Speaker to be a member of the House. In fact Article 59 (2) reads as follows:

(2) The Speaker may be elected either –
(a) from among persons who are members of the House of Representatives, but are not Ministers or Parliamentary Secretaries, or

(b) from among persons who are not members of the House of Representatives and are qualified for election as members thereof.

In situations of a close parliamentary majority (such as a one-seat majority), it is often the case that the person nominated for election as Speaker is not a member of the House so as not to disturb the situation of the majority party in Parliament.

For example, the election of the current Speaker was carried out after the prospective nominee resigned his parliamentary seat and was replaced by another member from the same party before he was elected unanimously by all the Members of Parliament.

The Deputy Speaker on the other hand has to be a Member of Parliament while serving as Deputy Speaker.[3] There is no option for the Deputy Speaker to be elected from among persons who are not members of the House.

The administration of Parliament is also set out by the Constitution of Malta by a direct reference to the person who globally is often termed the Secretary-General of Parliament. However, in line with Commonwealth traditions, this figure is referred to by the Constitution as the Clerk of the House.

The Constitution makes reference to this officer of Parliament by simply stating that 'There shall be a Clerk of the House of Representatives'[4] and that 'The office of the Clerk to the House of Representatives and the offices of the members of his staff shall be public officers.'[5]

Yet the Constitution does not indicate the functions, powers and status of the Clerk of the House and the offices of the members of his or her staff. As a matter of fact the Clerk of the House of Representatives is not only a member of the Civil Service but also subject to the regulations and status of the Civil Service falling within the remit and jurisdiction of the Principal Permanent Secretary (head of the Civil Service) and more specifically under the jurisdiction of the Permanent Secretary in the Office of the Prime Minister.

This anomalous situation persists where the Constitution regulates Parliament as a separate institution of the State but where the budget of Parliament is set by the Ministry of Finance and where the budgetary packet for Parliament in effect falls within the Office of the Prime Minister and parliamentary administration is seen as a department of government!

The Constitution sets out that:

> Parliament may make laws for the peace, order and good government of Malta in conformity with full respect for human rights, generally accepted principles of international law and Malta's international and regional obligations in particular those assumed by the treaty of accession to the European Union signed in Athens on the 16th April, 2003.[6]

Parliament is also empowered by the Constitution to determine by law 'the privileges, immunities and powers of the House of Representatives and the members thereof'.[7] However, the Constitution itself provides for three aspects of such privileges:

1   No proceedings, civil or criminal, 'may be instituted against any member of the House of Representatives for words spoken before, or written in a report to, the House or a committee thereof or by reason of any matter or thing brought by him therein by petition, bill, resolution, motion or otherwise'.[8] There have been calls for the removal of this privilege, and those taking this view cite occasions when third parties were mentioned specifically by name in Parliament without having any recourse to any legal protection to protect their reputation. However, it must be pointed out that this particular subsection of Article 65 can, according to the Constitution itself, only be changed by a bill which at the final vote thereon in the House would have the support of 'the votes of not less than two-thirds of all the members of the House'.[9]

2   Members of Parliament shall, for the duration of any session, be free from arrest for a civil debt unless that debt is also a criminal offence.

3   No process issued by any court in the exercise of its civil jurisdiction shall be served or executed within the precincts of the House or through the Speaker, the Clerk or any officer of the House.

The basic law of the land grants the House of Representatives the right to 'regulate its own procedure' subject to the provision of the Constitution itself.

Quorum in the House is also regulated by the Constitution, which covers the situation where at any sitting a member draws the attention of the presiding officer to there being an absence of quorum, which is set at 15 members. In such a case, if, after an interval as set out by the Standing Orders of Parliament, the presiding officer 'ascertains that a quorum of the House is still not present, the House shall be adjourned'.[10]

When a quorum was called it had been the custom that, after the elapse of the prescribed time (normally five minutes in the Standing Orders[11]), the Speaker would only ascertain the quorum if the question was raised again by the person who had first called for it. A recent ruling by the Speaker has determined however that, once a quorum is called, after the elapse of the prescribed time it is the Speaker who on his or her return to presiding over the House ascertains whether there is a quorum or not.

The majority rule is firmly laid down in the Constitution with regard to decision-making by the House. Article 71 (1) lays down very clearly that 'Save as otherwise provided in this Constitution, all questions proposed for decision in the House of Representatives shall be determined by a majority of the votes of the members thereof present and voting.'

A bill passed by the House shall only become law, according to the Constitution, when it is also assented to by the President. The Constitution however carries on to state that, 'When a bill is presented to the President for assent, he shall without delay signify that he assents.'[12]

The Constitution also regulates the summoning, prorogation and dissolution of Parliament, prescribing that there shall not be more than 12 months between the holding of one session of Parliament and another and that the House shall meet 'not later than two months after the publication of the official result of any general election'.[13]

It is the President who sets the date for the first meeting of Parliament after an election, and it is the President who may 'at any time by proclamation prorogue or dissolve Parliament'.[14]The maximum period of a Parliament is five years, calculated from the date of its first sitting. Beyond that, as a matter of law – by operation of the law – it is automatically dissolved.[15]

However, if Malta is in a time of war, Parliament may extend this five-year period from time to time for not more than 12 months at a time but not beyond more than an extension of a further five years.[16]

The Constitution also provides for a summoning by the President, on the opinion of the Prime Minister that an emergency has arisen which requires it, of a Parliament which had already been dissolved in a period where the ensuing general election had not taken place.

The Standing Orders

The Standing Orders provide us with more detail relating to the organisation of Parliament and its procedures. They deal in detail with, *inter alia*:

1 proceedings on the opening of a new Parliament or session;
2 sittings, quorum, adjournment and closure;
3 arrangement of business of the House;
4 the regulation of order in the House;
5 the carrying out of financial business;
6 the way divisions (votes) are taken;
7 the procedures for the passing of bills;
8 the regulation of committees of the whole House and of standing and select committees;
9 the summoning of witnesses;
10 the presentation of petitions and rules relating to the Speaker, Deputy Speaker and Deputy Chairman of committees, members, officers of the House and privileges of the House.

The Standing Orders provide for five Standing Committees of the Parliament of Malta. They are:

1 the Standing Committee on House Business, regulating the business of the House, presided over by the Speaker of the House;
2 the Standing Committee on Privileges, also presided over by the Speaker of the House;
3 the Standing Committee on Foreign and European Affairs, also serving as a scrutiny committee on European Union legislation and initiatives, presided over by a member representing the majority in the House;

4   the Standing Committee on Public Accounts, presided over, as in the tradition of the House of Commons of the United Kingdom, by one of its members from the opposition benches;

5   the Standing Committee on Social Affairs, presided over by a member of the majority benches of the House.

The House also appoints a number of select committees, which are specific to an issue or a number of issues and have a life which does not go beyond the life of each Parliament.

The Standing Orders themselves provide for what regulates the Malta Parliament if there is a lacuna in the regulation. Standing Order 197, which is regularly quoted by Speakers when the case arises, provides that:

> In all cases not provided for by these Standing Orders, resort shall be had to the rules, forms, usages and practice of the Commons' House of Parliament of the United Kingdom, which shall be followed as far as they can be applied to the proceedings of the House with due regard to the special nature of the Constitution.

Conclusion

As stated at the outset, the Parliament of Malta is a small unicameral Parliament in which the Members of Parliament are part-time and are expected to carry on with their professions and employment while serving as MPs. The pressures of parliamentary work and parliamentary time have markedly increased over the years, in particular since Malta became a member of the European Union in 2004. It is a Parliament which meets in the evening from 6 p.m. till 9.30 p.m., although there are occasional times when the committees meet at different times of the day.

A new parliamentary building is planned and, indeed, is currently under construction. This will be the first time that Parliament will have had its own home, since it has been sharing the Palace in Valletta (where it meets) with the President of the Republic's offices and official and ceremonial rooms.

Notes

1   Even more so if a party obtains the absolute majority (in the aggregate more than 50 per cent of all valid votes cast in that election) (Article 52 (1) of the Parliament of Malta).

2   The Constitution however states that the island of Gozo together with the islands of the Maltese archipelago other than the island of Malta must be established as one electoral division and cannot be separated (Article 61A (2) (a)).

3   Article 59 (3) of the Constitution of Malta: 'the House shall elect a member of the House, who is not a Minister or a Parliamentary Secretary, to be Deputy Speaker of the House'.

4   Article 64 (1).

5   Article 64 (2).

6   Article 65 (1).

7   Article 65 (2).

8   Article 65 (3).

 9 Article 66 (2).
10 Article 70 (1) and (2).
11 However, the majority side of the House often introduces a general procedure motion to regulate certain aspects otherwise normally regulated by the Standing Orders. For example, in this current legislature, the procedure motion in force lays down a period of 20 minutes for the ascertainment of the quorum.
12 Article 72 (2).
13 Article 75 (2) and (3).
14 Article 76 (1).
15 Article 76 (2).
16 Article 76 (3). This article has never had to be used.

9   Swaziland

The legislature of Swaziland – compromised hybrid

Susan Booysen

Swazi constitutional developments are . . . like a journey taken by the slowest of all animals, and which has the capacity to convince its beholders that it is different from that animal they might have seen a few minutes before – the chameleon to be precise. *It is ever changing but never really changing.*

(Hlatshwayo 2003)

Introduction[1]

Superimposition of authoritarian monarchism on to a template of modern representative democracy distinguishes the legislature of Swaziland. A range of reforms have not diluted the predominance of the monarchy and its associated autocratic control over legislative institutions. Opposition forces have been virulent, and at times, as in the present, international organisations have escalated pressure for change. Yet in the small and landlocked state in Southern Africa – its 17,364 square kilometres are largely surrounded by powerful neighbour South Africa – the Swazi monarchy's control has remained tight. The ethno-cultural homogeneity and small size of the population, concentrated in rural areas and suffering economic hardships, have in some respects facilitated oppression.

The Swazi system of government epitomises a fusion of traditional and modern, liberal-democratic institutions. Traditionalism, however, has provided the shell for monarchical executive authoritarianism. Whereas the 2005 constitution documents the constitution as the supreme law of the land, the hereditary King is the head of state and is regarded to be above the constitution. He has legislative, judicial and executive powers. The legislature's operations do not stray from the imposed will of the King and his associates. Members of parliament are elected through the tinkhundla system – the two-stage, controlled election of politically compliant, non-party candidates, introduced in 1979. The legislature is characterised by its fronting for authoritarian-monarchical rule. The authoritarianism is contested, by both a persecuted civil society and the banned opposition political parties. These 'terrorist organisations' are banned in terms of the Terrorism Act No. 3 of 2008. The opposition forces (parties, unions and social movements) are thus excluded from influence over the legislature. The result has been a legislature devoid of multipartyism and inter-party deliberations on policy and governance. Many progressive members of Swazi society have abstained from voting.

Policy-making and governance decisions in the Swaziland legislature are subordinate-to-the-King, contained affairs. Initiatives of policy and governance follow the King's directives, perceived or expressed – at present King Mswati III, previously King Sobhuza II. The King holds members of the legislature (and executive) directly to account – he summons them to the royal residence, and can dissolve parliament without stating his reasons (Mamba 2011). Policy initiatives by the legislature in this small and impoverished country are limited. In recent years the legislature has not seriously initiated any legislation dealing with any of the top policy issues in the country (Mlangeni 2011). By 2012 the Swazi economy was on its knees, jobs were being cut and youth unemployment was rife. The country lacked the funds to sustain health programmes, while its HIV infection rate was the highest in the world relative to population size. The socio-economic crisis was deepening, while parliament and the legislature were waiting for cues from the King.

The rest of this chapter takes stock of the prevailing legislative and other governance arrangements, the development of this set of institutions and practices over time, and specifics of the functioning and functionality of the Swazi legislature.

Institutional configuration and powers of the Swazi legislature

Legislative power in Swaziland is vested in the King-in-parliament. The King, as head of state with vested powers in terms of Swazi law and custom, keeps a circle of traditional advisers who constitute the powerful Liqoqo Supreme Council of Swaziland (PHR 2007, pp. 67–8). Officially the Prime Minister is the head of government, but along with the legislature he is a subject functionary to the King. The Prime Minister has executive authority only in as far as the King delegates it (see *Times of Swaziland* 2010). Instead of following the expected practice of appointing the Prime Minister from the ranks of elected members, the monarch has on several occasions chosen an *appointed* member of the House of Assembly.

The constitution (Section 64(3), 'Executive authority of Swaziland') specifies that, '(s)ubject to the provisions of this constitution, the king may exercise the executive authority either directly or through the cabinet or a minister'. Section 64(4b) elaborates that the King in his capacity as head of state has authority, in accordance with this constitution or any law, to summon and dissolve parliament. In Swaziland these provisions are used to exploit the King's final control over all formal aspects of Swaziland politics.

The bicameral parliament comprises the House of Assembly and Senate. The Assembly consists of up to 66 members. Of these, 55 members are directly elected by citizens in terms of the tinkhundla system. The King may appoint up to 10 members. The Speaker may be designated from outside parliament and thereby becomes an ex officio member, without voting rights. In terms of the 2005 constitution (implemented in the 2008 election) up to four women are to be elected to represent each of the country's four administrative regions. They are indirectly elected by the House from a shortlist supplied by the Election and Boundaries Commission. The Senate consists of 30 members. Assembly members elect 10 members of the Senate (half of whom must be women), and the King appoints another 20 senators.

The tinkhundla system allows candidates to run for parliament on the basis of individual merit and not group affiliation. Political parties and other organisations are banned from operating freely in the country and hence there is no formal opposition to monitor the executive (Mamba 2011). The tinkhundla system is a major tenet of the Imbokodvo National Movement (INM), the party that led Swaziland into independence in 1968. Mamba (2011) notes that the INM never disbanded when all other political parties were banned in April 1973. The present government in effect pursues INM policies. By default this renders Swaziland a one-party state.

These arrangements have an impact on the legislature's functionality vis-à-vis the executive. Control over the nomination and election processes of legislature members through chieftancy systems at the local level, and the banning of political parties combine with the King's direct executive control over the legislature to render it toothless. While political parties are outlawed and persecuted in the Swazi system, the Attorney-General declared in 2011 that political parties are free because 'the 1973 decree that banned them is no longer in existence' (the 2005 constitution is silent on this) (Rooney 2011). This was believed to have been 'a stunt though to accommodate pressure from the European Union (EU) on more democracy' at a time when Swaziland was desperate to access international loans to relieve fiscal difficulties (Mlangeni 2011).

Socio-economic and demographic context

Politics and the economy of an oppressive system at the time of writing were converging to build pressure for change – which could, among other things, alter the character of the legislature. International pressure was mounting on Swaziland to review its system of monarchical-executive oppression, and Swaziland's 2010–11 fiscal crisis gave rise to a convergence of factors that prompted the opening up of the system. Pressure also came from the United Nations, which attached civic education and governance components to a 2010 developmental loan agreement with Swaziland (UNDAF 2010). Amnesty International and the Human Rights Institute of the International Bar Association expressed concern that provisions in the Suppression of Terrorism Act No. 3 of 2008 were inherently repressive, breached Swaziland's obligations under international and regional human rights law and the Swaziland constitution, and were leading to violations of the rights of freedom of expression, association and assembly (Mlangeni 2011). The International Monetary Fund (IMF) stated that Swaziland was on the brink of economic collapse and risked social upheaval, should it be unable to curb fiscal excesses (Redvers 2011).

The socio-economic and demographic contexts (see Stuart 2009) help illuminate why it has been possible for the monarchical autocracy to continue with, among other things, its dominance of the legislature.

The 1.3 million Swazi people are about 75 per cent rural. Approximately 70 per cent of the population engages in subsistence agriculture (and 60 per cent of land is held in trust by the King). The World Bank classifies Swaziland as a 'lower middle income less indebted' country (*World Factbook* 2010), yet this status is belied by the abject poverty that defines the lives of a large proportion of Swazi people. In 2006, 69 per cent of the Swazi people lived well below the poverty level, estimated at Emalangeni 128 (about US$ 20 per month). An estimated 10 per cent of the population controls about 43 per cent of the wealth, according to the Ministry of Economic Planning and Development (Dlamini 2006, p. 168). The most advantaged in society frequently include the royalty, who are employed courtesy of the state. The 2008 estimate of unemployment was 40 per cent. Many Swazi men are migrant mine workers in South Africa. Their remittances sustain Swazi families. Swaziland is ethnically, linguistically and religiously largely homogeneous (Stuart 2009, pp. 466–7). The bulk of political arrangements in the country are also geared to build further elite advantage. Reports of government corruption abound (see for example SSN 2011). With a relatively high literacy rate in the country, many skilled professionals finding themselves excluded from these political arrangements, have self-exiled themselves and repatriated their skills elsewhere, mainly in South Africa. This has contributed to a civil society that is weak, fragmented and apathetic.

Despite infrastructural development the country is overwhelmingly dependent on South Africa. Income from the Southern African Customs Union (SACU), originating in South Africa, has over the years contributed roughly three-quarters of national income. Swaziland receives more than nine-tenths of its imports from South Africa and sends 60 per cent of exports there (*World Factbook* 2010). The manufacturing sector had been diversifying since the mid-1980s, but sugar and wood pulp remained among the important foreign exchange earners (others are chemicals and textiles). Mining also declined in importance, with only coal and quarry stone mines remaining active. SACU had previously contributed roughly 65 per cent of the national budget – this declined steeply in 2010–11.

Roots and emergence of the Swazi legislature

The Swazi state has been run by an absolute monarch for close to 40 years (also see International Crisis Group 2005, p. 1). Swaziland was formally a constitutional monarchy at independence. The independence constitution further concentrated substantial powers in the King and traditional monarchy. A landmark year was 1973: the independence constitution was scrapped and a system of non-party elections and elevated monarchical powers was initiated. Reforms from 2005 onwards brought change, yet retained the essentials. Throughout these times the Swaziland legislature took the form of a subjugated sideshow. In order to explore the fate of the Swazi legislature, the following text examines the main constitutional changes with relevance to the legislature, and resistance to the continuous exclusion of political parties from representation in the legislatures, and also explains the tinkhundla system.

The 1973 constitutional reforms

Swaziland 'is probably the last African redoubt when it comes to fundamental constitutional reform', notes Napier (2008, p. 9). It has undergone serial constitutional reform processes. The essentials of authoritarian rule and dominance of the hereditary monarchy (see Mzizi 2004) over the legislature, however, have continued.

Elections in mid-1964 preceded independence. In these elections the traditional Swazi leaders, including King Sobhuza II and his Inner Council, formed the INM, which capitalised on its close identification with the Swazi way of life. Four other parties, mostly to the left of the INM, also competed in the election. The INM won all 24 elective seats (Matsebula 1989).

The Swaziland Constitution Order of 1967 formed the basis for the independence government dispensation (Napier 2008), which also has institutional convergences with the present-day system. It recognised the Swazi King as head of state. The constitution established a bicameral parliament (libandla), which comprised a Senate and House of Assembly. The King was recognised, yet executive power at the time continued to rest with Her Majesty's Commissioner. The constitution catered for a prime minister, appointed on the King's prerogative. The Cabinet was to advise the King, and there was a consultative council, consisting of Her Majesty's Commissioner and his deputy. The King appointed one-quarter of the members of the National Assembly, and half of those of the Senate.

The 1972 election result made the INM realise that there was a budding opposition, even if the four seats of the Ngwane National Liberatory Congress (NNLC) were not posing any substantial threat. The royalists instituted drastic measures to safeguard future power. In the first set of post-independence reforms King Sobhuza II appointed the Royal Constitutional Commission (RCC) in 1973, with the brief to draft a new Swazi constitution. Utilising powers conferred upon the King, on 12 April 1973 Sobhuza repealed the 1968 constitution in an act that was generally seen as unconstitutional. Hlatshwayo (2003) notes that the independence constitution did not provide for its own repeal – only for amendment. The King and his associates argued that the preceding constitution was abrogated because it had failed to provide the machinery of good governance and the maintenance of peace and order, that it had introduced practices that were 'alien' to the Swazi people and that it was the cause of growing unrest, insecurity and dissatisfaction. The King's proclamation of 12 April 1973 (Proclamation to the Nation, paragraph 2(c), in Baloro 1994, pp. 25–6) observed:

> the Constitution has permitted the importation into our country of highly undesirable political practices alien to, and incompatible with, the way of life in our society and designed to disrupt and destroy our own peaceful and constructive and essentially democratic methods of political activity; increasingly this element engenders hostility, bitterness and unrest in our peaceful society.

The 1973 proclamation equipped the King with *absolute* executive, legislative and judicial power. He now ruled by decree, in council with the Cabinet. All political parties, meetings and public activities with party political intent were banned. In the new legislature the members enjoyed no visible constituency (Baloro 1994, p. 19). It would be elected through traditional structures, the tinkhundla. Commissions appointed by the King would subsequently repeatedly judge the tinkhundla system as being in the best interests of the Swazi people. The proclamation confirmed the bicameral parliament, including the House of Assembly, which now comprised 40 members elected by an electoral college in terms of the tinkhundla system (the King appointed a further 10 members). Under a declared state of emergency, opponents of monarchical authoritarianism were jailed and charged with sedition and high treason.

The tinkhundla and constitutional reforms up to 2005

Swaziland's tinkhundla system (created through the Parliament of Swaziland Order, 1978) provided the framework for the country's indirect election of members of the House of Assembly. The King said that the tinkhundla system was one that was written 'by the people themselves and for themselves' (Maseko 2007). Subsequent constitutional amendments would change the system in only minor respects.

Swaziland's four administrative regions – Manzini, Hhohho, Lubombo and Shiselweni – are subdivided into 55 political constituencies (tinkhundla). Each inkhundla (constituency) comprises several chiefdoms and is led by an indvuna yeNkhundla (elected official), who works together with each chief's representative (bucopho). Chiefs assume their positions on the grounds of heredity and are appointed by the King. Officials manage the day-to-day affairs of the chiefdom (PHR 2007), and voters in an inkhundla elect delegates to an electoral college. The college, in turn, elects members to the House of Assembly and Senate, in secret (in 2005 this process became more transparent). The process is overseen by an electoral committee (later replaced by a chief electoral officer) appointed by and answerable to the King.

The tinkhundla system lacked popular acceptance. Research has indicated popular discontent, fuelled by government corruption and growing poverty and unemployment. Participation in elections remained below 50 per cent of the registered voters (Stuart 2009, p. 496). Many enlightened Swazi people abstained, and organised civil society bodies took principled exception to the exclusion of political parties. Leaders of the People's United Democratic Movement (Pudemo) were brought to trial on charges of high treason, among other things. Constitutional reforms were demanded (Maseko 2007).

In 1991 King Mswati established the first of several committees to review the tinkhundla system. The first committee, the so-called Vusela I, headed by Prince Mahlalengangeni in 1991, conducted consultative political forums around the country (see Napier 2008). Youth and cultural organisations rejected the proposals. Vusela II reviewed the Vusela I recommendations, but pro-democracy groups equally rejected *its* findings. The Tinkhundla Review Commission (TRC, Decree No. 1 of 1992) and the Constitutional Review Commission (CRC, Decree No. 2 of 1996) followed. Owing to continuous entrenchment of the traditional structures and absolute powers of the King, including retention of the tinkhundla system, pro-democracy organisations dismissed these initiatives as well. A number of professionals resigned en masse from the CRC, which hence lacked competency and legitimacy. The Vusela committees also recommended that fundamental rights and freedoms be severely limited, to the extent that political parties would remain banned (CRC Report of 2001, in Maseko 2007).

The December 2001 Constitution Drafting Committee (CDC, Decree No. 1 of 2002) was the next effort to forestall the growing rejection of the monarchical-autocratic order. The disarray was exacerbated by the 2002 resignation of the Chief Justice and six judges of the court of appeal, as a result of government's failure to uphold orders issued by the judiciary (Stuart 2009, p. 464). Another round of tinkhundla elections followed in 2003. The report of the Commonwealth Expert Team encapsulated the concerns regarding legislative elections in abnormal conditions (Commonwealth Secretariat 2007):

> no elections can be credible when they are for a Parliament which does not have power and when political parties are banned. Whatever happens regarding the draft Constitution [of 2005] we hope that progress can soon be made to allow political parties and to introduce constitutional arrangements by which an elected Parliament and the Government which is drawn from it will have real power. We noted the serious concern regarding observation of the rule of law and the separation of powers, which are both key elements in any democratic arrangements.

Pressures for constitutional reforms from 2005 onwards

From 2005 on, candidates were nominated in *public* meetings in the tinkhundla process, followed by elections in two phases: by secret ballot and in terms of the first-past-the-post system. The only change brought by the 2005 constitution was that the King could no longer govern by decree. Pro-democracy groups continued to criticise the excessive monarchical powers and continuous restriction of political parties. The inclusion of a progressive bill of rights was a step forward (Maroleng 2003, pp. 3–5). However, as Maseko (2007, p. 7) points out, the constitution paid 'respect to the lofty principles of democracy, human rights, rule of law and good governance, such are then watered down by other provisions that give effect to the supremacy of the monarch, as opposed to supremacy of the constitution'.

More protests followed, and Pudemo leaders were charged with treason. Six political parties, including Pudemo and the NNLC, urged a boycott of the 2008 poll. A group styled the Umbane People's Liberatory Army set off bombs, and the Swaziland Federation of Trade Unions (STFU) and the Swaziland Federation of Labour (SFL) organised mass rallies. The Swaziland process of constitution-drafting remains incomplete, and the quest for party political competition and representation in the national legislative institution continues.

Legislative operations of the Swaziland legislature

The subordinate, and in many ways insignificant, position of the legislature in Swazi politics is evident in both the intra-parliamentary operations and the translocation of crucial legislative and constitutional deliberations from parliament to the royal quarters, in terms of both physical locality and functioning.

In Swazi politics the King's abode frequently substitutes for the legislative forum as the place where things happen. Historically, it was here that the INM was formed in 1964, and the Independence constitution was repealed in 1973. The 2005 constitution is commonly referred to as Swaziland's 'Cattle-Byre Constitution' because it was supposedly 'adopted by the people of Swaziland' at the royal cattle-byre. It is to the royal abode that the King summons members of parliament to come and account to him.

On the second front and intra-parliament, the King's dominance over the legislative institutions – the House of Assembly and Senate – is evident in both the 'extra-parliamentary' actions and the direct interventions in parliamentary matters. For example, when the Constitution Bill of 2005 was being debated by parliament the Prime Minister delivered a 'special message from the Throne'. This message directly influenced the parliamentary debate (Maseko 2007).

The following sections expand on the intra-parliamentary dominance of the King (the flip-side is the subjected position of the legislature), and then offers an overview of the legislature's position in relation to legislative and policy operations.

The King–Prime Minister–legislature hierarchy

On the level of generic legislative matters, parliament has the authority to make laws through bills. The constitution, however, vests legislative power in the King-in-parliament. The King exercises his executive power directly or indirectly, via parliamentary officers. The King appoints the Prime Minister, and the Deputy Prime Minister and other ministers after consultation with the Prime Minister. The Prime Minister and his deputy enjoy power only as delegated by the King (see *Times of Swaziland* 2010). In the aftermath of the 2008 elections, the recalling of known loyalist Sibusiso Dlamini to the position of Prime Minister was an indication of the King further securing his power.

The distribution of legislative power between the House of Assembly and Senate allows for multiple outcome variations. The constant, however, is that there is allowance for the King's will to prevail (see Constitution of the Kingdom of Swaziland 2005, articles 107, 112–17).

Generally bills require the approval of both Houses and the assent of the King. If the Houses cannot agree on a bill, the matter is referred to a joint sitting, where it can be adopted by a simple majority. If the King withholds his assent the matter is referred to a joint sitting, which can pass the bill with a simple majority and refer the bill back to the King for assent. However, this does not override the King's veto, since he may again refuse assent.

Bills dealing with financial and urgent matters cannot be delayed or amended by the Senate. Bills affecting traditional laws and customs can only be introduced in the Senate. If the House of Assembly fails to consider the bill it is sent to the King for assent by a two-thirds majority of senators. If the bill is not passed by the Assembly, a joint session of parliament is convened, which may pass the bill with a simple majority.

Policy and legislative performance of the Swazi legislature

Whereas the legislature concerns itself with the range of predictable policy and governance issues, it is overwhelmingly the King-in-council who determines government directions. The political orientation of Acts sheds light on the extent to which the legislature rubber-stamps royal directives, expressed or implied. The shrinking scope of parliamentary decision-making in the face of economic crisis, *circa* 2011–12, had an impact primarily on the King, but also on the dominated legislature.

The Suppression of Terrorism Act No. 3 of 2008 was a case in point. Aimed at suppressing dissent, it was tabled as urgent, and passed. Pudemo, the Swaziland Youth Congress (Swayoco), Swaziland Solidarity Network (SSN) and associated agencies were declared terrorist organisations. Consequential actions followed, such as the arrest of the Pudemo president. There have been some cases where the Swazi legislature exercised a touch more independence, however. A House select committee investigated the *Times Sunday* editor in 2007 after the newspaper criticised the Speaker for disallowing debate on constitutional amendments. The committee exonerated the editor, stating the constitutional right to freedom of expression. The Terrorism Act, however, had been an abrogation of precisely these constitutional rights.

The Swazi legislature has been unable to take decisive actions in the policy domains where it was most needed – particularly in terms of employment, health and the economy. The legislature did not present initiatives beyond the imperatives of the King. By 2011–12, the Swazi King had implored young Swazis to find employment in neighbouring South Africa. The IMF urged the Swazi government to reduce the size of the civil service. The government complied and then reversed the call, because it could not afford to pay departing employees. Civil servants were being paid late. The government was running out of money to buy the anti-retrovirals (ARVs) that were necessary to intervene in the HIV/Aids problem. The country was increasingly plunging into foreign debt. In 2012 parliament adopted a seemingly routine budget, yet without any certainty that it would be implemented. It appeared that, in the wake of this economic collapse, space might be opening up for change to more democratic governance, which had not existed before and which opposition parties and civil society could not wrench from the King and his compliant legislature.

In this context, Swaziland was simultaneously ceding some authority to international organisations of development assistance (see above). The Swazi government's 2010 agreement with the United Nations Development Assistance Framework (UNDAF) covered HIV/Aids, poverty and sustainable livelihoods, human development and basic social services, and governance. The agreement included attempts to promote the 'development of a supportive policy and legal framework for improved governance, increase of knowledge of rights by the people, enhanced gender equality as well as improved access to justice for all' (UNDAF 2010).

Conclusion

The story of the legislature of Swaziland is one of an institution that has stood in the shadow of an authoritarian monarchy. Its members were appointed by the King, or elected in a system that was guided by Swaziland's hereditary monarch, through the traditional chieftancy systems. The legislature was accountable to the King, rather than to popular constituencies. This tightly controlled system has prevailed for close to 40 years. By 2010–12 Swaziland's economy was caving in under the pressures of global and regional economic change, development aid was necessitated, and allegations of large-scale and high-level corruption abounded. International pressure for democracy and human rights grew steadily. These pressures combined with increasing internal resistance to erode the authority of the hitherto omnipotent King. It remains uncertain whether these pressures will combine to deliver a democratised legislature.

Note

1   I wish to thank Swaziland specialist Lindiwe Khumalo-Matse for her research assistance and for scrutinising a draft of the chapter.

References

Baloro, J. (1994) The development of Swaziland's constitution: Monarchical responses to modern challenges, *Journal of African Literature*, 38, pp. 19–34.

Commonwealth Secretariat (2007) Swaziland national elections 18 October 2003: Report of the Commonwealth Expert Team, Manzini, 18 October.

Constitution of the Kingdom of Swaziland 2005, http://aceproject.org/regions-en/eisa/SZ/CONSTITUTION%20OF%20THE%20KINGDOM%20OF%20SWAZILAND%202005.pdf (accessed 9 March 2010).

Dlamini, L. (2006) 'Interesting times' in the Kingdom of Swaziland: The advent of the new constitution and the challenge of change, in *Outside the Ballot Box: Preconditions for Elections in Southern Africa 2005/6*, http://www.osisa.org/resources/docs/PDFs/Outside_the_ballot_box_PEPSA.pdf (accessed 11 December 2010).

Hlatshwayo, N. (2003) Swaziland constitutional framework, Paper delivered at the Bridging the Political Divide workshop, Council of Swaziland Churches (CSC)/Southern African Conflict Prevention Network (SACPN), 21–23 June, Pigg's Peak Hotel.

International Crisis Group (2005) *Swaziland: The Clock Is Ticking*, Crisis Group Africa Briefing No. 29 (Pretoria/Brussels: International Crisis Group).

Mamba, V. (2011) Interview (electronic), 5 February.

Maroleng, C. (2003) Swaziland: The King's constitution, in *African Security Analysis Programme: Situation Report*, 26 June (Tshwane, South Africa: Institute for Security Studies).

Maseko, T. (2007) Constitution-making in Swaziland: The Cattle-Byre Constitution Act 001 of 2005, Paper presented at African Network of Constitutional Law Conference on Fostering Constitutionalism in Africa, http://www.publiclaw.uct.ac.za/usr/public_law/Nairobi/Maseko_ConstitutionMakingInSwaziland.doc (accessed 10 December 2010).

Matsebula, J. S. M. (1989) *A History of Swaziland* (Cape Town: Longman Southern Africa).

Mlangeni, B. (2011) Interview (electronic), 4 February.

Mzizi, J. B. (2004) The dominance of the Swazi monarchy and the moral dynamics of democratisation of the Swazi state, *Journal of African Elections*, 13 (1), pp. 94–119.

Napier, C. (2008) Africa's constitutional renewal? Stock taking in the 21st century, Paper, www.apsanet.org/~africaworkshops/ (accessed 12 January 2011).

Physicians for Human Rights (PHR) (2007) *Epidemic of Inequality: Women's Rights and HIV/AIDS in Botswana and Swaziland* (Cambridge, MA: PHR).

Redvers, L. (2011) Swaziland faces fiscal crisis: IMF, *Mail & Guardian*, 28 January – 3 February, p. 25.

Rooney, R. (2011) Free political parties lie exposed, Swazi media commentary, 30 January, http://swazimedia.blogspot.com/2011/01/free-political-parties-lie-exposed.html (accessed 4 February 2011).

Stuart, D. (2009) Swaziland, in D. Kadima and S. Booysen (eds), *Compendium of Elections in Southern Africa: 20 Years of Multiparty Democracy*, pp. 146–85 (Johannesburg: EISA).

Swaziland Solidarity Network (SSN) (2011) Latest information on Kuwait scandal exposes King, ssn-media-releases@googlegroups.com, 8 February.

Times of Swaziland (25 February, 2010) I'm the boss – PM, http://www.times.co.sz/News/14667.html (accessed 2 February 2011).

United Nations Development Assistance Framework (UNDAF) 2011–2015 (2010) Government of Swaziland and the United Nations, Royal Villas, Ezulweni, 8 March 2010.

Wanda, B. P. (1990) The shaping of the modern constitution of Swaziland: A review of some social and historical factors, *Lesotho Law Journal*, 6, pp. 137–78.

World Factbook (2010) CIA, https://www.cia.gov/library/publications/the-world-factbook/geos/wz.html (accessed 2 February 2011).

Part II
Semi-sovereign entities

10 Bermuda

Examining Bermuda's legislature: reflections on why size matters

Walton Brown Jr

Introduction

Bermuda's legislature is a policy-influencing or reactive legislature. Its Parliament was founded in 1620 and is one of the world's oldest. The island is officially designated a British overseas territory and has had internal self-government since 1684. It has evolved over the centuries to become a robust embodiment of democratic power, although such power is limited given its subordinate status to the United Kingdom as a colonial territory. It has a population of 68,679 living on 54 square kilometres.

There are two features contouring the political process that are a direct result of its size and structure: firstly, the influence of the executive over the legislature and, secondly, the structured minority position of the governing party in the upper chamber of Parliament. Other aspects of the legislature have parallels with systems rooted in Westminster-style democratic structures and have provided for a stable political structure throughout its history.

A brief history

When the Parliament was first established the vote was restricted to male property owners who had land of a specific minimum value. At emancipation, and with a black population somewhat larger than that of the white settlers, the Parliament amended the voting qualification to restrict black participation. After 1 August 1834, to vote for a member of assembly, one had to own property assessed at no less than £100, instead of £40, as previously required. To run as a member of Parliament, one had to own property valued at £400 instead of £200.[1] The ruling class justified this by claiming that most blacks lacked sufficient education and were not suited for civic responsibility, and that to enfranchise them immediately would only create social disruption. The most appropriate course to take, they argued, was gradually to groom blacks until they had reached an 'acceptable' level of political maturity. The rationale for this discriminatory practice was explained by the Colonial Office Under-Secretary, James Stephen:

> It seems to me that this is a grievance which time will redress, and that there
> may be a more general convenience and safety in allowance of the actual

supremacy of the whites for a while, to the legal extinction of it; and so to depart from it by degrees, than to reach the same end, by a more abrupt method.[2]

There would be no further change to either the structure of Parliament or voting qualifications until 1944, when property-owning women won the right to vote after a 25-year campaign by the Bermuda Women's Suffragette Society. The right for all citizens to vote would not come for another two decades. When Parliament issued a report of a joint select committee in 1960 concluding that there should be no further extension to voting rights, a grass roots campaign was launched called the Committee for Universal Adult Suffrage. This committee exerted sufficient pressure on Parliament for an abrupt change to be made with the commitment to extending the vote to all adults. Bermuda was set to move into the modern era.

While the vote was extended to all adults, first those aged 25 and older (in 1963), but then reduced to 21 in 1966 and then eventually down to 18 years of age (1989), there was a unique constituency structure created by having dual-seat constituencies. The context for this creation was racial politics, as was made clear by one of the members of Parliament, F. C. Misick and a staunch critic of this structure:

> The 18 two-member electoral districts now recommended have been so contrived as to achieve a precise racial result and ensure the election of 16 white Assemblymen. Such manipulation stultifies the full play of parliamentary democracy and the resultant 'elections' would be a complete travesty of the democratic process. The 16–20 distribution of Assembly seats is based upon the ratio of white to coloured voters. Though plausible, this apportionment will not stand critical examination.[3]

These constituencies were eventually abolished in 2002, and the island adopted 36 single-seat constituencies, with an average size of 1,200 eligible voters.

Government also moved to a Cabinet-style 'responsible' government in the 1960s, breaking away from the centuries-old practice of an absolute fusing of executive and legislative functions in the House of Assembly and upper house.

The current structure is that of a bi-cameral legislature. The upper house is the Senate and the lower house is the House of Assembly. There is a formal, written constitution. Bermuda is officially called a British overseas territory and is one of a small number of non-self-governing territories. In consequence, Parliament has power over most areas of governance except for defence, internal security and external affairs. These powers are reserved for the United Kingdom and are exercised either directly from London or through the UK's appointed governor. Bermuda's Parliament, therefore, is not supreme.

Political parties

Political parties are a comparatively recent phenomenon, emerging in the 1960s along with the introduction of democratic reforms. Two major parties exist – the governing Progressive Labour Party (PLP) and the United Bermuda Party (UBP), along with the fledgling Bermuda Democratic Party, formed by three defecting MPs from the UBP. The UBP governed the island from 1964 to 1998, winning every election fairly; and the PLP have held power continuously since 1998. These parties all occupy the same ideological terrain, and the differences relate more to style and emphases rather than a contestation between alternative visions of society.

A significant difference between the two main parties for decades was the structure of the electoral system. The UBP held the view that the dual-seat constituencies represented a fair and useful means of expressing popular sentiment and had no desire to alter it. The PLP long argued that the system was inherently unfair, as it had structured inequality built into it by creating electoral constituencies which varied wildly in terms of size. One of the first legislative changes introduced by the PLP after winning power was to create an electoral system of single-seat constituencies of comparable size.

Elections are held under the first-past-the-post system, where candidates with the largest plurality of votes are elected. While many countries using this system have seen parties winning the government with a minority of the popular vote, no party has ever won an election in Bermuda without securing at least 50 per cent of that vote. There has also never been a coalition or a minority government.

Bermuda's bi-cameral legislature

The House of Assembly consists of 36 elected members, called members of Parliament. With each constituency comprising approximately 1,200 voters, there is a comparatively high level of parliamentary representation. Almost any adult citizen can offer him- or herself for public office, although anyone who has pledged allegiance to another country is ineligible. The practical effect of this is that someone born in another country who has subsequently attained Bermuda status (shorthand for something akin to citizenship for voting purposes) is able to serve as an MP, but the Bermuda-born person who has acquired, say, American citizenship would be ineligible.

The House is typically the legislative chamber where legislation is introduced. Depending on the nature of the bill, it will either be debated on the House floor or presided over by the Speaker, or the House will resolve itself into committee for clause-by-clause consideration of the bill, with a committee chair. In the latter case, the committee would then report back to the House with the outcome of its deliberations. Once approved by the House the bill is then moved to the Senate.

Backbench or opposition MPs rarely initiate legislation. Rather, these members are primarily concerned with either supporting initiatives coming from their party colleagues in Cabinet or holding to the stances taken by the opposition party leadership. Again, this is in part a consequence of size. All parties hold caucuses prior to the weekly meeting in Parliament (when Parliament is in session) and arrive at party positions on each issue in advance. Where there are differences they are debated in caucus. With the small size of each caucus every member has an opportunity to contribute and shape the discussion. Those who are opposed to a bill are normally silenced by the imposition of the whip to ensure voting solidarity.

The parliamentary meeting schedule is light, with a maximum of seven months of a 12-month cycle. Other than legislation, much of the parliamentary time is taken up with congratulatory remarks and condolences, with MPs sure to acknowledge even minor celebrations, particularly when they occur in their electoral constituency; considerable time is also allocated to the motion to adjourn, allowing all members to raise issues and show the public their advocacy on specific matters.

During the 2009/10 parliamentary session, the House of Assembly met 31 times and for an average of six hours. The meetings are typically on Fridays, except for the budget debate, in which six sessions are concentrated within a two-week period. No MP attended less than 77 per cent of the sessions. During this same period, the Senate met 24 times for an average of four hours. These meetings are held on Wednesdays. No senator attended less than 80 per cent of the sessions.

The government leader, the Premier, is appointed by the Governor based on who, in his opinion, can best command the support of the majority of the MPs. It is not necessarily the person who leads his or her party to electoral victory. There is a subtle yet critically important issue here. All parties elect their own party leader; under normal circumstances the winning party will have their leader automatically appointed Premier by the Governor. In 2003, however, the Premier did not have the support of a majority of the elected members of Parliament – even after winning the election with a majority of seats. Faced with this the Premier was forced to resign as party leader and another leader was elected, one who had majority support and was therefore appointed Premier by the Governor.

The Senate consists of 11 appointed members: five appointed by the governing party, three by the official opposition, and three by the governor. These last three are termed independent, non-party-affiliated senators. In the upper house, then, the governing party is in a structured minority position. It is rare, however, for the Senate to reject legislation brought forward from the House. In 2004, Senate rejected a bill to introduce global positioning satellite technology to the taxi industry; and in March 2011 government was forced to suspend a debate on a special development order for a property developer when it became clear through independent senator comments that they would vote against the order. The government suspended the debate with a 'rise and report progress' measure and then set about redrafting the order to gain the necessary support.

As Bermuda's bi-cameral legislature is asymmetrical, the Senate's powers are effectively limited to delaying the passage of legislation. If the Senate votes against a bill it automatically reverts to the House for their reconsideration in the next parliamentary session. If the House approves it a second time it must be approved by the Senate as a mere formality. Any bill involving taxes cannot be rejected by the Senate. These two provisions are largely based on custom, and it is not clear what the outcome would be if senators acted contrary to this practice.

General elections must be called within five years of the date of the last election, but the Premier can call an election at any time during this interval. A vote of no confidence can also trigger an election. Premier Ewart Brown faced such a vote in July 2009 after he agreed a secret deal with the United States to bring four Uighur prisoners from Guantánamo Bay. The motion did not pass.

The executive

Executive power resides in Cabinet. All Cabinet ministers also serve as members of the legislature, although not more than 12 can be appointed from the House of Assembly, and at least one but not more than two must be appointed from the Senate.

As the primary policy-making and legislation-producing component of government, the Cabinet is the real locus of power. Patterned on the Westminster system, the Cabinet is actually granted greater power through the fusing of executive power with the legislature than it would have under the US-styled separation of executive and legislative branches. A bill initiated by a minister and presented to Parliament, for example, would be by the leadership of the governing party, submitted to a Parliament controlled by that same party, and under the party whip.

This structure takes on even greater significance when examined in a small parliament like Bermuda's. With only 36 MPs and a Cabinet of up to 12 Ministers from the House of Assembly, there is the potential that a third of the MPs will have already approved the bill in Cabinet. With a mere six additional votes required for passage, Cabinet is in a position to ensure its legislative agenda is carried out. At least this is the case under most circumstances.

Parliament in action

While Cabinet is the dominant political force – it sets all major policy and proposes almost all legislation – its authority rests upon the retention of the support of, and the resulting legitimacy from, Parliament, particularly the Cabinet's party colleagues who also sit in the House. In the absence of support – and therefore legitimacy – Parliament has demonstrated its ability to assert its power and lead the legislative process. Two examples, under two different leaders, are illustrative.

For many years, Bermuda had a policy banning the establishment of fast food franchises, after the KFC brand was set up in advance of any political discussion in the 1970s. In the 1990s, John Swan, while Premier, secured the licence to establish McDonald's, and the government later announced the decades-long policy of banning fast food franchises would be reviewed. Cabinet subsequently, and not surprisingly, announced that the policy would be relaxed and other fast food franchises would be allowed. In response to this, backbench members of the governing party formed an alliance with the opposition and passed legislation banning such franchises unequivocally, taking the power away from Cabinet in the policy-making arena.

In 2010, government brought forward a bill which would have allowed gaming on cruise ships. This was a contentious matter by a government that had already suffered a crisis of legitimacy among backbenchers over a series of earlier decisions. This matter was rejected by Parliament in an act of defiance and a matter of public embarrassment for government.

The House of Assembly has also shown that it is prepared to act contrary to the desires of the Premier, again when there is a crisis of legitimacy. A parliamentary tradition in Bermuda for many years had the Deputy Speaker automatically elected to the position of Speaker once that seat was vacated. In 1993, the Premier sought to change this by announcing his desire to have someone else as Speaker – an individual who would have been the first black Speaker. The person who was Deputy was of Portuguese ethnicity and would have been the first Speaker from this background. When the matter came for a vote in the chamber, the Clerk to the Legislature ruled that, since Parliament could not be in session until a Speaker had been elected, normal parliamentary rules did not apply and he would allow for a secret ballot, as was requested by some MPs. With the secret ballot allowed, members of the ruling party along with members of the opposition voted to elect the Deputy as Speaker, thereby rejecting the Premier's choice.

The Senate is meant to provide a sober second look at legislation; this is facilitated by its size and structure, giving it a less combative, more deliberative nature than the House of Assembly. The House is divided in half, with the opposition on the opposite side of the room to the government and its supporters. By contrast, the Senate chamber has 11 members sitting around a round table, where everyone sits while speaking – creating a very different set of dynamics. It is rare for the Senate to send back a piece of legislation, although it has done so. Typically, if there is a problem found with a bill or government senses it is likely to be rejected, the lead government senator on that bill will ask to 'rise and report progress', effectively stopping debate and allowing time for government to address, to the extent they can, these challenges.

It is important to note an aspect about the nature of the appointments to the Senate. Senators appointed by the political parties are typically persons who the party expects to run in the next general election, and the appointment is meant to enhance their electability. They are appointed to the upper house to increase their chances of getting into the lower house. The governor's three appointments are typically senior members of the business community or other areas of public life who have recently retired.

Where Parliament was once adjudged to be supreme, legislatures worldwide now have to adjust their modus operandi as a result of a number of changes. Bermuda confronts those same challenges, as well as an additional one:

1   Impact of disciplined parties. As political parties have matured and information can be more widely and easily disseminated there is no information vacuum. Those on the backbench expect information on all key issues as much as does the frontbench. This enhanced access to information coupled with the ease of holding meetings for the entire party executive and caucus on a regular basis provides the conditions for consensus building unlikely to occur in larger legislatures. The effect of this in Parliament is a greater demonstration of party unity on legislative initiatives. Paradoxically, though, what appears as a benefit for political parties – by having debates within the party caucus and not on the floor of Parliament – can just as easily send a message to the public that MPs are mere minions of the party hierarchy and do not have an independent voice. This creates a perception that Parliament is a rubber stamp of party

positions and not the bastion of vibrant democracy and intense debate some expect it to be.

2   Growth in scope and activity of government. Governments have become more expansive over time, taking on greater and greater responsibilities. As the executive branch works its way through issues there is a tendency to want to make important decisions on a time schedule that does not always align with the parliamentary schedule. Working through the parliamentary schedule can slow down the decision-making process, and in the current global economic and business climate this can lead to a loss of economic opportunity for a government. The response to this challenge is for the executive branch to try to find ways to make as many decisions as possible without having to go through the sometimes prolonged parliamentary process. The advantage is speed, but it can come at the price of pre-empting parliamentary oversight. One way to ensure parliamentary oversight but also expedite the decision-making process is to create a greater number of parliamentary committees. Bermuda currently has a number of committees that both facilitate the due diligence process and provide appropriate oversight. The Public Accounts Committee is chaired by a member of the opposition, and the committee is mandated to assess the financial management of any ministry. There is also the Private Bills Committee, which reviews mostly companies seeking to incorporate through specific legislation. In 2010 a joint select committee was established to look into the causes of violent crime. This work could be extended to other areas, such as sustainability and human rights, for example, which would strengthen democracy by having greater participation in the policy formulation process. The above notwithstanding, there will be times when the Premier and Cabinet will need to make important executive decisions quickly and Parliament be informed after the fact. An example of this recently in Bermuda was the quick decision to bail out a cash-strapped bank during the financial crisis.

3   Relevance of pressure groups. Pressure groups play a critical role in shaping democratic debate, and technology has to a considerable extent further democratized such groups through the power of the internet and social messaging. Online pressure groups – even when veiled in secrecy – have influenced national debates and continue to influence the decision-making process. In some respects, they can do more that even opposition parties in changing the expected outcome of proposed legislation. The power of such groups lies in both their numbers and their singularity of purpose. A large, diverse group speaking with one voice on a critical issue will probably have more impact than the predictable voice of an opposition party. This has been used with great effect on Bermuda's legislature when the issues related to the environment.

4   Role of the media. As the main conduit of information between politicians and the people, the media have more influence over how the public view issues than does the legislature itself. Bermuda's media, as is the case with the media everywhere, are often criticized for how they report the news and for not telling the story as the politicians would like it to be told. This creates an inevitable

suspicion and an obvious tension. But politicians fight a battle they cannot win when they focus their attention on the way the messenger delivers the message. With the plethora of media venues in print and online, legislators have an opportunity to share information in ways not possible even 10 years ago. This cannot but be an aid to effective governance.

5   Bermuda as a limited democracy. Perhaps the most salient issue on the political horizon for the Bermuda legislature to address is that of the practical consequence of it being a limited democracy. The people elect a government, but it only has the power to govern over a limited area – with the ultimate power held in London. The global landscape today requires that governments have more, not less, flexibility to meet challenges that often appear without notice. A legislature without responsibility, even indirectly, over its external affairs in a world rooted in globalization simply cannot be a genuinely effective legislature. A Cabinet, the embodiment of executive power, which can only address international issues after obtaining permission from the UK is a body poorly positioned to provide long-term effective leadership and good governance.

Conclusion

Bermuda's small size has created a legislature with a number of nuances as a result of that size: the relationship between the executive and legislature is of particular note, as is the minority position of the governing party in the Senate. In many other respects, it is a microcosm of the Westminster system: the fusing of the executive and legislative branches, the asymmetry of the bi-cameral structure, and the backbench/frontbench tension. It is not an ideal framework for effective governance given the obvious constitutional limitations, but what it does provide is the basis for progressive steps forward.

Notes

1   Cyril Packwood (1975) *Chained on the Rock* (Hamilton: Island Press), p. 185.
2   H. C. Wilkinson (1973) *Bermuda from Sail to Steam: A History of the Island from 1784 to 1901*, Vol. 1 (Oxford: Oxford University Press), p. 515, note 1.
3   *Journals of the House of Assembly*, June 1962, p. 310.

11 Gibraltar

The Gibraltar Parliament

Haresh K. Budhrani

Gibraltar is a British overseas territory, and the current relationship between Gibraltar and the United Kingdom is governed by the Gibraltar Constitution Order 2006, which came into effect on 2 January 2007. That Constitution provides for a modern relationship between Gibraltar and the United Kingdom and expressly 'gives the people of Gibraltar that degree of self-government which is compatible with British sovereignty of Gibraltar and with the fact that the United Kingdom remains fully responsible for Gibraltar's external relations'. The Constitution represents a process of evolution over the 300 years of British sovereignty over Gibraltar to its present non-colonial status but does not in any way diminish British sovereignty of Gibraltar. The United Kingdom retains its full international responsibility for Gibraltar, including for Gibraltar's external relations and defence.

The people of Gibraltar through their legislature, which consists of the Queen and the Gibraltar Parliament, as it has been known since 2007, exercise self-government. Section 32 of the Constitution confers upon the Parliament the power to 'make laws for the peace, order and good government of Gibraltar'.

While under Section 44 the executive authority of Gibraltar is vested in the Queen, that authority is exercised by the Government of Gibraltar, which comprises the Chief Minister and a Council of Ministers (not being fewer than four or more than 10 ministers) together with the Queen, who is represented in Gibraltar by the Governor.

The supremacy of the legislature is further underlined by the requirement that:

1   the Governor shall appoint as Chief Minister the elected member of the Parliament who in his judgement is most likely to command the greatest measure of confidence among the elected[1] members thereof; and
2   the ministers shall be appointed by the Governor, acting in accordance with the advice of the Chief Minister, from among the elected members of the Parliament.

The Gibraltar legislature is a unicameral system to which 17 members are elected for a four-year term, although the Chief Minister may at any time request the Governor to dissolve the Parliament. The Governor may not disregard the Chief

Minister's advice as to the dissolution of the Parliament unless he considers that the good government of Gibraltar requires him to do so (Section 38).

Members of the Parliament are elected by universal adult suffrage, the electorate comprising approximately 22,000 persons on the register of electors. In view of its small size both geographically (approximately 3 square miles) and in terms of population (approximately 30,000 inhabitants), Gibraltar is a single constituency for electoral purposes and voters are faced with a single ballot paper naming all the candidates who have been validly nominated.

However, under the Elections Act, each voter is entitled to vote for up to 10 candidates of his or her choice, the 17 candidates securing the highest number of votes being returned to the Parliament as elected members. The party securing a majority of those 17 seats forms the Government, and the leader of that party is appointed Chief Minister by the Governor.

Although the Constitution does not make specific provision for such an office, the leader of the party with the largest number of seats in the Parliament not forming the Government is known as the Leader of the Opposition and is accorded remuneration in that capacity.

The proceedings of the Parliament are presided over by the Speaker, who is appointed by the Parliament by a resolution (passed by a simple majority of its members) presented by the Chief Minister acting after consultation with the Leader of the Opposition. The Speaker may not be an elected member of the Parliament but he should be eligible for election to the Parliament.

The Speaker has neither an original nor a casting vote and, if upon any question before the Parliament the votes are equally divided, the Speaker is required to declare the motion lost (Section 43).

The Parliament is served by the Clerk and, in addition to the Clerk, the Principal Auditor and the Ombudsman are officers of the Parliament.

The Parliament's legislative power is exercised by bills passed by it and assented to by the Queen or by the Governor on her behalf. While the Governor usually assents as a matter of course to bills enacted by the Parliament and submitted to him, he has the power to reserve a bill 'for signification of Her Majesty's pleasure' which appears to him 'to be in any way repugnant to or inconsistent with [the] Constitution' or to withhold assent to any bill which appears to him 'to be in any way repugnant to good government or incompatible with any international legal obligation' unless he has been authorised by the Queen's Secretary of State to assent to it (Section 33). It is believed that this power has never been exercised by the Governor – certainly it has not been exercised since 1969.

The Governor also has power under Section 34 to initiate legislation if he considers that its enactment is necessary or desirable in the interests of any matter for which he is responsible (namely external affairs, defence and internal security) but only if, after consultation with the Chief Minister, it appears to him that the Government is unwilling to support the introduction into the Parliament of a bill for the purpose. Such legislative power may be exercised by the Governor by simply publishing the bill in the *Gibraltar Gazette* at least 21 days prior to assenting thereto.[2]

Subject to the foregoing, the Parliament enjoys the sole and full legislative power in Gibraltar but may not, except with the consent of the Governor, proceed on any bill which, in the opinion of the Governor, concerns a matter for which he is responsible under Section 47(1).

By Section 37(3) the Parliament is required to meet at least three times in any calendar year except a calendar year in which a general election is held, when there must be at least two meetings.

By Section 39 the Parliament is empowered to make, amend and revoke its own rules of procedure for the regulation and orderly conduct of its proceedings and the dispatch of business and, to that end, the Parliament has passed its own standing orders, which in large measure reflect the practices and procedures of the House of Commons at Westminster.

For the interpretation of its standing orders and, in the absence of a specific rule of practice or procedure within the standing orders, the Speaker invariably turns to Erskine May's *Parliamentary Practice* for guidance.

Being a parliamentary system based on the Westminster model, the Gibraltar Parliament may be fairly described as a policy-influencing legislature because, while it can either amend or reject measures proposed by the executive, it cannot, in practice, substitute any measure for policy of its own.

With the emergence of political parties in Gibraltar after the end of the Second World War and with the electoral system which has been in place since an earlier Constitution (the Gibraltar Constitution Order 1969), there has been a large element of 'block voting' by the electorate, in that all 10 votes tend to be cast for the preferred party rather than being split between individual candidates from the various parties or the independents contesting the elections. In short, the vast majority of those exercising their right to vote tend to vote for a government rather than for 10 MPs, and this inclination, as will be seen later in this chapter, does have a bearing on the make-up and the workings of the Parliament.

Elections have also increasingly focused on rival chief ministerial 'candidates', a phenomenon to which media coverage has in no small measure contributed and, indeed, it has led to a personalisation of the office. In fact, one might venture as far as to state that the Chief Minister is no longer the *primus inter pares* that Sir Robert Walpole was in the eighteenth century.

The electoral system and the tendency of the electorate to vote in 'block' always result in a Parliament in which, regardless of the extent of the contesting parties' respective popularity, the size of the majority in the Parliament reflects the 10 votes cast by the electors, with those securing the next seven highest number of votes forming the Opposition. This practice has, for several years, all but ruled out any representation (proportional or otherwise) in the Parliament by third parties or independents.

The fact that the party in Government has 10 of the 17 seats and that all 10 of those members are appointed to ministerial office means that there are no back-benchers in the Parliament other than those seven members sitting on the Opposition benches.

The consequence of this is that scrutiny of the acts (or omissions) of the executive or of the legislation brought to the House by the Government is limited to that by those forming part of the Opposition and, accordingly, their best endeavours can serve only to bring to the attention of the electorate or highlight what the Opposition perceives to be shortcomings on the part of the Government without directly influencing government policy.

By contrast, in a large legislature such as the House of Commons (not to mention those legislatures, including Westminster, which have a second or revising chamber) where a vast majority of MPs (even supporters of the Government) are not members of the executive, the power of scrutiny enjoyed by the legislature as a whole (even allowing for the fact that backbenchers within the governing party might tend to be less critical of the executive's actions and more forgiving of its omissions) would appear to be more effectively exercised and not infrequently influences the policy of the government of the day.

This is equally evident in the legislative process in that, while the Opposition members may sometimes succeed in persuading the Government of the merits of their arguments on matters of detail in one or two aspects of a bill in committee, the Government is hardly ever likely to be dissuaded from its intended course of action in a debate on the general principles of a bill introduced by it.

As a result, therefore, the conclusion, as far as the case of Gibraltar is concerned, is that size very definitely matters, particularly in (a) the absence of multiple constituencies and hence the lack of MPs' constituency interests and (b) the fact that the majority in the Parliament is made up of members of the executive.

Notes

1   Note the emphasis on 'elected' members in order to exclude the Speaker.
2   This power has not been exercised to date. Nor was a corresponding power under the previous Constitution ever exercised.

12 Guernsey

The States of Deliberation of Guernsey

Richard McMahon

History

The States of Deliberation are a unicameral legislature serving the British Crown dependency of Guernsey. Its origins lie in the steps taken in the sixteenth century to broaden the administration of Guernsey to include the clergy and the constables of the 10 parishes. This had previously been undertaken solely by the Royal Court, comprising the Bailiff and jurats, convening an assembly of the insular equivalents of the three French estates under the derived style 'Les États' (which explains its subsequent anglicisation to become the States). However, the principal legislature remained the Royal Court until well into the nineteenth century. By the end of that century, a small number of representatives were directly elected. The clergy's membership was abolished in the major constitutional reforms of 1948.[1] Those reforms also resulted in the participation of the jurats being ended, although direct parochial representation continued until the 2004 reforms.[2] In Hocart's detailed analysis of the historical developments up to 1948, he summarised the reforms as having 'transformed the States from a quasi-medieval assembly into a body combining the functions of a modern local council and a legislature'.[3] The States continue to exercise both legislative and administrative, or executive, functions.

Channel Islands – Guernsey

Electoral districts operate on parish boundaries, together with the splitting of St Peter Port roughly up the middle. The parish districts are:

1 Castel
2 Forest
3 St Andrew
4 St Martin
5 St Peter Port
6 St Pierre du Bois
7 St Sampson
8 St Saviour
9 Torteval
10 Vale

Membership

The present composition of the States of Deliberation is the Bailiff ex officio as non-voting Presiding Officer,[4] the two law officers of the Crown (HM Procureur, or Attorney-General, and HM Comptroller, or Solicitor-General), acting as non-voting counsel to the States, 45 people's deputies directly elected in seven electoral districts, or constituencies, across the island of Guernsey, and two representatives appointed from the members of the States of Alderney. The Alderney representatives are full members of the States and are entitled to vote on all matters. Whilst appearing to raise 'West Lothian'-type issues, the arrangements introduced after the Second World War under which Alderney is in fiscal union with Guernsey and the States of Guernsey take responsibility for the provision of specified major services in Alderney mean that the people of Alderney are inevitably interested in, and affected by, decisions reached by the States of Deliberation.[5]

Within the States of Deliberation party politics do not exist, members being free to vote as they please on each item of business. As every member is an independent and all play some role in government, there is no concept of collective responsibility, even within departments and committees. Dissension occurs without there being any requirement or even expectation that the member should resign from office.

Deputies are elected for four-year fixed terms. The most recent general election was in April 2008. Deputies entered into office on 1 May. Before taking office, members must take an oath and the oath of allegiance, or make such affirmations. Elections are held by secret ballot in accordance with the Loi relative au Scrutin Secret (1899). Electoral districts generally operate consistently with parochial boundaries: Castel, St Sampson and Vale are single-parish districts; the West comprises the four parishes of Forest, St Pierre du Bois, St Saviour and Torteval; St Andrew and St Martin combine to form a single South-East district; and St Peter Port is divided into two districts. Prior to the 2008 election the franchise was extended to 16- and 17-year-olds, and this new regime was used for the first time in that year. The States are considering whether to re-introduce island-wide voting for some of the members, as was the position between 1994 and 2000,[6] retaining the electoral districts for the majority of members, or even making the entire island a single constituency. Alderney representatives are selected at the States of Alderney's January 'annual meeting'.[7]

The States of Deliberation meet in the principal courtroom of the Royal Court, which is therefore configured for this dual purpose. Within the States Chamber, the Chief Minister and ministers sit facing the remainder of the Assembly on either side of the Presiding Officer in the seats otherwise used for court purposes by the jurats. If the Lieutenant-Governor, who is Queen Elizabeth II's personal representative in the Bailiwick of Guernsey, chooses to attend a meeting, as he is entitled to, although he does not participate, he sits on the right hand of the Presiding Officer. The other members occupy the seats within the body of the court, grouped by electoral district. The two law officers sit at separate tables facing the Presiding Officer. Proceedings are recorded and transmitted live on the local BBC radio station.

Under Article 7 of the 1948 Reform Law, the States have resolved to make rules of procedure of the States of Deliberation (the 'Rules of Procedure'), akin to standing orders. From time to time, they may vote to suspend any or all of them. Further, rules relating to the constitution and operation of States departments and committees (the 'Departmental Rules') have been made pursuant to the States Committees (Constitution and Amendment) (Guernsey) Law, 1991. Taken together, the 1948 Law and these sets of rules form the operational handbook of the States.

Departments and committees

The majority of functions are delegated by the States of Deliberation to departments and committees, in accordance with mandates[8] prescribed by the States, with other functions being conferred by extant legislation. In early May following a general election, the States hold elections for the purpose of choosing the membership of the departments and committees. Casual vacancies are filled as the need arises for the remainder of the four-year terms. There are no limitations placed on the number of occasions, consecutive or otherwise, on which an individual member may be elected to the same office.[9]

There are 10 governmental departments,[10] each comprising a minister and four other States members, one of whom is chosen as the Deputy Minister, plus up to two non-voting non-States members. The Chief Minister chairs the Policy Council, which also consists of the 10 ministers.[11] The States elect the Deputy Chief Minister from among the 10 ministers. A member is eligible to become Chief Minister only after having held the office of people's deputy for at least four years in the eight years immediately preceding the date of election.[12] The Chief Minister is not permitted to sit on any department or committee.[13] A minister may sit on one other department as an ordinary member, although in practice none has sought to do so, but may not chair or otherwise be a member of the Scrutiny or Public Accounts Committees.[14]

Political scrutiny of the activities of the governmental departments is undertaken on behalf of the States of Deliberation by the Scrutiny and Public Accounts Committees. This system was introduced in the 2004 reforms as a means of supplementing the parliamentary scrutiny otherwise undertaken by the full States of Deliberation. The Scrutiny Committee comprises a chairman and eight other States members, one of whom is chosen as vice-chairman. The Public Accounts Committee comprises a chairman and four other States members, one of whom is chosen as vice-chairman, plus four non-States members, all of whom are voting members. There is no bar on ordinary members who sit on departments also sitting on the Scrutiny and/or Public Accounts Committees. However, if those committees are engaged in scrutinising the activities of any department involving any membership overlap, the member concerned will withdraw from participating in the scrutiny process. In practice, the committees appoint smaller panels or sub-committees from within their membership for the purpose of carrying out particular reviews.

The Legislation Select Committee comprises a chairman and four other States members, one of whom is chosen as vice-chairman, plus up to two non-voting non-States members (and currently one such member is an advocate of the Royal Court of Guernsey). It is mandated to review all draft legislation prepared by the law officers of the Crown and their professional staff to ensure that it is consistent with the policy-based States resolutions prior to submission to the States of Deliberation for approval. Where there is an urgent need for a draft ordinance to be made, this committee is authorised to make it, and the measure is then laid before the States, under a form of negative resolution procedure, for them to consider taking steps to annul it, but without affecting anything done under it in the meantime.[15] A similar process applies to consideration of statutory instruments made by the departments and other bodies upon which the power to make subordinate legislation has been conferred.

The States of Guernsey are a single legal entity; the constituent parts do not have separate legal personality, although specific functions may be conferred on certain office-holders. The States act as employer of all established staff (i.e. civil servants), acting through the Policy Council, and for other public sector employees acting through various key departments. Functions relating to remuneration and conditions of service, including collective bargaining, are undertaken on behalf of the States by the Public Sector Remuneration Committee, the only one of the standing States committees that is not a 'parliamentary committee', comprising a chairman and four other States members, one of whom is chosen as vice-chairman, plus up to two non-voting non-States members.

Procedure

Meetings of the States of Deliberation are convened by the Presiding Officer through the publication of a 'Billet d'État', which contains the agenda of items to be debated. Meetings usually commence on the last Wednesday of each month, although the States do not meet in August or in the April during which a general election is held, and December meetings commence in the middle of the month. Depending on the amount of business at a meeting, it can be adjourned to the Thursday and then to the Friday and, where necessary, to another date. Each day commences with the Lord's Prayer and ends with the Grace, both recited in French by the clerk to the States, HM Greffier, or his deputy. There are six scheduled hours of sitting each day, split equally between the morning and the afternoon.

Unless there are any statements made with permission of the Presiding Officer under the Rules of Procedure, rule 8, at each meeting there is first an opportunity to put oral questions on notice to the Chief Minister, ministers and chairmen on anything not covered in the business in the Billet. Supplementary questions arising from the answer given may be permitted but need not be answered if the person being questioned thinks that any answer given might be inaccurate or misleading. The Presiding Officer may choose to curtail question time after 30 minutes.

The Billet lists the business for the meeting together with propositions thereon enabling the States to reach decisions. Draft legislation contained in an attached 'brochure' to the Billet is always listed first, the propositions being to approve the relevant 'Projets de Loi',[16] or bills, or, as the case may be, draft ordinances. Because the States will usually have debated the underlying policy on a previous occasion, there is frequently no further debate on these items of draft legislation. The absence of any apparent debate on the clauses in draft legislation may suggest that the States of Deliberation do not have a high regard for their legislative functions. However, it should be borne in mind that, following robust debate on the principles to be enshrined in legislation, the States formally direct two of their members, the law officers of the Crown, to prepare legislation to give effect to their policy decisions. During the drafting process, consultation with the sponsoring department is undertaken, and the department frequently engages in public consultation on the draft measure. Furthermore, the States have interposed the Legislation Select Committee, to which the task of reviewing draft legislation in detail is delegated, meaning that the States of Deliberation have no need to duplicate that exercise. However, because the committee meets in private, its scrutiny of draft legislation – indeed the overall legislative process – may be thought to lack transparency.

The other agenda items, or articles, in a Billet comprise reports emanating from the Policy Council, departments and committees. Such reports, other than reports of the parliamentary committees, generally have to be submitted to the Policy Council at least 11 weeks before a scheduled meeting of the States (although the Policy Council is permitted to waive this notice period).[17] This enables the Policy Council and, where there are financial implications, the Treasury and Resources Department to append their comments, if any, prior to the publication of the Billet d'État. Publication of the Billet generally occurs at least five weeks before the scheduled sitting of the States,[18] although shorter periods apply to the annual budget each December and at the discretion of the Presiding Officer.[19]

Debate

After an item of business is announced by HM Greffier, the Presiding Officer invites the minister of the department originating the report or, in the case of a report from the Policy Council, the Chief Minister (or another nominated representative) to open debate. Any two members may move an amendment to the propositions attaching to the item of business or seek to prevent or postpone debate on the matter by moving a 'sursis' (a delaying motion, which may also be coupled with a direction to provide an additional report). Some amendments and sursis have to be circulated no later than specified times in advance of the meeting.[20] The law officers frequently assist with the wording of these motions.

If an amendment is placed, the proposer of the amendment introduces it, after which it is formally seconded, with the seconder either choosing to speak immediately or reserving the right to do so later in the debate. The person who opened the debate is entitled to speak on the amendment immediately before the proposer replies to conclude the debate on it. Depending on the nature of the amendment, it might be feasible to debate it within the context of general debate, requiring minor modifications to the order of speeches in winding up. A member may seek a ruling from the Presiding Officer as to whether an amendment goes further than the original proposition and, where such a ruling is given, if not less than one-third of the members voting on it support a motion not to debate the amendment (or postpone its debate), the amendment will not then be pursued.[21] An alternative means of curtailing debate on an amendment or sursis is to test immediately after it has been moved and formally seconded whether there are seven or more members who wish to debate it.[22] If a sursis is moved, all other debate on the article ceases until the sursis has been debated and voted on. If carried, there is no further debate on the article at all.[23]

In relation to each debate, including a stand-alone debate on an amendment or sursis, unless the Presiding Officer rules otherwise, members are usually limited to a single speech.[24] There are, however, opportunities for those who opened debate on any matter to have the final word before that matter is put to the vote.[25] A member who has not yet spoken is able to propose that debate on any item be closed, subject only to the usual winding-up speeches, and when such a motion is proposed no debate on it is allowed; it is immediately put to the members by the Presiding Officer and carried if supported by two-thirds of the members voting thereon.[26]

When voting occurs, if there are two or more propositions, they may be voted on together or separately. Any member may request that a formal division by way of recorded vote (*appel nominal*) takes place; otherwise votes are taken *au voix*. The order of calling for members' votes on an *appel nominal* corresponds to their electoral districts and rotates by district for each meeting.[27] French is used for voting, so members supporting a proposition vote 'pour', those opposing it vote 'contre' and anyone abstaining announces 'Je ne vote pas.' There is no system of simultaneous electronic voting.

Requêtes

A requête is a form of private members' motion. It requires seven or more members to sign a petition which, rather than itself directing the preparation of legislation in any given policy area, usually calls for a named department to investigate a matter within its mandate and report to the States thereon at a later date. It is also the device by which members seek to reverse previous decisions of the States, usually, but not exclusively, of an executive nature. The Rules of Procedure, rule 17, provide special rules for the preparation of requêtes prior to their appearance as items of business in a Billet, enabling the Policy Council to solicit the views of interested departments and committees, and prescribe a structure for debate enabling the ministers and chairmen of those departments and committees to speak during both the opening and winding-up stages.

Motions of no confidence

Once members have been elected to departments and committees, the primary way of withdrawing that mandate from the chosen group of members is through moving a motion of no confidence in the entire department or committee.[28] The signatures of seven or more members are required, and thus the process is broadly comparable to a requête. The motion must contain the full details on which the petitioners propose that the lack of confidence should be determined and will be included in a Billet as soon as reasonably practicable. If successful, the minister or chairman and all the members of the department or committee are deemed to have tendered their resignations, triggering fresh elections to complete the unexpired portions of their terms of office. Similar procedures are available in respect of the Chief Minister and the Deputy Chief Minister.[29]

Conclusion

Guernsey is recognised by HM Government as being 'a long-standing, small democracy'.[30] Its parliamentary Rules of Procedure are not overly complicated, consistent with what is required for the governance of an assembly of independents in which constituents are numerically well represented. Consensus is achieved on a item-by-item basis through a legislative process that usually provides for debate on the principles underlying the measure separately from any debate on the draft legislation itself. Having agreed the policy direction, the States of Deliberation delegate consideration of the detail of draft legislation to the Legislation Select Committee, offering – at least in the eyes of supporters – an effective and efficient way of saving parliamentary time.

Notes

1 The Reform (Guernsey) Law, 1948 was enacted following consideration of the recommendations of the Committee of the Privy Council under the chairmanship of the British Home Secretary, James Chuter Ede, which reported in March 1947. The 1948 Law, albeit quite heavily amended, remains the principal source document of Guernsey's internal 'unwritten' constitution.
2 These reforms primarily affected the machinery of government but also covered the composition of the States of Deliberation. They resulted from consideration of the recommendations of a panel established by the States under the chairmanship of Advocate Peter Harwood (accessible at http://www.gov.gg/ccm/policy-and-hr/machinery-of-government/report-by-the-harwood-panel-which-was-published-in-november-2000.en).
3 *An Island Assembly* (1988). Details of the post-1948 developments and the present structure are contained in Ogier, *The Government and Law of Guernsey* (2005).
4 The Deputy Bailiff substitutes when the Bailiff is absent or otherwise unable to preside. Traditionally, the three longest-serving deputies are appointed to fulfil duties as acting Presiding Officer as necessary. The similar position of the Bailiff of Jersey acting as President of the States Assembly has been reviewed by a panel under the chairmanship of Lord Carswell, which reported on 6 December 2010 (http://www.gov.je/Government/Pages/StatesReports.aspx?ReportID=491), so further consideration about the composition of the States of Deliberation may follow.
5 Perhaps here it should be noted that the States of Deliberation of Guernsey are a separate legislature from those of Alderney and Sark, the smaller islands of the Bailiwick of Guernsey. Alderney and Sark each conduct elections on the basis of their single, island-wide constituencies. The States of Alderney are constituted by a president and 10 other

members, all directly elected by universal suffrage. The Chief Pleas of Sark are constituted by the Seneschal ex officio as president, the Seigneur, who may speak but may not vote, and 28 conseillers, all of whom are directly elected by universal suffrage. Both islands hold elections for half their members every two years. The States of Alderney and the Chief Pleas of Sark have the same degree of legislative competence for their islands as the States of Deliberation have for Guernsey, save that criminal justice legislation is enacted on behalf of the entire bailiwick solely by the States of Deliberation.

6   The 1948 reforms introduced the office of conseiller, 12 members elected by the States of Election (an electoral college) for staggered six-year terms. The Reform (Election of Conseillers and Minor Amendments) (Guernsey) Law, 1993 replaced this method of election by direct universal suffrage from the islands of Guernsey and Alderney. The 'experiment' was short-lived: only one full election, one partial election to fill the six seats of those whose terms of office were initially for three years only, and one by-election took place before the office was abolished.

7   Section 41 of the Government of Alderney Law, 2004, as amended. See also generally the States of Guernsey (Representation of Alderney) Law, 1978, as amended.

8   Accessible from http://www.gov.gg/ccm/navigation/government/states-members-and-committees/mandates-and-memberships/.

9   Departmental Rules, rule 8.

10   Commerce and Employment; Culture and Leisure; Education; Environment; Health and Social Services; Home; Housing; Public Services; Social Security; and Treasury and Resources. Prior to the 2004 reforms of the machinery of government, there were more than 40 committees of the States of Guernsey.

11   An alternative departmental representative may substitute at any meeting.

12   Rules of Procedure, rule 20(2A).

13   Departmental Rules, rule 3(2).

14   Ibid., rule 4(3).

15   Article 66(3), Reform (Guernsey) Law, 1948.

16   These measures require royal sanction from the Queen in Council, involving submission through the UK Ministry of Justice.

17   Rules of Procedure, rule 2(1)(a).

18   This period was increased from 19 days with effect from September 2010, designed to permit members longer to digest the reports contained therein, consider whether any amendment or sursis is needed and prepare for debate.

19   Rules of Procedure, rule 1(4), which could be used where the urgency of the situation requires. An alternative means of proceeding should an emergency exist and be formally declared by the Emergency Powers Authority (comprising the Chief Minister, the Minister of the Home Department and one other minister appointed from a panel of five, with substitutes permitted if anyone is unavailable) would be for that authority to make use of its regulation-making powers under the Emergency Powers (Bailiwick of Guernsey) Law, 1965, as amended, which confers wide-ranging legislative powers, subject to any regulations made being laid before the States as soon as may be thereafter.

20   Rules of Procedure, rule 13(2) and (3). Within a system of consensus government by committees, advance notice enables proper consideration by the department in question of the issues raised.

21   Ibid., rule 13(6).

22   Ibid., rule 13(4). The Presiding Officer asks members who wish to debate the amendment to stand.

23   Ibid., rule 13(5), although if a sursis is moved after general debate has commenced the person entitled to reply at the end of general debate may still exercise that entitlement (rule 13(7A)).

24   Ibid., rule 12(3).

25   Ibid., rule 12(1).

26   Ibid., rule 14(1).

27_Ibid., rule 14(2A).
28 Ibid., rule 18.
29 Ibid., rule 19, save that the petition is addressed to the Presiding Officer instead of the Policy Council.
30 Framework for developing the international identity of Guernsey, 18 December 2008, paragraph 3 (see page 1292 of Billet d'État XV of 2008, accessible from http://www.gov.gg/ccm/policy-and-hr/billets—resolutions/2008/-billet-dtat—-xv-2008-november.en).

References

Hocart, R. (1988) *An Island Assembly – the development of the States of Guernsey 1700–1949* (Guernsey: Guernsey Museum and Art Gallery).

Ogier, D.M. (2005) *The Government and Law of Guernsey* (Guernsey: States of Guernsey).

13 Jersey

The States of Jersey

Michael de la Haye

The States Assembly

Jersey has a unicameral legislative assembly known as the States of Jersey, the word 'States' having derived from the French word *États*, signifying the three estates (the court, the clergy and the people) from which the Assembly was originally composed. The powers and duties of the States were most recently defined in the States of Jersey Law 2005 and the Standing Orders of the States made under that Law.

Jersey is a self-governing Crown dependency and not part of the United Kingdom. The States Assembly is one of the oldest legislatures in the Commonwealth, with minutes being recorded as far back as 1524. The functions of the Assembly, as Jersey's legislature, are primarily legislative, but the Assembly also has considerable executive powers, including the appointment of the Chief Minister and ministers, who are entrusted with executive authority for the day-to-day government of the island. The States Assembly has full legislative authority within the bailiwick, save that the adoption of primary legislation (called 'Laws') is subject to sanction by the Queen in Council. As a Crown dependency the island is dependent on the forces of the Queen for its defence, although since the liberation from Nazi occupation in 1945 the island has faced no significant military threat.

The States Assembly comprises 53 elected members and 5 non-elected members: a total membership of 58. The 53 elected members (from a voting population in 2008 of 55,198 – with a turnout of 44.1 per cent in the island-wide senatorial election in 2008), despite the different methods of their election, all have an equal right to speak and vote. There are three categories of elected member, namely:

- 12 senators, serving for a term of six years;
- 12 connétables, one for each of the island's parishes, serving for a term of three years; and
- 29 deputies, serving for a term of three years.

The first of the non-elected members is the Bailiff of Jersey, who is appointed by the Crown and is President of the States. The Bailiff acts as its Speaker and has no political power. In the Assembly, as Speaker, the Bailiff has the right to speak, but this is customarily only exercised for the purpose of managing the proceedings and preserving order. The Bailiff has no casting vote, and if the votes on a matter are equally divided it is determined in the negative. The Deputy Bailiff, who discharges the functions of the Bailiff in the event of the latter's absence or incapacity, is also a Crown appointee but is not actually a member of the States even though he is able to undertake all the Bailiff's role when the Bailiff is absent.

There are four other non-elected members of the States Assembly, namely the Lieutenant-Governor, who is Queen Elizabeth II's personal representative in Jersey and as such attends States meetings as the representative of the Crown but takes no part in debates, the Dean of Jersey, the Attorney General and the Solicitor General, who each have a right to attend and speak but not to vote. Traditionally they speak on matters falling within their area of responsibility. Additionally the Attorney General and Solicitor General (who do not normally attend the Assembly together) may be called upon to advise the Assembly on legal aspects of the matter that is under consideration.

Public elections

Elections for senators, connétables and deputies have, to date, been held every three years, when the term of six of the 12 senators and all 12 connétables and 29 deputies expires. In the past the elections for senators and connétables have taken place in October, with an all-island constituency for senators and parish-based voting in each of the 12 parishes for connétables.

The elections for deputy have been conducted by electoral district, and have taken place in November. Most electoral districts return a single member; others return two, three or four members, according to population. Connétables are elected as head of their parish administration by the voters of their parish. The States Assembly has recently agreed that from 2011 all elections will be held on the same day and for a common four-year term of office, with a reduction over time from 12 senators to eight senators and a consequential reduction in the elected membership of the Assembly from 53 to 49.

The same electoral register serves for all three types of election. With the ability to vote for a number of senators, one connétable and one or more deputies it could be argued that the individual Jersey voter has more parliamentary representatives to call on than in almost any other jurisdiction.

Political parties

The States of Jersey do not currently operate on a party political basis. There is no formal restriction on the establishment of political parties in the island but, in recent years, few parties have been created and at the time of writing only one party is active and only one elected member is a member of that party. Although more political parties may emerge in the future, most candidates for election at present stand on their own individual merits and publish a personal manifesto. Elected members do, from time to time, form themselves into informal groups to pursue common interests, but generally every one of the members acts and votes independently of the other members.

This is not to say, of course, that there is no political controversy in the island. Issues inflame and divide the community in Jersey as they do elsewhere – preserving the island's unique way of life and natural beauty, how to deal with an ageing population and run a productive economy while preserving the island's environment, achieving value for money in public administration, actions to minimise material and social deprivation, the level of taxation, and many others. On each issue people will group on every side and the politicians will divide. But on the next issue the groupings will be different, and the political adversary of yesterday may be the ally of tomorrow.

The work of the States Assembly

The States Assembly meets on a fortnightly cycle between January and July and again between September and early December. Each fortnightly meeting lasts for one, two or three days, and on average the Assembly meets for some 50 to 55 days a year. All meetings are held in the States Chamber, which was first opened in 1887 and which has changed little over the last 120 years apart from the installation of certain equipment such as sound recording and an electronic voting system.

On each meeting day the business of the Assembly starts in French to reflect the island's French tradition. After the formal entry of the Bailiff, the Greffier (Clerk) calls the roll of members in French, and this is followed by prayers read in French by the Dean of Jersey. All members are invited to join in the Lord's Prayer.

After these formalities the business normally continues in English, although any member can, if he or she so wishes, address the Assembly in French. The first two hours of each fortnightly meeting are allocated to questions, with up to two hours of oral questions with notice, followed by two 15-minute periods of oral questions without notice. Two ministers answer questions without notice at each meeting, with the Chief Minister answering at every second meeting. If there are any statements on matters of official responsibility these follow question time before the Assembly moves to consideration of public business. This represents the great majority of the Assembly's business. Decision-making in the States Assembly is by way of a proposition (or 'projet'), which is either a proposition of legislation or a business proposition which requires some definite action to be taken. Propositions are usually presented to the States by ministers, but individual members also have almost unlimited scope to present propositions on their own behalf.

The system of government

While the States Assembly serves as the island's legislature, with some executive powers, the day-to-day administration of the island's government has, since December 2005, been entrusted to a Chief Minister and nine ministers – all drawn from the States – who sit together as a Council of Ministers. Ministers are assisted by assistant ministers (also drawn from the States), but the total number of assistant ministers cannot exceed 13, thereby ensuring that the Chief Minister, ministers and assistant ministers (collectively referred to as the 'Executive') are always in a minority in the Assembly.

The Chief Minister, ministers and assistant ministers must all be members of the States. Ministers have legal responsibility for matters falling within their portfolio, and they must operate within the annual budget voted to their department by the Assembly. In addition they must obtain the approval of the States for new legislation and major capital projects, and will not normally embark on major new policies without States approval. Each new Council of Ministers must, within four months of its appointment, bring to the States for debate a draft strategic plan setting out the main policies which it wishes to pursue during its term of office, and once the plan is approved ministers are expected to work within this policy framework.

Members who are not in the Executive can be appointed as members of a scrutiny panel or of the Public Accounts Committee (PAC). There are currently five scrutiny panels covering all aspects of ministerial responsibilities, and each has dedicated subject areas. States members can serve on up to two panels at a time. Each panel can have up to five permanent members and can also appoint other non-Executive members to a sub-panel to review a particular topic. The panels, which have similar functions and powers to select or scrutiny committees in other parliaments, scrutinise the existing and proposed policy of the Executive, review draft legislation and conduct reviews on matters of public importance.

The PAC seeks to improve the efficiency and effectiveness of public administration, usually by examining and holding hearings on reports prepared by Jersey's Comptroller and Auditor General. The chairman of the PAC must be a member of the States, but the remaining membership of the committee – which must be at least four members and is currently eight – is split equally between members of the States and persons who are not. All nominations for membership must nevertheless be approved by the Assembly.

The appointments process

Every three years, immediately following the elections for senators, connétables and deputies, the 53 (49) elected members meet to appoint a Chief Minister. All 53 (49) members of the States are eligible to stand for this position. Members who wish to be selected must give advance notification of their intention to stand and, after addressing the Assembly and being questioned individually, a ballot or ballots are held until one candidate receives the support of a majority of members.

The Assembly reconvenes three days later to appoint ministers. The newly appointed Chief Minister sets out a list of their nominations for the nine ministerial positions, but it is then open to any other member of the States, without notice, to nominate alternatives. If alternative nominations are made for a particular ministerial position a ballot or ballots are held. In a largely non-party political system there is no guarantee that the ministers appointed will be the Chief Minister's nominees, and the Chief Minister may therefore have to work with one or more ministers who were not his or her preferred nominees. After their appointment ministers cannot be dismissed by the Chief Minister alone and can only be removed from office by the States, although since the introduction of ministerial government in December 2005 only one minister has ever been removed from office in this way.

After the appointment of ministers the Assembly moves to appoint the chairmen of the five scrutiny panels, the Public Accounts Committee and the Privileges and Procedures Committee (this Committee is responsible for matters such as the procedures and operation of the Assembly, members' facilities, the code of conduct for elected members and members' remuneration). These positions are open to all members who are not ministers, and nominations are made by any member of the States, with a ballot or ballots being held to select a chairman if there is more than one nomination for a particular position.

At the third meeting after the elections the various chairmen who have been appointed nominate the members of their panels and committees. Any member of the States is free to propose alternative nominations, and a simple first-past-the-post ballot is held if there are more nominations than the number of places available.

Role of individual members

When ministers present propositions to the States Assembly for approval their proposals are subject to the scrutiny of the other members in open debate. In addition there are very few procedural restrictions on individual States members, be they ministers or not, bringing propositions to the Assembly for debate, and members have significantly more opportunities to pursue cases than in many other Commonwealth parliaments. They may also submit up to five written questions for each meeting, table up to two oral questions with notice and ask questions without notice during each meeting. Individual members may also present petitions on behalf of constituents and seek a debate on the subject matter of the petition.

Conclusion

Before December 2005 government in Jersey was organised on a committee basis, and all 53 elected members were able to serve on one or more of the 14 committees that existed at that time. Committees covered every area of government activity in Jersey, and each one consisted of a president and between four and six other members. Through their work on committees all States members could participate in executive decision-making in a particular area.

The introduction of the ministerial/scrutiny system in December 2005 has, for the first time, led to a clear distinction between those members who are appointed to the Executive and those who are not. Nevertheless, as outlined, the Assembly as a whole retains wide-ranging powers in addition to the traditional functions of a legislature, one of the most significant of which is undoubtedly the power to appoint and dismiss ministers.

After only a relatively short period of time it is probably still too early to pass a definitive judgement on the operation of the new system of government, although it is of interest that in a review of the new system conducted by the Privileges and

Procedures Committee in 2007 very few of those consulted wished to revert to the former committee system. Those who support the new system consider that co-ordination between government departments has been improved and decision-making streamlined. In addition many point out that the establishment of the five scrutiny panels and a PAC with proper administrative support has introduced a level of formal scrutiny that did not previously exist. Those who are critical of the new system consider that the distinction between those who serve as ministers or assistant ministers and those who do not has caused a division between members and left some members feeling isolated from the business of government.

In the coming years the new system of government will undoubtedly evolve and be amended in the light of experience. It is nevertheless likely that, for as long as there is an absence of a formal party system in Jersey, the consequential need to find consensus on issues between independent members will mean that the Assembly will retain a strong role in limiting the power of the Executive and holding it to account.

References

Standing Orders of the States of Jersey 2005 (Chapter 16.800.15), www.jerseylaw.je.
States of Jersey Law 2005 (Chapter 16.800), www.jerseylaw.je.

14 The Isle of Man

Tynwald

Jonathan King

Historical and constitutional background

The legislature of the Isle of Man, Tynwald, claims to be the world's oldest parliament in continuous operation. Tynwald traces its roots back to administrative structures put in place by the Vikings, and it chose to celebrate its millennium in 1979 (Quayle 1990). With the decline of Norse influence the kingship of Man passed between England and Scotland. By the fourteenth century the overlordship of the English Crown was established. From 1405 to 1765 the title 'King of Man' (in the sixteenth century restyled 'Lord of Man') was held by the Stanley family and their heirs, the Dukes of Atholl. In 1765 the lordship was revested in the English Crown, with the result that today the Isle of Man acknowledges the sovereignty of Queen Elizabeth II as Lord of Man.

The Lord of Man is represented in the Isle of Man by a Lieutenant Governor. Before 1980 the Governor had a direct day-to-day role in both the executive and the legislature. By the end of a period of significant constitutional reform in the 1980s and 1990s (Ramsay 2000) most of the Governor's former executive responsibilities had been transferred to the Chief Minister and Council of Ministers, while his responsibilities within the legislature had been transferred to the President of Tynwald. The Governor (and occasionally the Lord of Man herself or another member of the royal family) retains a ceremonial role in presiding over the annual open-air sitting of the legislature at Tynwald Hill in the centre of the island, during which primary legislation which has been enacted in the preceding 18 months is promulgated and persons having a grievance relating to a public matter which cannot otherwise be resolved have the right to present a petition for redress to the Lord of Man or her representative.

Much Manx statute law is based closely on English models. In the Manx courts, English decisions are generally persuasive in the absence of any Manx precedent to the contrary. In 2001 the Isle of Man enacted its own Human Rights Act, similar to the UK's Human Rights Act 1998, which incorporates the provisions of the European Convention on Human Rights into Manx law. The most significant differences between Manx and English law today are in the areas of taxation and company law (Rawcliffe 2009). Westminster enactments can be extended to the Isle of Man by Queen Elizabeth II in Council. Areas in which Westminster legislation is routinely extended include defence, immigration and nationality.

Where matters internal to the island are concerned, Tynwald prefers to legislate for itself, and this is normally the procedure followed. Legislation made in the island is passed to the UK for scrutiny prior to the granting of royal assent. This scrutiny is undertaken by officials in the Ministry of Justice, acting on behalf of the Secretary of State for Justice in his capacity as a Privy Councillor. A procedure exists to amend a bill at any stage after receiving suggestions from the Privy Council (House of Keys 2009, Standing Order 4.16), although this is seldom used, as any differences tend to be resolved informally during the drafting process.

The relationship of the Isle of Man to the European Union is set out in Protocol 3 to the Treaty of Accession 1972 by which the United Kingdom became a member of what was then the European Economic Community (see 'Chapter appendix'). Under this relationship the island is neither a member state nor an associate member of the European Union. It is also worth emphasising that, although the island's relationship with the EU is through the UK, the Isle of Man is an internally self-governing dependent territory of the Crown and is not part of the UK.

The resident population of the Isle of Man rose from just over 47,000 in 1961 to 80,000 in 2006 (Isle of Man Government Treasury 2007). The total number of members of Tynwald is 35 (see Table 14.1). With only 2,286 residents per legislator on average, Manx residents enjoy a high degree of access to their parliamentary representatives.

Procedures exist for anyone with an interest adversely affected by a matter on the Tynwald order paper to attend a sitting and present his or her case before the relevant motion is debated. The person claiming a distinct interest is required to submit in advance a written statement, or 'memorial', setting out why he or she should be heard. If this is accepted, the person is given an opportunity to present his or her case orally in Tynwald Court, either in person or through a lawyer. Members of Tynwald have the opportunity to ask questions about the statement. When they have finished questioning the memorialist they return to their order paper and debate the motion itself (High Court of Tynwald 2010b, Standing Order 8.2). This is not just a theoretical procedure but has been used three times since the 2006 general election. In July 2007 Tynwald Court heard a memorial from John Maddrell, a resident of Port Erin, objecting to a proposal that a café in a local beauty spot be sold by the Port Erin Commissioners to central government. In December 2009 Peter Canipa objected to a proposed compulsory purchase from him of land needed for a road-widening scheme. In October 2010 Stephen Hamer, as Chairman of Michael Commissioners, objected to a proposal to build a new doctor's surgery in the neighbouring local authority area, Jurby.

Composition and functions of the three chambers

The House of Keys comprises 24 members (MHKs), directly elected by voters aged 16 and above for a five-year fixed term. The most recent general election to the Keys was held in September 2011, with the next scheduled for 2016. The island is divided into 15 constituencies, some of which return one member, some two and some three:

Ayre (1 seat)
Castletown (1 seat)
Douglas East (2 seats)
Douglas North (2 seats)
Douglas South (2 seats)
Douglas West (2 seats)
Garff (1 seat)
Glenfaba (1 seat)
Malew and Santon (1 seat)
Michael (1 seat)
Middle (1 seat)
Onchan (3 seats)
Peel (1 seat)
Ramsey (2 seats)
Rushen (3 seats)

The House of Keys is one of the few legislatures which have tried proportional representation and reverted to 'first past the post'. An independent commission chaired by David Butler reported in 1980 recommending a single transferable vote system to provide for equality of voting rights and an end to the possibility of election on a minority vote. A reformed system was put in place in 1982 and used for the general elections in 1986 and 1991, but the changes were reversed for the general election in 1996 (Kermode 2009, pp. 88–9).

The Legislative Council comprises 11 members, known as MLCs. As indicated in Table 14.1, eight of these are indirectly elected by the House of Keys in two overlapping groups of four. The last elections to the Legislative Council were in 2008 and 2010; the next will be in 2013 and 2015. The elected members and the Lord Bishop have a vote, while the Attorney General has no vote and the President only a casting vote. This means that for most purposes the number of voting members of the Legislative Council is nine and the majority required to carry a vote is five.

Tynwald Court comprises the two branches, the House of Keys and the Legislative Council, sitting together. Sitting separately, the function of the two branches is the consideration of primary legislation. Sitting together as Tynwald Court they exercise the other functions of the legislature in relation to policy, finance and secondary legislation. Questions may be asked and statements made in all three chambers.

Sittings of Tynwald Court are held once a month from October to July, scheduled to commence on a Tuesday and continuing into Wednesday and Thursday depending on the volume of business and the extent of debate. Sittings of the branches separately are held on the intervening Tuesdays and normally last for one day only. When breaks for Christmas, Easter and the TT period are taken into account the total number of sitting days each year is around 40. In all three chambers, every member is expected to attend throughout and to vote for or against every motion (although the Speaker is entitled to abstain in the House of Keys).

Table 14.1 Composition of the Manx legislature

		Tynwald Court		
House of Keys		*Legislative Council*		
Members of the House of Keys	24	Directly elected by residents over the age of 16. Fixed five-year term. Speaker, elected from among the 24, acts as impartial presiding officer when House sits alone but speaks and votes freely in Tynwald Court.	President of Tynwald	1	Elected by the members of Tynwald from among their number just before a general election. Presides over both Legislative Council and Tynwald Court. Casting vote in both Chambers.
			Lord Bishop of Sodor and Man	1	Can speak and vote.
			HM Attorney General for the Isle of Man	1	Can speak but not vote.
			Elected members of the Legislative Council	8	Elected by the House of Keys in two overlapping groups of four, each with a different five-year term offset from the Keys election cycle.

There is no restriction on any member's right to speak on every motion and at any length.

The voting rules in Tynwald Court reflect the supremacy of the House of Keys. As with bills (see below), so with policy and financial motions the Legislative Council can delay a proposal but does not have a veto. Under the normal procedure the votes of the two branches are cast simultaneously but counted separately. If a motion is to carry it needs the support of a majority in both branches (13 in the Keys and 5 in the Council). If carried in the Keys but defeated in the Council it can be brought back at a later sitting for a 'combined vote', which can be carried with the support of 17 members overall (High Court of Tynwald 2010b, Standing Order 3.19).

All the proceedings of Tynwald Court are broadcast on Manx Radio and can therefore be heard not only in the Isle of Man but also internationally over the internet. In the House of Keys, oral questions are broadcast on Manx Radio, but the consideration of primary legislation is not. No proceedings of the Legislative Council are broadcast. Every word spoken in the public sittings of the three chambers since the late nineteenth century has, however, been transcribed and published. Proceedings since October 1997 are available on the Tynwald website (www.tynwald.org.im). In 2008 the Office of the Official Report, or Hansard office, in the Isle of Man, adopted pioneering voice recognition software which has improved both the speed and the efficiency of production (Rodan 2008).

The structure of the executive

Most candidates for the House of Keys stand, and most members serve, as political independents. After a general election, the House first sits alone to swear in the members and to elect a Speaker. A sitting of Tynwald Court is then held to nominate a Chief Minister. The Chief Minister, once appointed by the Governor on the nomination of Tynwald Court, has the right to appoint up to nine other members to form the Council of Ministers. Members of either branch may be nominated as Chief Minister or appointed as ministers. For example, the Chief Minister in February 2011, Tony Brown MHK, appointed all his ministers from within the Keys. His predecessor, however, was a member of the Legislative Council.

The Governor in Council (that is, the Governor on the advice of the Council of Ministers) appoints other members of the Keys and Council to 'membership of departments' and to other executive roles, including the chairs of statutory boards such as the Manx Electricity Authority and Isle of Man Post Office. There are nine departments, each of which may have up to four additional 'members'. It is, therefore, possible for the Council of Ministers to offer some executive role to every member of Tynwald, should it wish to do so. In practice, despite notable exceptions, most elected members of Tynwald (other than the President, Speaker, Chief Minister and ministers) usually hold one or more executive roles simultaneously. For this reason the system is sometimes described as one of 'government by consensus'.

The system is finely balanced. Collective responsibility is for the most part accepted within the Council of Ministers, although circumstances exist in which a minister may speak and vote against the Council on particular issues (Kermode 2001, pp. 298–9). With 10 members in total, the Chief Minister and Council of Ministers do not form a majority in the House of Keys (13), nor in Tynwald Court (where most votes require the support of 13 in the Keys and 5 in the Council), nor in the Legislative Council (where under the current disposition no minister sits). In practice 'members of departments' are expected to support proposals put forward by their own minister. With a combination of the Council of Ministers and its 'members', a department can normally carry a vote, but this is not guaranteed.

Seating in the House of Keys is organised by constituency and in the Legislative Council by seniority. Nevertheless, elected members of Tynwald who are not ministers or presiding officers sometimes refer to themselves as 'backbenchers' – even if they hold one or more executive role. This reflects the fact that, although expected to vote with their own department, they are considered free to speak and vote against proposals emanating from other departments.

Members' remuneration is linked to their roles as presiding officers or in the executive. With the exception of the Bishop and the Attorney General, to whom different arrangements apply, all members receive a basic salary which is linked to a particular point in the middle of the pay scale for the Isle of Man civil service. Since April 2008 the sum has stood at £36,441 per year. To this basic amount is added an enhancement of 80 per cent for the Chief Minister, 60 per cent for the Speaker, 50 per cent for the President and ministers, 40 per cent for 'members of the Treasury', 30 per cent for 'departmental members' and 10 per cent for chairmen of statutory boards. There is also an annual sum for expenses, which since April 2008 has stood at £6,178 per member.

Prior to the 2011 election, two political parties had members in Tynwald: the Manx Labour Party, with two members, and the Liberal Vannin Party, with one. The Manx Labour Party played a full part in the executive, one of its members being a minister and the other a 'member of the Treasury'. Liberal Vannin, on the other hand, eschewed any executive office, advocating a clearer distinction between executive and scrutiny roles (Kermode 2009, pp. 408, 414). Following the 2011 election Liberal Vannin had three members, and the remaining 21 members were all independents.

A motion to redesign the remuneration structure to take more account of members' scrutiny roles was debated in Tynwald on 19 January 2005 but was defeated. Meanwhile many members continue to combine an executive role within one or more departments with a scrutiny role in relation to others.

The influence of the legislature

The influence of the scrutiny role played by individual members in relation to the action (or inaction) of the executive can be seen in all three chambers across the full range of parliamentary activities.

Primary legislation

Each of the three chambers has its own set of standing orders and its own distinct role in the legislative process. A bill is first introduced into either the House of Keys or the Legislative Council. If it passes its stages in the branch in which it starts, it is sent to the other branch and goes through a generally similar procedure (although first reading is a formal stage in the Keys, whereas it is debated in the Council). By convention government bills are today introduced in the Keys, with the Council acting as a revising chamber. If amendments are made in one branch to which the other does not agree, a 'conference' or private meeting may be held between representatives of the two branches in order to resolve the dispute (for a recent example see House of Keys 2010). If a dispute cannot be resolved then ultimately the Legislative Council can only delay a bill, a procedure existing under the Constitution Act 2006 (and previously under the Isle of Man Constitution Act 1961) for the will of the Keys to prevail.

Once the Keys and Council have agreed on a text, the bill is sent to the Privy Council for agreement. A letter is sent to the Lieutenant Governor permitting him to give royal assent on behalf of the Queen. The bill must be signed in Tynwald Court by a quorum of each branch before being submitted finally for royal assent. The giving of royal assent is then publicly announced in Tynwald Court. That is not the end of the procedure, however. Every Act must also be promulgated on Tynwald Hill within 18 months; otherwise it ceases to have effect. This traditional requirement is now enshrined in the Promulgation Act 1988.

Secondary legislation

Some secondary legislation is subject to Tynwald approval. Orders made under such powers are debated by Tynwald Court. Orders are rarely voted down, but there have been cases where an order has been delayed following serious concern in the Court (a recent example was the debate in May 2008 on the Road Transport Act 2001 (Revocation of Schedule 2) Order 2008). Other secondary legislation is subject to a negative resolution procedure. There was a rare example of an annulment motion on 16 July 2009. Following the debate the Rules of the High Court of Justice 2009 were not, in the event, annulled.

Implementation of policy resolutions

Policy motions are regularly tabled by individual members for debate in Tynwald Court. The Government is not strictly speaking obliged to fulfil every action requested of it by Tynwald Court. The principle was agreed by Tynwald in February 2004, and reaffirmed in April 2009, that 'a resolution of the Court on any matter related to Isle of Man Government policy supersedes or supplements any previous resolution on the same matter and Government must respond positively to such resolutions'. That said, it is rare for the Manx Government overtly to refuse to adopt one of Tynwald's policy resolutions, many of which are expressions of opinion in any event.

Petitions for redress of grievance and other committees

Petitions for redress of grievance which are presented to the Lord of Man or her representative on Tynwald Day may, if they are in order, be picked up by a member for debate in Tynwald Court: typically on a motion that a committee be formed to investigate the matter and make recommendations. To be in order, a petition must relate to a matter of public interest. As a result, a number of public policy areas have been investigated by 'petition' committees, for example health service complaints procedures, police complaints procedures and legal aid in family matters.

Temporary ad hoc investigative committees, known in the Isle of Man as 'select committees', are regularly established to look not only at petitions for redress of grievance but also at other matters proposed by individual members. Membership of these committees is decided by Tynwald Court by secret ballot. Ministers occasionally serve on select committees, but such committees are more often made up of backbenchers.

There also exist four permanent committees of Tynwald Court, or 'standing committees', with a scrutiny function. These are: the Public Accounts Committee to oversee the use of government funds; the Standing Committee on Economic Initiatives to look at initiatives and legislation of the European Union, international agencies and states, and economic factors generally; the Standing Committee on Constitutional Matters to report on the Council of Ministers' policy and approach to matters of constitutional importance, and any treaties, international agreements and so on; and the Scrutiny Committee to review secondary legislation and to follow up on the implementation of Tynwald decisions.

The Standing Orders of Tynwald Court provide that oral evidence heard by committees should be heard in public unless the committee determines otherwise. Oral evidence heard in public is transcribed and published in full.

Committees of Tynwald or the branches can be given powers under the Tynwald Proceedings Act 1876 to compel the attendance of witnesses or the production of documents. Evidence given to committees is protected under the Tynwald Proceedings Act 1984, which ensures that an answer by a person to a question put by a parliamentary committee is not admissible in evidence against him or her in any civil or criminal proceedings.

Tynwald and external affairs

As a dependency of the British Crown the Isle of Man relies on the United Kingdom for its defence and for representation internationally. In 2007 an international identity framework was agreed between the Isle of Man and the UK, confirming that the Isle of Man has an international identity which is different from that of the UK, and that the UK supports the principle of the Isle of Man further developing its international identity (Isle of Man Government 2009, paragraph 11). Nevertheless the relationship with the UK remains of central importance.

Within the Manx political system, lead responsibility for maintaining and developing the relationship with the UK in the round is held by the Chief Minister, while specific policy matters are taken forward between departments and their

UK counterparts. The island's overall approach to external matters is summarised in the following Tynwald resolution of 18 February 2010:

> That Tynwald requests that the Council of Ministers continue to pursue the Island's constitutional development by promoting and vigorously defending the Island's autonomy in relation to its internal affairs, seeking to extend the Isle of Man's influence over external issues affecting the Island through the further development of the Isle of Man's international identity, and seeking additional ways in which the Island can represent itself more effectively on the international stage.

Members of Tynwald from time to time seek to influence through public proceedings in Tynwald the approach taken by the Chief Minister and other ministers in their negotiations with UK counterparts on specific issues. Examples include debates in April 2009 on the reciprocal healthcare agreement with the UK, in December 2009 on territorial waters, and in March 2010 on the Sellafield nuclear installation in the North-West of England.

Although the Isle of Man is not a sovereign state and is therefore ineligible for membership of the Commonwealth, the Manx legislature is a member in its own right of the Commonwealth Parliamentary Association (CPA). Participation in CPA activities gives members of Tynwald regular opportunities to meet and share experiences with parliamentarians from the British Islands and Mediterranean Region (BIMR) of that association, and from further afield across the Commonwealth. Much benefit has been derived from this (Winterbottom 2002). The annual BIMR conference of the CPA was held in the Isle of Man in May 2010.

For the same reason, Tynwald also values highly the place reserved for it within the British–Irish Parliamentary Assembly. That assembly's plenary conference in November 2010 was held in the Isle of Man.

The future

A thousand years old it may be, but Tynwald does not stand still. In closing, it is worth noting a number of developments which have the potential to change the operation of this ancient but still developing institution.

There are three proposals agreed in principle by Tynwald Court but not yet in place which are likely to have a significant effect on the Tynwald Court's capacity to scrutinise the executive. These are the introduction of a Tynwald Auditor General, a Tynwald Commissioner for Administration (or Ombudsman), and a statutory access-to-information regime. At the time of writing, legislation to establish the first two of these has been passed by the House of Keys and the Legislative Council, while the third is listed in the Government's legislative programme.

In 2010 the House of Commons Justice Committee made recommendations which could lead to the streamlining of that part of the legislative process concerned with the granting of royal assent (see House of Commons Justice Committee 2010, Vol. 1, pp. 20–24).

In June 2010 a committee of Tynwald was established to assess the implications and benefits of establishing a system of standing committees relating to the work of government departments. The committee's report (High Court of Tynwald 2010a) was debated in January 2011. Although the committee's recommendations were subject to some amendment during the debate, the principle of establishing a new system along departmental lines was approved. At the time of writing work is under way to put this new system in place.

The composition of the Legislative Council is a perennial topic of debate, the existing system having been criticised by a number of MHKs as 'undemocratic'. The latest reform proposal – a bill which proposed a move to a directly elected second chamber – foundered in June 2009. Nonetheless, others may follow, while the possibility of course exists of further evolutionary development.

References

High Court of Tynwald (2006) *Report of the Select Committee on Scrutiny and the Functions of the Public Accounts Committee*, http://www.tynwald.org.im/papers/reports/2005-2006/r0027.pdf (accessed 23 November 2010).

High Court of Tynwald (2010a) *Report of the Select Committee on the Committee System 2010–2011*, PP167/10, http://www.tynwald.org.im/papers/reports/2010-2011/r0010.pdf (accessed 17 February 2011).

High Court of Tynwald (2010b) *Standing Orders of Tynwald Court: Consolidated Edition with All Amendments Incorporated*, February, http://www.tynwald.org.im/papers/standing/tso.pdf (accessed 23 November 2010).

House of Commons Justice Committee (2010) *Crown Dependencies: Eighth Report of Session 2009–10*, HC 56–I–II (London: Stationery Office).

House of Keys (2009) *Standing Orders of the House of Keys: Consolidated Edition with All Amendments*, December, http://www.tynwald.org.im/papers/standing/kso.pdf (accessed 17 February 2011).

House of Keys (2010) *Marriage and Civil Registration (Amendment) Bill: Report of the Delegation Elected by the House on 25th May 2010*, http://www.tynwald.org.im/papers/reports/2010-2011/r0005.pdf (accessed 24 November 2010).

Isle of Man Government (2009) Memorandum submitted to the House of Commons Justice Committee, October, in House of Commons Justice Committee, *Crown Dependencies: Eighth Report of Session 2009–10*, HC 56–II (London: Stationery Office), Ev 68.

Isle of Man Government Treasury (2007) *Isle of Man Census Report 2006*, GD5/07, http://www.gov.im/lib/docs/treasury/economic/census/censusreport2006.pdf (accessed 24 November 2010).

Kermode, D. G. (2001) *Offshore Island Politics: The Constitutional and Political Development of the Isle of Man in the Twentieth Century* (Liverpool: Liverpool University Press).

Kermode, D. G. (2009) *Ministerial Government in the Isle of Man: The First Twenty Years 1986–2006* (Douglas: Manx Heritage Foundation).

Ministry of Justice (2010) *Government Response to the Justice Select Committee's Report: Crown Dependencies*, Cm 7965.

Quayle, R. (1990) The Isle of Man Constitution, in V. Robinson and D. McCarroll (eds), *The Isle of Man: Celebrating a Sense of Place*, pp. 123–32 (Liverpool: Liverpool University Press).

Ramsay, A. (2000) Tynwald transformed, 1980–96, in J. Belchem (ed.), *A New History of the Isle of Man*, Vol. 5: *The Modern Period 1830–1999*, pp. 185–206 (Liverpool: Liverpool University Press).

Rawcliffe, R. (2009) *No Man Is an Island: 50 Years of Finance in the Isle of Man* (Douglas: Manx Heritage Foundation).

Rodan, S. (2008) Voice recognition technology: A touch of the future in the Isle of Man, *The Parliamentarian: Journal of the Parliaments of the Commonwealth*, 84 (4), pp. 322–3.

Winterbottom, D. (2002) *Charles Kerruish: Manx Politician and Commonwealth Parliamentarian: A Political Biography* (Douglas: Manx Heritage Foundation).

Chapter appendix

Protocol No. 3 annexed to the Act of Accession of the Kingdom of Denmark, Ireland and the United Kingdom of Great Britain and Northern Ireland to the European Economic Community and the European Atomic Energy Community 1972.

Article 1

1   The Community rules on customs matters and quantitative restrictions, in particular those of the Act of Accession, shall apply to the Channel Islands and the Isle of Man under the same conditions as they apply to the United Kingdom. In particular, customs duties and charges having equivalent effect between those territories and the Community, as originally constituted and between those territories and the new Member States, shall be progressively reduced in accordance with the timetable laid down in Articles 32 and 36 of the Act of Accession. The Common Customs Tariff and the ECSC unified tariff shall be progressively applied in accordance with the timetable laid down in Articles 39 and 59 of the Act of Accession, and account being taken of Articles 109, 110 and 119 of that Act.

2   In respect of agricultural products and products processed therefrom which are the subject of a special trade regime, the levies and other import measures laid down in Community rules and applicable by the United Kingdom shall be applied to third countries.

Such provisions of Community rules, in particular those of the Act of Accession, as are necessary to allow free movement and observance of normal conditions of competition in trade in these products shall also be applicable.

The Council, acting by a qualified majority on a proposal from the Commission, shall determine the conditions under which the provisions referred to in the preceding sub-paragraphs shall be applicable to these territories.

Article 2

The rights enjoyed by Channel Islanders or Manxmen in the United Kingdom shall not be affected by the Act of Accession. However, such persons shall not benefit from the Community provisions relating to the free movement of persons and services.

Article 3

The provision of the Euratom Treaty applicable to persons or undertakings within the meaning of Article 196 of that Treaty shall apply to those persons or undertakings when they are established in the aforementioned territories.

Article 4

The authorities of these territories shall apply the same treatment to all natural and legal persons of the Community.

Article 5

If, during the application of the arrangements defined in this Protocol, difficulties appear on either side in relations between the Community and these territories, the Commission shall without delay propose to the Council such safeguard measures as it believes necessary, specifying their terms and conditions of application.

The Council shall act by qualified majority within one month.

Article 6

In this protocol, Channel Islander or Manxman shall mean any citizen of the United Kingdom and Colonies who holds that citizenship by virtue of the fact that he, a parent or grandparent was born, adopted, naturalised or registered in the Island in question; but such a person shall not for this purpose be regarded as a Channel Islander or Manxman if he, a parent or grandparent was born, adopted, or naturalised or registered in the United Kingdom. Nor shall he be so regarded if he has at any time been ordinarily resident in the United Kingdom for five years.

The administrative arrangements necessary to identify those persons will be notified to the Commission.

Part III
Sub-national entities

15 Hong Kong

The Hong Kong Legislative Council – where politics matters more than size

Lam Wai-man

Hong Kong as a partial democracy

Before returning to China in 1997, Hong Kong had been a British colony for over a hundred years. During British colonial rule, Hong Kong remained a partial democracy, with its colonial governor appointed by the British government, and who ruled with the Executive Council, which played an advisory role. The Legislative Council,[1] established in 1843, was also only an advisory body.

Priding itself on being an executive-led system under which the executive leads the legislature, the colonial government had not introduced universal suffrage for the seats of the Legislative Council until 1991, when Hong Kong was well along the way of political transition. In the 1991 Legislative Council election, among the 60 seats of the Legislative Council, 18 were returned by universal suffrage via geographical constituency elections. The other seats were filled by official or appointed members, or legislators returned by indirect election via functional constituencies composed of small circles of business people and professionals. In 1995, the number of Legislative Council seats allocated for universal suffrage increased to 20.

Hence, before the political handover, the Legislative Council in Hong Kong was limited in influence as a result of its advisory nature, and hardly represented the popular will, since only a restricted number of Legislative Council members were elected by universal suffrage. Pro-democracy political parties, although enjoying popularity among the people, could hardly become the majority in the Legislative Council because of the composition and methods of election of the legislature.

Development, composition and methods of election

Owing to the political rows between the last Hong Kong governor Christopher Patten and China, the last colonial legislature was dissolved in 1997. The Provisional Legislative Council formed upon the dissolution of its predecessor – and which lasted until 1998 – had 60 members, who were elected by the 400-member Selection Committee. The same committee also elected the first Chief Executive (CE) of the Hong Kong Special Administrative Region (SAR) under the rule of China. Only four among the 60 members were from moderate pro-democracy political parties.

The first Legislative Council election in Hong Kong was held in 1998. Table 15.1 illustrates the composition and methods of election of the various terms of the Legislative Council in Hong Kong since 1998. As of today, Legislative Council members are returned in one of two ways: from five geographical constituencies consisting of around 3.4 million registered electors, each electing four to eight seats and making up a total of 30 members, and from 28 functional constituencies[2] of only around 230,000 registered electors, who represent predominantly business interests and secondary professional interests, also electing 30 members. Eligible voters include naturalized persons and designated legal entities such as organizations and corporations (Loh 2006). The Election Committee that elected 10 and 6 members to the Legislative Council for the terms 1998–2000 and 2000–04 respectively was composed of 800 members, who also elected the second term of the Chief Executive.

Constitutional powers

Under Article 73 of the Basic Law,[3] the mini-constitution of Hong Kong, the Legislative Council has the constitutional powers to enact, amend or repeal laws, examine and approve budgets, approve taxation and public expenditure, monitor the work of the government, endorse the appointment and removal of the judges of the Court of Final Appeal[4] and the Chief Judge of the High Court, receive and handle complaints from the public, impeach the Chief Executive if he or she has committed a serious breach of the law or for dereliction of duty, and summon persons to testify or give evidence. So, theoretically, the Legislative Council is granted the main powers pertaining to a modern legislature for it to carry out its functions.

Nevertheless, the Basic Law has also imposed significant constitutional constraints on the powers of the Legislative Council. These clauses, along with the composition and methods of election of the Legislative Council as outlined, have curtailed the functioning of the Legislative Council since the political handover to China. This will be further explained later.

Table 15.1 Composition and methods of election of the Hong Kong Legislative Council

	Geographical constituencies	Functional constituencies	Election Committee	Total
1998–2000	20	30	10	60
2000–04	24	30	6	60
2004–08	30	30	0	60
2008–12	30	30	0	60
2012–16	35	35	0	70

Institutions and mechanisms

Although it is a small legislature composed of 60 members, the Hong Kong Legislative Council is a well-developed legislature including a division of labour, a leadership structure, a committee system, and an extensive network of formal and informal rules and norms. Institutionally and procedurally, it is well equipped to exercise proper functions.

Legislative power

With regard to the legislative power of the Legislative Council, both the government and Legislative Council members may introduce new legislation, or bills to amend or repeal existing legislation and proposed bills. The process of law enactment involves three readings of a bill in the Legislative Council. In the second reading, the Legislative Council may allocate a bill to a bill committee for detailed scrutiny. A bill committee considers the principles, merits and provisions of the bill concerned, and may propose amendments. The maximum number of active bill committees is limited to 16 at any one time.

Nevertheless, the Basic Law has also imposed certain constraints on the legislative power of Legislative Council members. First, under Article 74 of the Basic Law, members can initiate bills through the mechanism of private members' bills only if the bills do not relate to public expenditure or political structure or the operation of the government. The written consent of the Chief Executive is required before bills relating to government policies are introduced. This explains why, since the political handover, an absolute majority of the bills introduced into the Legislative Council for deliberation have been government bills (Lui 2007, p. 44). A second constraint is the 'split voting procedures'. Different from the passage of bills introduced by the government, which requires only a simple majority vote of the Legislative Council members present, the passage of motions, bills or amendments to government bills introduced by Legislative Council members requires a simple majority vote of each of the two groups of members present: members returned by functional constituencies and those returned by geographical constituencies (Annex II, Basic Law).

Controlling public expenditure

With regard to controlling public expenditure, the Finance Committee of the Legislative Council has the power to approve or disapprove the annual proposed government budget and additional expenditure requested by government departments. In addition, the Public Accounts Committee considers reports of the Director of Audit on the accounts and the results of value-for-money audits of the government and other organizations which are within the purview of public audit. It may invite government officials, senior staff of public organizations, and any other person to attend public hearings to give explanation, evidence or information if necessary.

Scrutiny of government

In carrying out another important legislative function of scrutiny of the government, the Legislative Council has established 18 non-permanent panels relating to the policy functions of the bureaus to deliberate on specific policy areas.[5] These panels also examine issues of wide public concern referred to the Legislative Council, and give views on major legislative and financial proposals before they are introduced into the Legislative Council.

Another mechanism is the select committee. The Legislative Council may by resolution appoint one or more select committees for in-depth consideration of matters or bills. Under the Power and Privileges Ordinance, the Legislative Council may summon, as required when exercising its powers and functions, persons concerned, including government officials, to testify or give evidence. A select committee, as soon as it has completed consideration of the matter or bill referred to it and reported to the Legislative Council thereon, will be dissolved. If summoned, a person must appear before the committee and testify under oath unless the Chief Executive decides against that in light of security and vital public interests. An example of a select committee is the one that was appointed to inquire into matters relating to the post-service work of Leung Chin-man[6] (2008).

Through questions, debates and motions Legislative Council members can also monitor the work of the government. Questions may be posed in Legislative Council meetings and the Chief Executive's question-and-answer sessions during which the Chief Executive answers questions about issues of public concern and public policies. Questions are intended to seek information on government actions on specific problems and policies, and to monitor the effectiveness of the government. Debates take place on the Chief Executive's annual policy proposal (policy address debate), annual government budget proposal (budget debate), and all the motions raised during the Legislative Council meetings.

Other mechanisms

As stated above, despite the small size of the Hong Kong Legislative Council, it is well developed, with institutions, mechanisms, and rules and norms. Along with the above structures, the Committee on Members' Interests is established to maintain the Register of Members' Interests, and to consider any complaints lodged against Legislative Council members' registration and declaration of interests or their failure to do so. It also considers matters of ethics of Legislative Council members. When a motion to censure a Legislative Council member under Article 79(7) of the Basic Law has been made, an investigation committee may be established to follow up on the matter. The Committee on Rules of Procedure reviews the rules of procedure of the Legislative Council and the committee system. Lastly, the Legislative Council Redress System aims to receive and handle complaints from citizens who are aggrieved by government actions or policies. It also deals with public representations on government policies and legislation and other matters of public concern. Under this system, Legislative Council members take turns to be on duty each week to oversee the system and meet with complainants.

Politics matter: constitutional, political and institutional constraints

Despite being a well-developed body, the Legislative Council has suffered from three main types of constraints on its power and performance not only when seeking to exercise its legislative functions, control public expenditure and scrutinize government, but also with regard to representation, legitimization, and education and recruitment since the political handover.

First there have been *constitutional constraints*. For example, Article 73 and Annex II of the Basic Law curtail the Legislative Council's legislative power and performance as well as unity, and dampen its ability to monitor the efficacy of the government.

As many have argued, the constitutional constraints on the Legislative Council have been imposed to keep the Legislative Council weak so as to maintain a strong executive (Li 2007). Indeed, *political constraints* constitute the second type of constraint on various functions of the Legislative Council, such as legislative, scrutiny of government, representation and legitimization. Contrary to governance being a legislative-led model, both the Hong Kong government and Beijing have stressed that it should follow the executive-led principle. Donald Tsang, Hong Kong's second Chief Executive, wrote: 'The political system established under the Basic Law envisions the Hong Kong SAR to practice "executive-led" government. The Chief Executive is the head of the SAR and leader of the SAR government' (Tsang 2006, p. 4). Similarly, at the celebrations of the fifth anniversary of Hong Kong's return to China, former Chinese President Jiang Zemin said that 'the executive-led structure should be further strengthened' (*People's Daily*, 1 July 2002). In practice, the Basic Law gives supreme power to the Chief Executive relative to the legislature (Articles 48–51, Basic Law). Any winning candidate for the office of Chief Executive has to declare that he or she is not a member of any political party (CE Election Ordinance, Cap 569, s. 31), thus preventing the candidate from being politically affiliated with and responsible to any political parties in the Legislative Council, and major political parties in the Legislative Council could never become ruling parties in the executive.

Institutional constraints – the third type of constraint – have divided the Legislative Council and hampered its performance. These include both the composition of and the method of election to the Legislative Council. Legislative Council members are returned through elections from geographical and functional constituencies, both of which are very different on electoral principles, electoral methods, and composition of registered electors. Generally speaking, members from functional constituencies are relatively pro-establishment, pro-Beijing and pro-business, while members from geographical constituencies are relatively pro-democracy, pro-grassroots and representative of the public in Hong Kong. Functional constituency elections have long been criticized as undemocratic, and their continued survival has dampened the representation and legitimacy of the Legislative Council (Loh 2006).

In addition, fragmentation in the Legislative Council has been serious, and this makes it unable effectively to challenge the executive in unity of strength. Besides the division of the 60 Legislative Council members into geographical and functional categories, recent research also shows that the members belong variously to six political parties and nine political groups, and are officially unaffiliated with any political organizations, the so-called 'independents' (SynergyNet 2009, pp. 42–3).

Despite this, based on the decision of the Standing Committee of the National People's Congress of China on Hong Kong's constitutional development made on 26 April 2004, the ratio between Legislative Council members returned by geographical constituency and functional constituency elections should be half to half (*China Daily*, 26 April 2004).[7] So, although the number of seats in the 2012–16 Legislative Council will be increased from 60 to 70, functional constituency elections will not be abolished in the near future, and the ratio between the two types of members will remain the same.

Assessing performance

Legislative power

On the whole, the Legislative Council is supportive of government business despite the occasional scenes of verbal or physical opposition staged by pro-democracy Legislative Council members as dramatic devices to catch public attention. Rowena Kwok's study that covers the period 1998–2003 found that, in the 1,943 instances of votes during the period under study, a great majority of the votes (82.4 per cent or 1,602) were unanimous. Only 233 (12 per cent) votes involved 'divisions'.[8] This indicates that most of the policies that the government hoped the legislature would endorse were supported and duly voted into law by the Legislative Council (Kwok 2006, pp. 405–06).

Because of the restrictions on private members' bills, an absolute majority of the bills since the political handover to China have been put forward by the government, and this has weakened the Legislative Council members' legislative power to initiate bills, to challenge existing government policies or to push for any substantial policy change. Ma Ngok's study shows that, in 1995–97, a total of 53 private members' bills were tabled, making up 23.2 per cent of all the bills tabled in the Legislative Council (228) during the period. In 1997–2004, a total of 29 private members' bills were proposed; only 10 were allowed to be tabled. Nine were ruled out of order on grounds of involving public expenditure or operation of government, and four needed the consent of the Chief Executive because they involved government policy. For the other six, the members who initiated the bill decided not to pursue it, as the bill involved public policy or public expenditure. Altogether 12 private members' bills were tabled and all were passed, but they constituted only 2.6 per cent of the total bills (456) tabled in 1998–2004 (Ma 2007, pp. 117–18).

Regarding the power of the Legislative Council in amending legislation, the above study also found that it has diminished since 1997. The success rate of Legislative Council members' amendments before and after 1997 is very different: 71 per cent in 1995–97, 14.7 per cent in 1998–2000, and 10.9 per cent in 2000–04. Nevertheless, the success rate of proposed government bills before and after 1997 is almost identical: 92.9 per cent in 1995–97, 91.9 per cent in 1998–2000, and 97 per cent in 2000–04; so is the success rate of government amendments before and after 1997: 96 per cent in 1995–97, 99 per cent in 1998–2000, and 99 per cent in 2000–04 (Ma 2007, p. 119).

A legislature will be more powerful if it acts in unity. Nevertheless, in the case of Hong Kong, as analysed above, fragmentation has been serious. Kwok's study discussed above confirms the functional constituency members' pro-government voting inclination, which has safeguarded the passage of government motions and served as a bulwark against geographical constituency members' articulation of public aspirations. Among the 233 votes which involved divisions, 171 instances involved opposite votes, meaning that, when a majority of the functional con- stituency members had voted 'no', a majority of the geographical constituency members had voted 'yes' and vice versa. Most of the instances concerned matters broadly political (64 per cent), while 22 per cent dealt with matters that were largely economic (Kwok 2006, pp. 406–07).

Controlling public expenditure

In a similar vein, when the major political parties in the Legislative Council are united in opposing the government's funding requests, they can force the govern- ment to make policy concessions.

For example, in 2001, the government was forced to withdraw a HK$177 million bird flu compensation and loan package when a majority of the Legislative Council members were opposed to the package because it was not providing financial assistance for poultry workers but for their bosses. In December 2006, the government was compelled to drop its plan to introduce a sales tax, which was unpopular with the public and major political parties in the Legislative Council. Overall, the Legislative Council was more effective in monitoring the government's expenditure and revenue-raising plans than in initiating alternative policies and monitoring the work of the government (Lui 2007, p. 49).

Scrutiny of government

The restrictions on private members' bills and split voting as stipulated in the Basic Law have adversely affected the Legislative Council's performance in scrutinizing the work of the government.

With these restrictions, motion debates as a tool of Legislative Council members to give pressure to the government have also become ineffective as a result particularly of the split voting mechanism. Indeed, the political and ideological differences between the geographical constituency and functional constituency members on a range of matters such as constitutional development, democratic governance, public accountability, and social and economic fairness have prompted the latter to use their legislative powers to block the passage of motions moved by the former. In 1998–2004, the Legislative Council had 287 motion debates. Among the 99 motions vetoed, 50 of them had received simple majority support but were vetoed because of the split voting rule. For example, the motion debate moved by Emily Lau on 8 October 2003 calling on the Chief Executive to step down was voted down by functional constituency members (Ma 2007, p. 119). In 2004–08, the Legislative Council had 209 motion debates, and 38 were vetoed for the same reason, whereas in 2008–09, likewise, five motions were vetoed out of 59 (SynergyNet 2009, p. 64).

Questioning is another tool of Legislative Council members to monitor the work of the government, which, however, has had relatively little success. In 2000–04, the total number of questions asked by members was 2,411 (Ma 2007, p. 115). In 2008–09, it was 597. The average number of questions asked per year is similar (SynergyNet 2009, pp. 45, 51).

Having said that, however, it should be noted that motion debates and questioning still serve some purpose, even if only as 'tactics of shame'. They can usually arouse public attention and put pressure on government officials. In some instances, government officials may withdraw their proposed legislation or policies. A notable example is the government's proposed national security legislation in 2003, which had aroused substantial opposition from, firstly, the pro-democracy legislators and, next, the general public. The proposed legislation was later withdrawn. Another example is the decision of the members of the Legislative Council to repeal the order signed by the Chief Executive in Council on the expansion of a landfill that would encroach on a country park in 2010. The government has subsequently decided not to take the matter to the court in view of the political pressure from the Legislative Council and the public opinion.

Regarding select committees, in 2000–04 two select committees were set up, namely the Committee on Building Problems of Public Housing Units, and the Committee on the Handling of the SARS Outbreak by the Government and the Hospital Authority. On the other hand, no select committee was established during the 2004–08 period. At present, there is the Select Committee to Inquire into Matters Relating to the Post-Service Work of Mr Leung Chin-man, established by the 2008–12 Legislative Council.

Representation

Despite the fact that half of the members of the Legislative Council are elected by functional constituencies and have only a restricted mandate, the other half of the members – elected by universal suffrage via geographical constituencies – are representative of the public. In this sense, the Legislative Council represents the people and enjoys a degree of legitimacy, although it is constitutionally less powerful than the executive, has little policy influence, and has, as outlined, suffered from other political and institutional constraints on its powers and performance.

Functional constituency elections in Hong Kong have long been criticized for their unfairness and undemocratic nature. Although some people consider the arrangement a good way to protect business interests and maintain political stability in Hong Kong, the process is hardly representative of the people of Hong Kong in any modern sense. They represent certain special interests and thus, when compared to geographical constituencies, they look utterly – and unfairly – over-powerful. The combined registered electorate for all functional constituencies for the 2008 Legislative Council elections was 230,000 and the electorate chose 30 legislators, whereas the geographical electorate, which stood at 3.4 million, also returned 30 legislators. There are also many other problems associated with the arrangements, such as unclear functional classification, illogical groupings of functions, and different sizes of functional constituencies (Loh 2006).

Elections in Hong Kong, including Legislative Council elections, have been run in a clean, orderly and fair way. Political parties have the legal right to participate in elections and have been keen to do so. In this sense, the Legislative Council's electoral arrangements are open and fair in providing access to every political party to the Legislative Council on the basis of competition. Nevertheless, the fact that no majority political party in the Legislative Council could become the ruling political party in the executive has hindered it from fully realizing its platforms in government policies. This may be considered as an obstacle for the Legislative Council to becoming fully representative of the causes of political parties.

Legitimation

Although the Legislative Council is well developed, which illustrates the cosmopolitan and modern character of Hong Kong, it serves few political legitimization purposes such as resolving disputes. In fact, owing to the functional constituencies arrangement, the Legislative Council itself has been the source of political disputes. The ongoing disagreements between the pro-establishment functional constituency members and pro-democracy elected members, and between the government and the elected members, have damaged the image of the Legislative Council, and weakened the efficiency and effectiveness of government policy making. A poll conducted in September 2008 showed that 26 per cent of the respondents were satisfied with the performance of the third Legislative Council (2004–08). Nevertheless, 30 per cent of them felt dissatisfied, whereas 36 per cent stated 'half–half'.[9]

Moreover, the fact that the pro-democracy elected members in the Legislative Council remain a permanent opposition has also created a lot of frustrations among them and led to an escalation of political conflicts both inside and outside the Legislative Council. For instance, early in 2010, the Civic Party and the League of Social Democrats had initiated a campaign – in essence a 'referendum' – to call for support from the people of Hong Kong for universal suffrage. In actuality, this was only a by-election to fill five legislative seats left vacant by the resignation of pro-democracy councillors who asked for universal suffrage in 2012. The move led to severe criticisms from the Chinese authorities, the Hong Kong government and pro-establishment figures in Hong Kong, which further worsened the image of the Legislative Council and the authorities. Nevertheless, it aroused substantial public discussion on the problems of functional constituency elections and the slow pace of democratization in Hong Kong, and so at the very least had an educational effect in this regard.

Education and recruitment

Political parties in Hong Kong have been organized on the political cleavage of whether they are pro-establishment and pro-Beijing or pro-democracy since the Tiananmen crackdown in Beijing in 1989. Although Hong Kong does not operate on a high degree of political autonomy under Chinese rule as expected, the fact that the Legislative Council still functions relatively properly and that political groups and parties of different orientations are free to participate in elections is laudable. Such political space enables the political parties to continue to advocate their causes and contribute to the policy process both inside and outside the Legislative Council. Their presence, political platforms and action serve demonstrative and educational values to the public and the governments. In particular, the pro-democracy elected Legislative Council members have strived to bring matters of constitutional reform and social and economic fairness to the forefront in Legislative Council meetings.

Political parties in Hong Kong are different in their capacity of recruitment, while those parties which have attained seats in the Legislative Council usually perform better in this regard. Over the years, we have seen the gradual building up of strength of the Democratic Alliance for the Betterment and Progress of Hong Kong, a pro-Beijing political party, and the Democratic Party, a pro-democracy party. Recently, the League of Social Democrats, because of its relatively radical political stance and charismatic leaders, has also become popular among the young. It is foreseeable that, in the years to come, the increasingly intensified debates on Hong Kong's constitutional reforms will further strengthen the role of the Legislative Council political parties in recruitment and political leadership.

Conclusion

This chapter has examined the power and performance of the Hong Kong Legislative Council, with consideration of its composition, election methods, constitutional powers and institutional mechanisms, as well as of the constraints under which it functions. Overall, the Hong Kong Legislative Council is small but well developed. It includes a division of labour, a leadership structure, a committee system, and an extensive network of formal and informal rules and norms. Institutionally and procedurally, it is well equipped to exercise proper functions. Nevertheless, political circumstances and conditions have rendered it constitutionally less powerful than the executive, with little policy influence (greater if it acts in unity), and it suffers from a number of political and institutional constraints on its power and performance. Despite that, the Legislative Council represents the people and enjoys legitimacy to some extent, and is relatively effective in controlling public expenditure. In the years to come, it will continue to play important educational and recruitment functions. In that sense, it can still be classified as a policy-influencing legislature.

Notes

1 Hong Kong Legislative Council website, http://www.legco.gov.hk/english/index.htm.
2 They include: (1) accountancy; (2) agriculture and fisheries; (3) architectural, surveying and planning; (4) catering; (5) commercial (first); (6) commercial (second); (7) district council; (8) education; (9) engineering; (10) finance; (11) financial services; (12) health services; (13) Heung Yee Kuk (representatives of each rural committee and is a statutory advisory body representing establishment interests in the New Territories of Hong Kong); (14) import and export; (15) industrial (first); (16) industrial (second); (17) information technology; (18) insurance; (19) labour; (20) legal; (21) medical; (22) real estate and construction; (23) social welfare; (24) sports, performing arts, culture and publication; (25) textiles and garments; (26) tourism; (27) transport; (28) wholesale and retail.
3 Basic Law website, http://www.basiclaw.gov.hk/en/basiclawtext/index.html.
4 The Court of Final Appeal is the highest appellate court in Hong Kong. Under the Basic Law, it has the final adjudication power on the local laws. See http://www.judiciary.gov.hk/en/index/index.htm.
5 The panels include: Administration of Justice and Legal Services; Commerce and Industry; Constitutional Affairs; Development; Economic Development; Education; Environmental Affairs; Financial Affairs; Food Safety and Environmental Hygiene; Health Services; Home Affairs; Housing; Information Technology and Broadcasting; Manpower; Public Service; Security; Transport; and Welfare Services.
6 Leung is a retired senior civil servant. After a 12-month 'sterilization period' after retirement, in 2008, he submitted an application for approval, which was subsequently granted, to take up a job offer by New World China Land. The issue caused an uproar as a result of the widespread suspicion that the job offer was made in return for Leung's favours granted to the consortium in 2004.
7 http://www.chinadaily.com.cn/english/doc/2004-04/26/content_326436.htm.
8 A 'division' enables individual Legislative Council members' votes to be recorded. In the case of non-division voting, there is no record of how individual members have voted (Kwok 2006, p. 405).
9 Hong Kong University Public Opinion Poll (HKUPOP) website, http://hkupop.hku.hk/.

References

Kwok, R. Y. F. (2006) *Functional Representation in Hong Kong's Legislature:Voting Patterns and Political Implications*, *Asian Survey*, vol. 46, no. 3.
Loh, C. (Ed) (2006) *Functional Constituencies: A Unique Feature of the Hong Kong Legislative Council* (Hong Kong: Hong Kong University Press).
Lui, Percy Luen-tim (2007) 'The Legislature', in: Lam Wai-man, et al. (eds) *Contemporary Hong Kong Politics: Governance in the Post-1997 Era*, pp. 39–58 (Hong Kong: Hong Kong University Press).
Li, Pang-kwong (2007) 'The Executive', in: Lam Wai-man, et al. (eds.) *Contemporary Hong Kong Politics: Governance in the Post-1997 Era*, pp. 23–38 (Hong Kong: Hong Kong University Press).
Ngok, Ma (2007) *Political Development in Hong Kong: State, Political Society, and Civil Society*, Hong Kong: Hong Kong University Press.
SynergyNet (2009) 'Voting Studies of the HKSAR Legislative Council 2008–2009', SynergyNet, Hong Kong, 4th October 2009 www.synergynet.org.hk
SynergyNet (2012) 'Review of the Governance Performance of the HKSAR Government 2012 – 15 Years of HKSAR Governance: Retrospect and Prospect', SynergyNet, Hong Kong, June 2012, www.synergynet.org.hk
Tsang, Donald (2006) 2005–06 Policy Address (Hong Kong: Hong Kong SAR Government).

16 Nunavut (Canada)

Nunavut – size matters, but so does culture[1]

Graham White

Size has long been recognized as a key factor in understanding legislatures (Hedlund 1984; White 1990). Certainly, anyone familiar with the Legislative Assembly of Canada's newest territory, Nunavut, will readily agree that its scale – 19 members, representing roughly 30,000 people – profoundly affects its operations and its effectiveness.

However, this by no means implies that size is the defining feature of the Nunavut legislature, or even the most significant. This chapter argues that, while as elsewhere size matters in Nunavut, its legislature must be understood as a complex interaction of factors, including but not limited to size, and culture.

As a preliminary, when speaking of size, Nunavut is on one dimension the ultimate outlier among the jurisdictions included in this collection. The membership of its legislature may be small, as befits a small population, but Nunavut is geographically immense, encompassing more than 2 million square kilometres – roughly the size of Western Europe.

Were Nunavut a sovereign entity it would rank among the largest countries in the world. This is more than an intriguing factoid; as discussed below, Nunavut's physical geography has a direct and substantial bearing on its legislature.

The Nunavut legislature: a thumbnail sketch

Nunavut came into existence in 1999, when the Northwest Territories was divided roughly in half following a far-reaching comprehensive land claim settlement between the Government of Canada and the Inuit, the indigenous people of the eastern Canadian Arctic. Canada's three northern territories enjoy less extensive jurisdictional powers than its provinces; they are best understood as 'proto-provinces'. At the same time, Canada's subnational governments – territories and provinces alike – rank among the powerful in the world vis-à-vis the central government, so that the Government of Nunavut (GN) has authority over, among other policy fields, health, education, social welfare, renewable resources, internal transportation, civil and corporate law, and municipal government; it shares jurisdiction with the national government in a number of policy fields, including justice, economic development and environmental protection. Although the GN is heavily dependent on the national government for its revenue, the great bulk of which comes in unconditional grants, it does possess extensive taxation powers, encompassing personal, corporate and sales taxes plus a panoply of licence and user fees. In short, despite its diminutive size and (in Canadian terms) secondary constitutional status, the GN – and hence its legislature – exercises close to the range of powers enjoyed by many sovereign states.

Although the GN's existence can be traced back to the Inuit land claim agreement, it is what is termed a 'public' government, that is, the right to vote and to run for office is open to all residents meeting standard residence and (Canadian) citizenship requirements, and its programmes and services are delivered to all residents, Inuit and non-Inuit. While this may seem unremarkable – what else can government be besides public? – it stands in significant distinction to various 'Aboriginal self-government' regimes emerging throughout the Canadian North, which may entail substantial exclusionary provisions. Still, with Inuit constituting roughly 85 per cent of Nunavummiut (the people of Nunavut), the GN is very much an Inuit government.

The 19 members of the unicameral Legislative Assembly (MLAs) are elected via a single-member plurality electoral system. They follow the central precepts of Westminster cabinet-parliamentary government, the most critical of which is the fundamental constitutional principle that governments gain and retain power by maintaining the 'confidence' of the House, confirmed by winning the crucial votes. Thus the Assembly exhibits such typical elements of British-style 'responsible government' as cabinet solidarity, a politically neutral Speaker, Question Period, and a primal distinction between government bills and private members' bills (though, as discussed below, distinguishing bills in this fashion misses more important aspects of the legislative process).

The Nunavut Legislative Assembly, however, is not a typical Westminster parliament. Its most notable departure from conventional British practice lies in the absence of political parties. In what is styled 'consensus government', all candidates, including incumbent cabinet ministers, run for election or re-election in their constituencies as independents. Following each election, the Speaker is elected by secret ballot of all MLAs, and the cabinet (typically the premier and seven ministers) is chosen in a similar process. The premier assigns ministers to portfolios and may shuffle but not dismiss them; that prerogative is reserved for – and has indeed been exercised by – the legislature. Cabinet solidarity and ministerial responsibility – hallmarks of the Westminster system – prevail, but the premier's capacity to impose his or her will on cabinet is far more constrained than in party-dominated parliaments. The Nunavut Assembly has no analogue of another standard feature of parliaments characterized by party politics: a disciplined official opposition party whose prime objective is to replace the sitting government. A 'regular members' caucus, composed of all MLAs save the Speaker and those in cabinet, meets daily when the House is sitting and forms something of a loose unofficial opposition aimed at fostering cabinet accountability. It plays a significant coordination and communications role among MLAs and from time to time influences policy but it is far removed from a disciplined, party opposition. Another distinctive feature[2] of the Nunavut legislature is the institution of 'caucus': a regular, closed-door meeting of all MLAs, including the Speaker, to discuss issues. While cabinet remains the primary policy- and decision-making body, caucus does make some decisions and, more significantly, serves as a key vehicle for establishing positions and resolving conflict.

For its size, the Legislative Assembly of Nunavut provides its members with a significant level of services and support staff. MLAs also participate in a substantial and active committee system. Nunavut MLAs are among the best paid of Canadian legislators, though it is important to recognize that living costs can be several orders of magnitude higher in Nunavut than in Southern Canada. MLAs' indemnity permits them to leave their previous employment and serve as full-time legislators; they receive generous accommodation and travel allowances (all but the three local MLAs must travel to Iqaluit, the capital, by air and must live there during sessions) plus other substantial perks. MLAs are assigned small but well-appointed personal offices in the legislative building. The legislature has a small but highly professional full-time bureaucracy devoted to supporting the MLAs administratively, pro- cedurally and politically. Headed by the Clerk of the Assembly, the staff consists of: procedural advisers, including a law clerk; officials to manage payroll, MLA travel and expenses and other administrative matters; and experienced, politically neutral researchers, backed by a substantial library with a professional librarian, who provide both raw information and analytic papers to members on a confidential basis and also staff committees. The Assembly maintains a corps of professional translators who not only translate documents but also provide simultaneous interpretation for House sittings and committee meetings. (The role of Inuktitut, the Inuit language, is discussed below.) All told, the full-time Assembly staff number 26, administering a budget of $Cdn 12.9 million (roughly 9.7 million euros) in 2010–11.[3] Full Hansard coverage of all House proceedings is provided in English and Inuktitut on a contract basis by an external firm; preliminary debate transcripts are available to MLAs and the public within hours of adjournment. Nunavut has the only fully bilingual Hansard in Canada beyond the national Parliament. Sittings are broadcast live throughout the territory.

The services and facilities mentioned above are available to all MLAs, but some, such as research assistance, are understood as largely the preserve of the regular members. Ministers have extensive resources not available to the regular members: the extensive bureaucracies of the departments they head plus the usual range of central agencies. They are also entitled to hire personal political staff to look after all manner of political and policy tasks. The political staff of ministers and of the premier are housed in the legislative building but are part of the executive rather than the legislature.

In the dozen years since its inception, the committee system of the Nunavut legislature has gone through a number of permutations as adjustments are made to try to find the most effective set of committees to cover the GN's many policy sectors and administrative processes with only 10 private members. Whatever their structure and mandate, however, the committees have been active and have made their mark. For example, they hold public hearings, in Iqaluit and throughout Nunavut, that substantially influence government policy initiatives (in some cases derailing them altogether) and they produce detailed and often critical assessments of government actions and policies. Although the committees foster accountability and facilitate public input to the governmental process they are primarily reactive; only rarely do they develop or initiate policy proposals of their own. As of early 2012 there were five standing committees: two sectoral committees, Social Wellness and Community and Economic Development with five members apiece (plus three designated substitutes); two broad, government-wide committees, the Committee on Legislation and the Committee on Oversight of Government Operations and Public Accounts, with all 10 regular members as members; and one internal committee, Rules, Procedures and Privileges, comprising five MLAs. The last-named committee has one minister serving on it; on none of the others are ministers members.[4] From time to time, temporary committees are struck to look into issues of special import.

With the absence of political parties and the pressures they impose on legislators to adopt common policy and political stances, Nunavut MLAs are strongly focused on their constituencies for reasons both altruistic and self-interested. Size very much reinforces this tendency in that the average Nunavut constituency has barely 1,500 people and no more than 800 or 900 eligible voters; several have fewer than 700 (Nunavut's demographic profile is heavily skewed towards youth). Virtually no one in Nunavut lives outside clearly delineated (if often very small) communities, so that 11 of 19 MLAs represent single communities, seven constituencies comprise two communities, and one has three. An independent boundary commission established in 2010 recommended adjustments to constituency boundaries, including an increase of the size of the Assembly to 22 members (Nunavut 2011 Electoral Boundaries Commission 2011). The commission's recommendations were passed into law late in 2011 and will be in place for the next election, expected in 2013.

Given the numerical preponderance of Inuit, it is hardly surprising that the great majority of MLAs since the creation of Nunavut have been Inuit: 15 of 19 in the first (1999) election, 17 of 19 in 2004 and 14 of 19 in 2008. Correspondingly, cabinet has one, or at most two, Qallunaat (non-Inuit) ministers; both premiers have been Inuit – politically, it is hard to imagine a Qallunaat premier. Typically of Nunavut, but in sharp contrast to other legislatures in Canada and elsewhere, only one MLA has come from the legal fraternity – former premier Paul Okalik – whereas several hunters and frontline municipal employees (truck drivers, labourers and the like) have been elected. Few MLAs emerge from professional occupations as is common in legislatures in Canada and elsewhere. Many MLAs have experience in municipal governments and Inuit political organizations and it is not unusual for defeated or retired MLAs to return to such posts. Only once (at the time of writing) have there been more than two women MLAs. In the 2008 election only one woman was elected, though she was subsequently chosen as premier (and two women won by-elections after the general election). Most Inuit MLAs have been fluent in both English and Inuktitut, though a few have been unilingual Inuktitut speakers; very few of the Qallunaat MLAs have had passable Inuktitut skills let alone fluency.[5]

Size matters in the Nunavut Assembly

Scale unquestionably plays a substantial role in the workings of the Nunavut Legislative Assembly. First and foremost, the non-partisan 'consensus' government regime, which frames so much of the legislature's operations, would only be possible in a relatively small Assembly. In principle, a legislature of any size could be wholly composed of independents, but in practical terms it is hard to imagine a substantially larger one without stable factions and parties. Given the small scale of the Nunavut legislature, the absence of parties holds significant advantages. With only 19 MLAs the talent pool is already very limited but at least all MLAs can be considered for cabinet positions. This would not be the case in a party system, where a cabinet of six to eight would have to be constructed from a legislative contingent of (say) 10 to 12, necessarily including some second- or third-rate talent while excluding able MLAs from non-government parties. (This analysis is premised on the deeply ingrained Canadian preference for single-party governments, reflecting only the most limited experience of coalition cabinets.) Another advantage of the absence of parties to a jurisdiction like Nunavut is that the critically important relationship it must maintain with the national government is not imperilled by the prospect that control of the territorial and national governments might rest in the hands of parties of differing political stripe. (Some Nunavut MLAs – and ministers – have strong and well-known links to national parties, but this is very different from party control of the GN.)

The larger point here is that elements of legislative structure do not exist in isolation; they are closely intertwined, influencing and being influenced by one another.

In all legislatures structured along cabinet-parliamentary lines, the ratio of cabinet to non-cabinet members is of substantial import (White 1990). In Nunavut close to half the MLAs are in cabinet; the eight-minister cabinet, which consistently votes as a bloc on government policy, faces a disparate group of 10 regular members. Most formal votes are pro forma and carry unanimously (reflecting, if necessary, extensive backroom politicking on controversial matters), but the essential calculus is that cabinet needs only to attract the support of one or two regular MLAs to assure victory should a genuine division occur.

By no means, however, does cabinet get its way on all policies and initiatives. Nearly 95 per cent of government bills are passed, but over the years several major government legislative initiatives have either been fundamentally altered or entirely rejected by MLAs. Ministers are well aware that they owe their positions to the regular members and that they can be removed at any time, as indeed some have been. In addition, all ministers – the premier included – are subjected to a 'mid-term review' roughly two years after each election in which formal votes may be held to confirm or replace them.

Various formal and informal procedures can be understood as a function of the legislature's diminutive size. By way of illustration, MLAs' speeches on legislation, most motions, and government spending estimates are not subject to time limits; House rules permit every MLA, including ministers, to make a two-and-a-half-minute statement on any topic at the start of every sitting day. Convention assures that any MLA who wishes to ask a question in Question Period can do so, although with a one-hour limit to Question Period there is no guarantee that MLAs can ask all the questions they might want on any given day.

Size is also linked to the Assembly's scrutiny function. Each government department's spending estimates are reviewed, in often agonizing detail, by all MLAs in Committee of the Whole rather than having responsibility parcelled out to shadow ministers ('critics' in Canadian parliamentary parlance) assigned to keep tabs on specific departments. In part this reflects MLAs' unwillingness to give up their prerogative to examine any and all aspects of government. Whether the all-MLA Committee of the Whole approach is superior to the delegation of the scrutiny function to specialized departmental critics is not the issue here; the point is that size enables and fosters a group rather than an individual approach.

The Nunavut legislature's size makes possible a highly unusual practice: holding full sessions in communities outside the capital. Like their counterparts in larger parliaments, Nunavut's legislative committees regularly travel about the territory, gathering information and advice through public hearings and visits to important government and private-sector projects. Precious few legislatures, however, transport all members and senior staff plus all manner of technical paraphernalia to a community hundreds of kilometres away, bringing government directly to the people in a remarkably direct fashion. Several times in its first few years this is precisely what happened in Nunavut, though the practice has atrophied recently, in large measure as a result of the substantial costs involved.

A final point, reflecting both the size and the non-party character of the Nunavut legislature, is that astute and able individual MLAs can wield unusual influence – for good and for bad. As few as one or two bloody-minded MLAs can prove seriously disruptive to the operation of the legislature, since it is so strongly premised on universal acceptance of consensual norms rather than the formal rules which, in larger legislatures, greatly constrain the capacity of individual members to cause trouble. That such behaviour has not characterized the Nunavut Legislative Assembly by no means implies that it is not vulnerable. More generally – parties or no – interpersonal dynamics loom much larger in legislative politics in small legislatures such as in Nunavut.

But culture matters too[6]

As with several of the other jurisdictions analysed in this volume, geography looms large in shaping Nunavut politics, through its effect on political culture. As noted at the outset, despite its tiny population, Nunavut encompasses a huge land mass. Yet sheer expanse is less significant than the character of the land. Nunavut's climate is among the harshest on earth, with long, brutally cold winters. Natural resources that other societies take for granted are unknown – trees cannot grow and any form of agriculture is out of the question. Until only two or three generations ago virtually all Inuit were nomadic, coping with almost unimaginably difficult living conditions. Thus this unique and unforgiving – though bountiful in its own way – land has powerfully influenced the character and political culture of the Inuit. In particular, and at the risk of unduly simplifying a rich, complex culture, Inuit are non-confrontational and value harmony in the group; they emphasize teamwork, sharing, cooperation and the willingness to subsume individual preferences to the needs of the group; they are exceptionally adaptable and pragmatic; they prize the wisdom of elders and are respectful in interpersonal relations – it is rude not to pay attention when someone is speaking, worse still to interrupt. The Inuit worldview is holistic and thus quite different from the compartmentalized epistemology of Western thought; among other things, this entails a lack of distinction between the private and public spheres. When it comes to politics, Inuit – in common with many indigenous peoples – prefer consensual to majoritarian decision making, dislike divisive adversarial politics (including formal votes), prefer extensive public participation and community control of leaders to delegation of power to political representatives (and thus concentrated power), and find formal processes and rigid hierarchical organizations distasteful.

Such traditional Inuit values are not easily accommodated in the large, impersonal institutions that characterize modern governments, including the GN. Indeed, in many instances traditional Inuit political culture conflicts directly with the imperatives of modern government. A long-time goal of Inuit political leaders was the creation of a jurisdiction dominated numerically by Inuit whose government would strive not only to represent and promote Inuit interests but also to operate according to Inuit cultural values. Early on the GN committed itself to following, in both policies and operations, the precepts of Inuit Qaujimajatuqangit (IQ: 'that which has been long known by Inuit' – the Inuit cultural worldview). The desire to incorporate Inuit culture into Nunavut's governing institutions is nowhere more pronounced than in its legislature.

That it has been difficult to make significant headway in terms of incorporating IQ into the GN is not to deny the importance of culture in the legislature. Cultural symbols are prominent in the trappings of the legislative chamber, in which members' desks are arrayed not in the standard parliamentary rows of opposing benches but in a circle (a common arrangement among North American indigenous peoples). The chamber features seats reserved for elders on the floor of the chamber, sealskin trim on MLAs' desks and visitors' seats, a mace fashioned by Inuit carvers from a narwhal tusk,[7] and other manifestations of Inuit culture. Of far greater substantive import is the extensive use of Inuktitut in House and committee proceedings. Although few of the Inuit MLAs lack fluency in English, debate usually carries on in Inuktitut, with simultaneous translation into English for members and visitors who do not understand it. A legislature where debates take place in the local language may seem unexceptional, but in the Canadian context it is little short of remarkable that a major subnational legislature should function other than in English or French, the two national official languages. The dominance of Inuktitut in the Assembly is more than symbolic; as elsewhere, language in Nunavut is a key transmitter and preserver of culture. The opportunity for Inuit MLAs to express themselves and place their ideas in a conceptual framework rooted in Inuit worldviews and traditions is highly significant.

It would be easy to interpret the non-party 'consensus' government that characterizes the Nunavut Assembly as a direct manifestation of traditional Inuit culture. The reality, however, is a good deal more complex. Consensus government in Nunavut was in effect inherited from the NWT in 1999, when the latter was divided into Nunavut and a residual NWT. Little thought or time was devoted to the possibility of introducing a party system when the government of the new territory was being designed; Inuit are nothing if not pragmatic and, since the existing NWT consensus system was both familiar and functioned satisfactorily, the Inuit leadership focused its attention on more pressing issues. The possibility of grafting a territory-wide vote for the premier on to the NWT system, which would have fundamentally transformed it into something quite different from Westminster-style responsible government, was briefly mooted but never seriously pursued.

The origins of consensus government in the NWT lie less in the influence of Aboriginal political culture than in the exigencies of everyday legislative politics, as practised by Aboriginal and non-Aboriginal members alike.[8] Moreover, consensus government, as practised in Nunavut and the NWT, is a far cry from the consensual decision making that characterized the small bands of Northern indigenous peoples in days past. That said, if consensus government was not created to accommodate indigenous culture, their congruence has undoubtedly contributed to the success and the continuation of the non-party regime. Finally, while a solid argument can be mounted that political parties continue to be rejected in Nunavut at least in part because the implications of a party system – confrontation, division, over-heated rhetoric, and the like – run directly contrary to traditional Inuit culture, a quick glance to the east raises questions about this interpretation. The Inuit of nearby Greenland, who share many of the cultural traits of Nunavut Inuit, have for many years embraced political parties in their politics.

Within the legislature, cultural influence is unquestionably at work. The MLAs' preference for thrashing out tough issues in the less formal – and private – vehicle of caucus rather than in public debate in the chamber has obvious cultural resonance. House debate is by no means devoid of criticism or disagreement, but a good deal of conflict is dissipated in caucus before issues reach the chamber. Among other things, Inuit pragmatism inclines members to prefer reaching a solution than scoring political points through attention-grabbing speeches. The cultural expectation of respectful personal relations plays out in remarkably civil debate in the House. Almost all MLAs are typically present in the House at any given time and are usually listening to what their colleagues have to say; heckling is not unknown but it is limited in extent and generally mild in nature; so too points of order and privilege – bogus or genuine – are uncommon. As of 2012, no MLA had yet been 'named' (temporarily ejected from the chamber) by the Speaker for unparliamentary language or disruptive behaviour. Southern Canadians, used to the constant din, catcalls and mean-spirited heckling of the national House of Commons and the provincial chambers, are immediately struck by the calm civility of the Nunavut Assembly. Another manifestation of respectfulness towards others is the almost universal willingness of MLAs to give unanimous consent to colleagues' requests to permit them to finish their daily personal statements when the 150 seconds allotted to them runs out (as often happens). Indeed, it is so deeply ingrained that one instance where unanimous consent was denied attracted significant media attention. To be sure, not all is sweetness and light among MLAs: serious hostility, hard feelings and direct confrontation certainly occur, but usually behind the scenes, rather than in the public forum of the Assembly.

The influence of Inuit culture on legislative practices extends well beyond trappings and decorum into power relations. The continued preference for 'consensus government' and its (relatively) diffuse power clearly owes a good deal to Inuit cultural precepts. The reluctance of Inuit MLAs to support the notion of the premier choosing and dismissing ministers, despite the clear legal authority that already exists for such a practice, is telling in this regard. So too is the widely accepted norm that, despite the obvious political advantages to MLAs in bringing forward private members' bills, this is simply not done; only one private members' bill has ever been introduced in the Nunavut Assembly. A distinctive type of bill has also emerged: a 'House bill' – one dealing with internal Assembly matters, brought forward under the authority of the Management and Services Board, defended by the Speaker and vetted by the full caucus prior to introduction. That MLAs adopted this sensible, if highly unusual, practice seems consistent with the harmonious teamwork prized by Inuit.

Conclusion

Even small legislatures can be highly complex. As this chapter has attempted to demonstrate, this is certainly true of the Nunavut Legislative Assembly. Its small scale directly affects virtually all aspects of its operation, from the fundamental (the non-party 'consensus' system) to the important (the nature of interpersonal relations) to the trivial (the ability of all MLAs to make personal statements every day). Yet precisely the same thing could be said – and the identical illustrations cited – about the influence of culture. Disentangling the relative importance of size and culture for understanding the Nunavut legislature is an all-but-impossible task. Moreover, it is pointless: in the Legislative Assembly of Nunavut, size matters, but so too does culture.

Notes

1 My thanks to Alex Baldwin, for information and insight and for correcting several errors in an earlier draft.
2 'Distinctive' but not unique. The Nunavut Assembly closely follows the model established in the Northwest Territories (NWT) in the mid-1980s and which still prevails in the truncated NWT (White 1991).
3 Nunavut, Office of the Legislative Assembly (2010), A-2; these figures exclude eight full-time staff equivalents and $Cdn 2.6 million for independent officers of the Assembly such as the Chief Election Officer and the Languages Commissioner.
4 The powerful Management and Services Board sets Assembly budgets and oversees Assembly administration. This is not, however, a legislative committee in the conventional sense. A three-member Striking Committee recommends committee assignments.

5   On the use of Inuktitut in the Assembly, see Okalik (2011).
6   The issues discussed in this section are examined more extensively in White (2006).
7   The narwhal is a small whale native to the Arctic, with a single ivory tusk.
8   The pre-division NWT legislature was composed, in roughly equal proportions, of MLAs who were Inuit, non-Aboriginal, and Dene-Metis (the indigenous peoples of the western reaches of the territory); see White (1991).

References

Hedlund, R. (1984) Organizational attributes of legislatures: Structure, rules, norms, resources, *Legislative Studies Quarterly*, 9 (1), pp. 89–103.

Nunavut 2011 Electoral Boundaries Commission (2011) *Report*.

Nunavut, Office of the Legislative Assembly (2010), *Business Plan 2010–2013*.

Okalik, P. (2011) Inuktitut and parliamentary terminology, *Canadian Parliamentary Review*, 34 (4), pp. 22–4.

White, G. (1990) Big is different from little: On taking size seriously in the analysis of Canadian governmental institutions, *Canadian Public Administration*, 33 (4), pp. 526–60.

White, G. (1991) Westminster in the Arctic: The adaptation of British parliamentarism in the Northwest Territories, *Canadian Journal of Political Science*, 24 (3), pp. 499–523.

White, G. (2006) Traditional Aboriginal values in a Westminster parliament: The Legislative Assembly of Nunavut, *Journal of Legislative Studies*, 12 (1), pp. 8–31.

17 Scotland

Britain devolved –
the Scottish Parliament

Mark Shephard

Unlike many of the legislatures covered in this book, the Scottish Parliament (SP) is different in that it is both quite new and also a devolved legislature representing a nation within a state. The Scottish Parliament was created in 1999 following a successful referendum in 1997 on devolution for Scotland. The Scottish Parliament has 129 members (MSPs), is unicameral, and meets in the Scottish Parliament buildings in Holyrood, Edinburgh. Elections have been held every four years (1999, 2003, 2007, 2011),[1] using the mixed member proportional voting system – 73 MSPs elected via plurality voting to represent 73 constituencies within Scotland, and 56 MSPs elected to represent eight Scottish regions (seven MSPs per region) using regional party lists that correct in part disproportional party outcomes from the first-past-the-post constituency success of parties in each region.

One of the core advantages of the Scottish Parliament, as a relatively new institution, has arguably been the benefit of hindsight prior to design and implementation of the institution. A consultative steering group comprising a cross-party mix of pro-devolution party representatives ultimately concluded that the founding principles of the Scottish Parliament should be openness, accountability, the sharing of power, and equal opportunities. When the roles and functions of the Scottish Parliament are assessed, these principles often provide the lens through which the body is assessed. In this chapter an assessment is made as to how well the Scottish Parliament has performed according to these criteria bearing in mind the operative comparative framework inherent to this comparative endeavour concerning the legislative roles and functions that legislatures fulfil. However, before this, it is important to start by considering the extent of the Scottish Parliament's constitutional authority and the state of constitutional flux that devolution in the UK helps facilitate.

Constitution in flux

The exercise of power and influence of the Scottish Parliament has ultimately been constrained by the 1998 Scotland Act, which stipulates that all Acts passed by the Scottish Parliament must be limited to those areas where it has competence. This means that it cannot legislate on matters that are reserved to the UK Parliament and Government, and must not contradict Convention rights or Community (EU) law. Reserved areas are enumerated and currently include: international relations, defence, national security, fiscal and monetary policy, immigration and nationality, drugs and firearms, regulation of elections, employment, company law, consumer protection, social security, regulation of professions, energy, nuclear safety, air transport, road safety, gambling, equality, human reproductive rights, broadcasting and copyright (McGarvey and Cairney 2008, p. 2).[2] Everything else such as health, education, law and home affairs, police, prisons, local government, transport, environment, agriculture, fisheries, forestry, sport and arts are devolved domains for the Scottish Parliament. However, the distinction between reserved and devolved is not clear cut, as many reserved issue domains have exceptions, for example, while energy is a reserved power, the Scottish Parliament can encourage energy efficiency provided it does not engage in prohibition or regulation. There are also grey areas of control, for example, while the UK Government may be responsible for energy, in the case of nuclear power planning permission for new nuclear power stations is a devolved matter for the Scottish Government. While the Scottish Parliament cannot currently legislate in areas that are not devolved (although see below for likely changes), the UK Parliament can legislate in devolved areas on behalf of the Scottish Parliament when the SP gives its consent (legislative consent motions, LCMs, also known as 'Sewel motions') and even when it does not. For the first three parliamentary sessions (1999–2011) considerably more legislation has been realised via LCMs than was anticipated at the outset. However, this is not quite as simple as it seems, as a fairly large proportion of the LCMs only relate to clauses within UK bills and so comparisons of the number of LCMs versus the numbers of bills enacted in the Scottish Parliament are not strictly comparative. Moreover, in some cases the legislation resulting from LCMs can in fact entail the granting to Scottish ministers of devolved powers for reserved matters.

Recent developments such as the 2007 electoral success of the pro-independence party the Scottish National Party, minority government and the associated need for deal-making, and practical issues of best constitutional practice and subsidiarity (decision making at the most appropriate level) have meant that the Scottish Parliament is likely to gain substantial new powers from Westminster by 2015. The Scottish Parliament established a Commission on Scottish Devolution (the Calman Commission) in 2008, with the remit:

> To review the provisions of the Scotland Act 1998 in the light of experience and to recommend any changes to the present constitutional arrangements that would enable the Scottish Parliament to serve the people of Scotland better, improve the financial accountability of the Scottish Parliament, and continue to secure the position of Scotland within the United Kingdom.
>
> (Commission on Scottish Devolution 2009, p. 3)

The Calman Commission made a number of recommendations in 2009, and the Conservative/Liberal Democrat Government at Westminster looks likely to implement many of its recommendations.

Since devolution, Scotland has had the (unused) power to raise or lower income tax by 3 pence in the pound. Under the latest Scotland Bill (published in late 2010 and based on many of the proposals of the Calman Commission), it looks highly likely that the UK Treasury will deduct 10 pence from income tax in Scotland, giving MSPs the power to decide how to raise this cash instead. This is a significant development for the powers of the Scottish Government and Scottish Parliament, as (unlike with the plus or minus 3 pence power) action will have to be taken *within* Scotland to maintain the status quo, as Scotland's block grant from London would be cut to reflect the loss of income tax coming from Scotland. On top of this Scottish ministers are likely to be given additional borrowing powers to manage short-term cash flows. In addition to more powers over tax and borrowing, the Scottish Parliament is likely to be given the power to legislate in reserved areas where the UK Parliament agrees. This has a very practical application of saving time (the UK Parliament can be slow to react and timetable Scottish needs) and money (lawsuits) when emergency legislation is required to solve problems such as those exposed by the 2009 *Somerville* v *Scottish Ministers* case.[3] Other powers likely to be devolved include: stamp duty, landfill tax, deprived areas fund, some aspects of the oversight of elections (especially for the Scottish Parliament), controls over air weapons, speed limits, and drink-driving limits (HM Government 2010).

Specific proposals in the Scotland Bill for improving Scottish parliamentary oversight of the UK Government include the expectation that the UK Cabinet minister with responsibility for Scotland (currently the Secretary of State for Scotland) would appear before the Parliament to be questioned about the UK Government's legislative programme. In addition, all the leaders (conveners) of the Scottish Parliament's committees look likely to be given a further opportunity to meet with and question the UK minister. To facilitate reciprocity and connectivity with Westminster, the First Minister looks likely to fulfil a comparable role in the UK Parliament. Moreover, where responsibilities interact on an issue between Westminster and Holyrood, the UK Government is recommending that both parliaments should be able to hold both governments to account. For LCMs, the expectation is that one or more Scottish MPs will sit on the relevant public bill committee, and that they should then be eligible for invitation by the relevant Scottish Parliament committee scrutinising the legislative consent memorandum to account for matters. In addition, MSPs and MPs (and indeed MEPs) are expected to be encouraged to establish administrative arrangements that facilitate better interaction between the institutions on matters of interest that overlap. At the EU level, Scottish ministers and Scottish Parliament committees are expected to be proactive and timely in identifying EU issues of concern with the UK Government. There are also a number of UK Government recommendations on the Scottish Parliament's committee system, and these will be addressed in more depth below with an evaluation of the performance of the Scottish Parliament on openness, accountability, the sharing of power, and equal opportunities.

The proposed changes are not all about power extension for the Scottish Parliament, however. In some cases, the UK Government has justified why it proposes to re-reserve areas which had in part been devolved to the Scottish

Parliament by the Scotland Act 1998, for example the regulation of health professions and insolvency. Also, some areas that looked as though they were going to be devolved now look as though they will not in the short term, for example aviation tax and the aggregates levy (HM Government 2010, pp. 12–13). Interestingly, the UK Government also plans to tighten Section 31 (1) of the Scotland Act 1998 to make it clear that MSPs (and not just the Government) should have to justify that proposed legislation is within the Parliament's legislative competence.

In sum, devolution is clearly a constitutional arrangement subject to much flux, and the Scottish Parliament looks likely to benefit from an overall extension of powers, particularly over tax and budgeting responsibilities. One reason for this extension is the recognition by both the Commission and the UK Government that while the devolution settlement in Scotland has been 'a remarkable and substantial success' there is a need to correct the 'imbalance between power and responsibility within the existing Scotland Act' (Michael Moore, *Hansard Ministerial Statements*, 30 November 2010, col. 70WS). In the remainder of this chapter analysis is directed towards how well the Scottish Parliament has performed on accountability, power sharing, openness and equal opportunities, bearing in mind the constitutional context and constraints of the political system.

Power sharing and accountability

In the debates surrounding the establishment of a Scottish Parliament, it was clear that there were hopes that the Scottish Parliament would be stronger in relation to government than the UK Parliament. To this end, and also because of the absence of an upper chamber, emphasis was placed on creating 'strong' committees that not only combined powers of legislative initiation, scrutiny and investigation, but could engage with the legislative process at an early stage.

Two different types of committees are used in the Scottish Parliament. Mandatory committees are established under the Parliament's Standing Orders with defined remits and include: equal opportunities; European and external relations; finance; public audit; public petitions; standards, procedures and public appointments; and subordinate legislation. The subject committees are established at the beginning of each parliamentary session and are roughly designed to reflect the briefs of the Scottish Government's ministers. In Session 3 they have included: economy, energy and tourism; education, lifelong learning and culture; health and sport; justice; local government and communities; rural affairs and environment; and transport, infrastructure and climate change.

The main contrast with Westminster is that committees in Scotland not only combine powers to scrutinise legislation (Westminster's public bill committees) with powers to conduct enquiries (Westminster's select committees), but also have additional powers of legislative initiative – the right to introduce committee bills. On top of this, committees invariably enter the legislative process earlier than in Westminster, as it is the committees and not the chamber that first consider the general principles of legislation.[4] As a result, McGarvey and Cairney (2008) contend that committees in Scotland have often been touted as having more powers at their disposal than any one Westminster committee. Kaare Strom's (1998) research on parliamentary committees in European democracies supports this contention, especially the earlier engagement of the committees in the legislative process and the additional rights of legislative initiative.

However, a distinction needs to be made between theoretical power and de facto power. Strom (1998) also notes that committee power is contingent upon control of the timetable and ability to access information, and there are practical limitations here that have an impact upon the scrutiny and influence of the government as well as the capacity of the committees to be proactive. Control of the timetable, as well as access to information, has largely favoured the governing parties (especially in 1999–2007, when Labour and Liberal Democrats had a majority) and their legislative agenda. This is compounded by tight whipping and party unity (Keating 2010) and sheer workload given the combined expectation of legislative scrutiny, initiative and inquiry (Shephard 2010). In turn there has been very little initiation and success of committee bills. In the first session (1999–2003) three committee bills were passed, while only one was passed in the second session (2003–07). Even minority government and less government legislation in the third session have had little impact on committee bills, as only two have passed (2007–11). Moreover these two did not result from existing committees, but from the work of committees specifically established to examine areas which required legislation.

The realisation of committee powers is also hampered by the number of MSPs, and by the connected issue of the number of MSPs per committee. Compared with larger parliaments like that of the UK, the Scottish Parliament has considerably fewer politicians to do committee work. At the outset, the learning curve of the Scottish Parliament was quite steep, as by early 2001 the committee system was overhauled to reduce the numbers of politicians on a committee typically from 11 to seven MSPs per committee (Carman and Shephard 2009, p. 23). While this reduction in number helped reduce the number of committees MSPs had to sit on (making one per MSP the norm and not two per MSP and so increasing time for committee work), it also arguably increased the competition for places per committee, thereby increasing the power of parties over MSPs and their behaviour (Carman and Shephard 2009). Exacerbating party control still further in 2001 was the introduction of 'substitute' committee members with voting rights who could stand in for absent colleagues. Arguably less aware of the issues facing the committee, substitutes are more likely to rely on party cues than other cues such as knowledge of a topic.

However, Keating suggests that the legislative power of MSPs should not be underestimated when the size of government majorities has only ever meant at best very slim government majorities in Parliament (2010, p. 133) and, by extension of this logic, even slimmer majorities at best in committees. Even more of a problem for minority government, this means that in order for the Government to get its way it has to do deals with MSPs. Indeed, there is some evidence to suggest that concessions are made to MSPs by the Government, even when the Government has a majority. Extensive and detailed work by Shephard and Cairney (2005) of amendments by committees to government legislation reveals that many of the amendments passed by the Government in its name are actually inspired by MSPs in committee. MSPs are often asked to withdraw amendments on the understanding that the Government will consider and even address amendments using its greater access to resources and legal advice to make the amendment(s) workable.

The Scottish Parliament not only shares power with the Scottish Government, but shares it with Westminster too. And not only does Westminster decide in reserved policy areas, but it can decide policy in devolved areas and alter the powers of Scottish ministers and the Scottish Parliament, albeit that the usual courtesy is to ask for the Scottish Parliament's consent. LCMs chiefly entail instances of the Scottish Parliament giving its consent for Westminster to pass legislation on matters that are devolved to Scotland. In the first and second sessions there were 39 and 38 instances of legislative consent respectively. In the third session there were slightly fewer at 30 (Scottish Parliament 2011). While some have expressed concerns that LCMs have not been used sparingly (as was promised) and that the Scottish Parliament has been ducking power and responsibility especially on more controversial issues such as gay rights (see for example Hassan and Warhurst 2002), others have disaggregated LCMs to illustrate that most are the product of legislation tangled between reserved and devolved domains (Cairney and Keating 2004). One of the problems of LCMs is that in passing power to Westminster to decide the Scottish Parliament loses control over the timetable, success and final shape of the legislation (Keating 2010).

Power sharing is further hampered in part by the consequences of collective responsibility, Westminster-style party politics, electioneering and the electoral system. The principle of collective responsibility is derived from the Westminster system and means that government ministers (who are in turn MSPs) must agree in public on the actions of the Government (even if in private they might disagree). Those ministers disagreeing with the Government in public usually either have to resign or are removed from government. Overall, this makes for strong cohesive parties.

The role played by party politics and electioneering is neatly illustrated by the case of the inter- and intra-party dealings of the parties over the passage of the budget in 2011. To gain a majority of votes for passage of the 2011–12 budget, the minority Government of the SNP had to bargain with the other parties in the Parliament. Despite the need for quite substantial cuts to address a £1.3 billion reduction in funds, a number of concessions were offered to all the main players, and eventually the Conservatives and Liberal Democrats voted with the SNP to get the budget passed. Even though Labour worked with the SNP to negotiate deals that it wanted, the party ultimately voted against the budget, arguably for electoral reasons. Since the Conservative and Liberal Democrat coalition Government at Westminster is not popular in Scotland (it has the lowest level of regional support at 25 per cent, ICM Poll, February 2011), there was a certain electoral logic for the May 2011 Scottish Parliament elections for the Labour Party not to be seen to be on the side of the unpopular Conservatives and the Liberal Democrats. Moreover, because the SNP secured the support of the Conservatives and Liberals to pass the budget, Labour gained a potential electoral advantage over the SNP in being able to sell itself as the main left-of-centre party least associated with the unpopular policies of the coalition Government in London. Indeed, Labour MSPs David Whitton and James Kelly were quick to add their support to the Green MSP Patrick Harvie's quip that the Tory-led budget cuts were delivered in Scotland by blue Tories, yellow Tories and tartan Tories (*Official Report*, 9 February 2011, cols 33091, 33093, 33107).

Of course, a different interpretation of the 2011 budget is that power sharing did take place. Just because Labour and the Greens did not vote for the budget, three parties did vote together. Moreover, the SNP did engage in discussions and did deliver concessions to parties across the political spectrum. For instance, the Conservatives arguably gained some ground on policies for supporting employment growth and private investment in housing development, and the Liberal Democrats arguably gained additional apprenticeships, and an extension of a post office diversification scheme. Thus the final vote can be seen as indicative of the breadth of power sharing that occurred to secure the passage of the budget, and ultimately the survival of the minority Government.

Much has been made of the capacity of a minority government to pass legislation. In the first two parliamentary sessions (1999–2003 and 2003–07) the Labour–Liberal Democrat Executive passed 50 and 53 bills respectively. Halfway through the 2007–11 session, the SNP minority Government[5] headed by First Minister Alex Salmond was derided by Labour's Michael McMahon as being 'work-shy' for only managing to pass seven pieces of legislation (Peterkin 2009). However, legislation takes time to pass through legislative stages, and as with the first two sessions more is enacted in the last two years than in the first two years. Indeed, by the end of the 2007–11 session the SNP minority Government had managed to pass 52 pieces of legislation (Morgan 2011). Most legislation continues to derive from the Government, and concerns over the sessions have been raised that Parliament has been a 'conveyor belt' for the Government at the expense of committee and member bills. In Session 3, there were only two committee bills and six member bills. Of course, quantity says nothing about quality, and in the case of the Government Cairney (2009) has argued that the majority of legislation passed by the SNP up to September 2009 was not manifesto commitments, but reactions to existing commitments or upcoming events such as the Commonwealth Games.

Under the minority SNP Government, the Parliament (or, more accurately, parties) has had greater ability to exercise influence to secure deals. Whereas the Labour and Liberal Democrats voted together 99 per cent of the time in the second session (2003–07), effectively blocking the need for deals with non-governing parties, in the third session (2007–11) the strongest plenary coalitions were between Labour and the Liberal Democrats (56 per cent) and the SNP and the Conservatives (55 per cent). While cohesion within parties is arguably even stronger under minority government, coalitions between the parties are much more varied and depend upon the issue under consideration.[6] This means that the minority SNP government has had to work with multiple parties to secure deals to get legislation passed. Under minority arrangements, the Government has been forced to work more with the opposition to get anything done. In the first couple of years this meant some interesting non-delivery and posturing as the parties wrestled with how to deal with minority government. However, in the last two years it has become increasingly apparent that consensus building has been possible, even if consensus depends on finding cross-party legislation and problems that can command majorities in the Parliament. Of course, this means that big SNP manifesto commitments such as local government taxation reform and independence for Scotland have proved notoriously difficult to move forward.

Aside from minority government, another reason for strong intra-party unity is that the electoral system used for the Scottish Parliament helps exacerbate and strengthen intra-party control over MSP voting behaviour in Parliament. Indeed, as Keating (2010) contends, those elected from the party list are under strong pressure to conform to the party line, as the party determines the order of names on the party list at each election. Those MSPs who meander from the party line risk being demoted down (or indeed off) the party list, making re-election more difficult.

Another issue for many small legislatures is that of the sheer breadth of the subject remits of committees. To get around the small number of politicians available to serve on committees, subjects covered per committee are often conflated. Whereas in Westminster, for example, education and culture are split across two committees, in Scotland they are conflated. This is not an anomaly, as the same is true for other subjects such as transport and climate change. Compounding this point still further is that these comparisons are between Scottish committees with powers to scrutinise legislation, conduct inquiries and introduce legislation. The examples above from Westminster are of select committees which primarily conduct inquiries – legislative (general) committees are a separate entity. Consequently, not only do Scottish Parliament committees invariably do more (powers and subjects), they do this with over five times fewer politicians (Carman and Shephard 2009, p. 23).

Given the small pool of parliamentarians this places greater turnover pressure on committee memberships than it does in larger legislatures. Indeed, continuity of committee membership was recognised by the Calman Commission as a serious issue for the effective operation of Parliament:

> We believe that, if committees are to be effective in fulfilling their dual-purpose role (conducting inquiries and scrutinising legislation), they need to build up expertise in the subject-matter over time, and this requires a relatively low rate of turnover of members. It also helps committees to act as an effective counterweight to the Executive if their conveners are seen as figures of influence and status. In practice, however, the ideal of continuity has been undermined by regular rotations of members of all parties, usually prompted by internal party re-shuffles. The upshot is that only a small minority of committee members appointed at the beginning of a session are still members by the end of the session; and conveners (and deputy conveners) change with around the same frequency as other members.
>
> (Commission on Scottish Devolution 2009, p. 222, para. 6.35)

Given the sensitive political context,[7] the Commission arguably had little room for recommending increasing the number of parliamentarians and it settled for calling on parties to limit rotation as much as possible. This is quite difficult in small, multi-party legislatures, as ministerial promotion or demotion or any intra-party reorganisation triggers a cascade of rotations. Contrasting Westminster committees with Holyrood committees, Shephard (2010) finds that rotation is highest in the Scottish Parliament. The recommendation of the Calman Commission, and the subsequent position of the UK Government (HM Government 2010), has been to acknowledge the problem of turnover, but to offer precious little on how to solve it. Ultimately it depends on how serious one is about facilitating an operating climate in which the Parliament can match its theoretical expectations. All the evidence suggests that 129 MSPs are too few in number for the Parliament to meet dual-purpose expectations (which both Calman and the UK Government (HM Government 2010) argue should be kept) and that this issue will probably be revisited in the future.

Rotation, low numbers per committee, breadth of remit, and dual-purpose roles of committees also play a role in reducing the capacity of the Parliament to hold the government accountable. This is made worse if committee focus is reaction to government legislation. The Calman Commission found this problem to be particularly acute in some cases:

> Another practical difficulty that has arisen is one of legislative overload on particular committees and hence on their ability to strike a balance between legislative scrutiny and proactive inquiry work. This was particularly a problem in Session 1, when a raft of law reform and justice-related legislation dominated the work programme of the Justice and Home Affairs Committee to such an extent that it was eventually replaced by two separate Justice Committees (with identical remits), while a number of other subject committees also found their ability to undertake substantial inquiries of their own choosing heavily constrained by the volume of legislation.
>
> (Commission on Scottish Devolution 2009, p. 222, para. 6.37)

To gain a comparative sense of how this compares and contrasts with Westminster, Shephard (2010) examined committees with similar remits in both Holyrood and Westminster and found that committees in Holyrood produced far fewer inquiries than comparable committees in Westminster.

To address issues of overload and to ensure flexibility, the Calman Commission and subsequently also the UK Government (HM Government 2010) have recommended that committees be given the power to establish sub-committees without the need of full parliamentary approval (Commission on Scottish Devolution 2009, p. 223, para. 6.43). How this would work in practice, particularly if it became widespread, without increasing the number of MSPs is not clear. The 2001 committee reorganisation is evidence enough of what happens if MSPs sit on too many committees at any one time.

On accountability, there have been additional concerns that the Parliament is not always treated in accordance with the expectations and demands of the Ministerial Code. In January 2009, Presiding Officer Alex Fergusson asked the Standards, Procedures and Public Appointments Committee to investigate the issue of the policing of what is said both in chamber debates and during exchanges at question times. Following a string of points of order on the 'veracity' of what is said, Fergusson expressed concern that the highest standards of probity, scrutiny and accountability were being undermined. Like the UK Ministerial Code, the Scottish Ministerial Code calls on ministers to give accurate and truthful information to Parliament. Under both systems, those 'knowingly misleading' Parliament are expected to resign. The upshot has been that the Standards, Procedures and Public Appointments Committee has recommended a number of improvements to the highlighting and request for corrections, as well as greater transparency and publicity of corrected inaccuracies. It remains to be seen whether the codes of conduct will be changed to reflect these recommendations. Of course, it is invariably quite difficult to ascertain not only accuracy but also whether ministers 'knowingly mislead'. Compounding the problem is that it is up to the First Minster to decide the fate of ministers. However, the SNP did alter the Ministerial Code in 2008 to establish an independent advisory panel of past presiding officers who could investigate and advise on matters relating to the Ministerial Code. Although it is early days, this has arguably altered the balance of power away from the Government and towards the Parliament, as the Alex Fergusson actions above illustrate.

Openness and equal opportunities

The Scottish Parliament has worked really hard to connect with the Scottish public and has responded comparatively quickly to address issues relating to the need for probity of its members. It has a very good website that not only includes a verbatim report of chamber and committee business, but even enables those who are interested to see exactly what expenses MSPs claim for and how much is claimed on a month-by-month basis. The website is so transparent that the level of detail you can search for ranges from monies spent on evening meals to the costs of key cutting. Indeed, had Westminster operated a system as transparent as that put in place in the Scottish Parliament (2005–06 onward), it is highly likely that much of the damage of the MPs' expenses row could have been avoided.

McLaverty and Morris (2007) argue that the Scottish Parliament has been particularly proactive in seeking public engagement with the Parliament through the petitions system, although ultimately constraints on the legislative agenda and the remit of the Scottish Parliament set by Westminster do mean that there are limits to participatory democracy in Scotland. Petitions have to fall within the responsibilities of the Scottish Parliament, and guidelines and procedures have been introduced to discourage serial petitioners who clogged the process in the beginning. Across the first three sessions (1999–2011), there have been 1,390 admissible petitions. For 2009–10 there were 77 petitions lodged with the Public Petitions Committee (Scottish Parliament 2010: 77).

Just because there is a petitions system provided, it does not mean that this is recognised, used or supported by the public, or indeed is representative of the public. Petitioning is clearly a minority activity and, in presenting findings to the Petitions Committee, Mark Diffley of Ipsos MORI expressed concerns that 'the public are generally uninformed about the Scottish Parliament's public petitions process, as well as about the role of the Parliament more generally' (Public Petitions Committee, *Official Report*, 19 May 2009, col. 1781).

Moreover, if we examine those who do take part, it is clear that petitioners do over-represent the usual suspects, the white middle class (Carman 2009, p. 13). The Parliament has reacted to this finding by doing more to publicise its work. This has included efforts at physical outreach such as meetings outside Parliament, visits to schools, and redesigning of promotional materials and the website. In an effort to reach more young people (and address a specific petition on this very point) there has also been enhanced connection and engagement using new technologies.

Surveying petitioners of the Scottish Parliament, Christopher Carman (2010) found that expectations of the process were greater than evaluations of the process and that, for participatory forms to work, it is not enough just to provide a petitions system for the public to engage with the Parliament, but that perception of fairness of process needs some attention, as only 36 per cent of those responding thought that their petition was handled fairly. Of course, what is considered fair and what is considered successful are highly subjective. The Petitions Committee itself regularly provides examples of 'successful' petitions in its annual reports. For example, one petitioner:

> called on the Scottish Government to produce new guidelines on vitamin D supplementation for children and pregnant women and to run an awareness campaign to ensure that people know what level of vitamin D supplements they should be taking. As a result of this petition the Scottish Government agreed to a co-ordinated programme of action with NHS Health Scotland to produce guidance on vitamin D and ensure health professionals give out correct and consistent advice to pregnant women and new mothers in relation to vitamin D.
> (Scottish Parliament Public Petitions Committee 2010, para. 9)

Success is also difficult to assess, as there is no way of knowing in full what legislation is blocked, amended or even introduced because of petitions. What is important about the petitions process is that an avenue exists in the Scottish Parliament for public engagement and capacity for redress on issues that matter and that otherwise might get missed by the politicians.

As well as petitions, visits to the Parliament are actively encouraged. In the first full year of access to the Scottish Parliament (2005–06),[8] there were 355,047 visits, including 6,025 from schools and further education colleges (Scottish Parliament

2006, pp. 151–2). By 2009–10, interest in the Parliament had not abated, as there were 411,105 visitors, including 12,478 from schools and further education colleges (Scottish Parliament 2010, p. 119). MSPs also conduct outreach sessions in communities and schools, and in 2005–06 there were 116 MSP visits to schools (Scottish Parliament 2006, p. 153). For 2009–10 there were 400 outreach events in schools and colleges (Scottish Parliament 2010, p. 120).[9]

At the outset, the Scottish Parliament also worked hard to connect with the public by holding committee meetings outside the Parliament. In 1999–2000, for example, there were 361 committee meetings held in the first parliamentary year and 27 (7 per cent) of these were held outside the Parliament in locations around Scotland (Scottish Parliament 2000). In 2009–10, there were 370 committee meetings, and eight (2 per cent) of these were held outside the Parliament (Scottish Parliament 2010). While the number of meetings outside the Parliament has gone down, and is likely to continue to stay low because of economic circumstances and budget constraints, such attempts to connect with individuals and groups in Scotland, particularly those in remote areas, are a credit to the ideals of those who designed the Parliament. Benefits of such contact are multi-faceted and include the ability to connect with and include hard-to-reach groups, as well as the advantage of the information such groups can provide. This is arguably of most importance for the Rural Affairs and Environment Committee given the physical distance from Edinburgh for many affected by this brief as well as the distance from the MSPs in terms of their formative careers and training (Shephard *et al.* 2001).

Even the Calman Commission noted how much effort had been given to openness in the case of the committees:

> Committees conduct the large majority of their business in public, with private sessions normally restricted to consideration of draft reports and to house-keeping matters such as considering lines of questioning or deciding on candidates for the post of committee adviser. Inquiries are launched with public calls for evidence, and much of the time involved taken up with hearing oral evidence from the principal relevant interests. As a result, committee reports are substantially evidence-based.
>
> (Commission on Scottish Devolution 2009, p. 221, para. 6.31)

One criticism on openness (for that matter, power sharing and accountability) that did arise in the Calman Commission was that organisations could do with more time to react to legislative proposals:

> A regular complaint from organisations that take an active interest in new legislation is the lack of time available between publication of amendments to Bills and the proceedings at which they are debated and decided – and hence the amount of time available to such organisations to consider the implications of amendments and to make representations to MSPs about them.
>
> (Commission on Scottish Devolution 2009, p. 225, para. 6.48)

While time periods between legislative stages have been extended in the past to address this problem, both the Commission on Scottish Devolution (2009) and UK Government (HM Government 2010) recognised that more time needed to be given to Stage 3 (whole chamber – see note 3) consideration of amendments and reflection upon these. At the moment, the final vote invariably takes place at the end of Stage 3 and this is literally moments after the consideration of some often quite important last-minute amendments. Consequently, it had been suggested that Stage 3 be subdivided into a Stage 3 for amendments and a new Stage 4 for final passage of legislation, giving both the legislature and other interested parties time to reflect upon the changes being proposed before final passage of legislation. Given additional concerns that substantial changes were being made at Stage 3 without due reflection, both the Commission on Scottish Devolution (2009) and the UK Government (HM Government 2010) recommended that any MSP be permitted to propose at Stage 3 that parts of a bill be referred back to committee at Stage 2 for further consideration. The intention was not only to make the Parliament more open to public and outside group scrutiny, but to improve power sharing and accountability. However, the Standards, Procedures and Public Appointments Committee reported that 'there is adequate flexibility within the current rules for a four stage process to be used if required and recommends that the Stage 4 procedure proposed should not be progressed' (Scottish Parliament Standards, Procedures and Public Appointments Committee 2010, para. 95). The report was approved by the Scottish Parliament on 29 September 2010.

Equal opportunities are the final principle of the Scottish Parliament. This principle is reflected in the fact that there is a mandatory committee devoted to equal opportunities which not only considers and reports on matters relating to equal opportunities, but checks on what goes on in the Parliament to make sure that equal opportunities within the Parliament are adhered to. To achieve this, the committee gets involved in legislation where equal opportunity issues arise and also promotes mainstreaming of equal opportunities and awareness across all committees. Moreover, equal opportunities are broadly defined in the Standing Orders of the Parliament as:

> the prevention, elimination or regulation of discrimination between persons on grounds of sex or marital status, on racial grounds or on grounds of disability, age, sexual orientation, language or social origin or of other personal attributes, including beliefs or opinions such as religious beliefs or political opinions.
>
> (Standing Orders, Rule 6.9.2)

This has given an institutional legitimacy to the quest for anti-discriminatory legislation and practices. Even if more controversial legislative measures have been farmed out to Westminster through LCMs (see above), the mandatory presence of equal opportunities in the Scottish Parliament provides important institutional constraints for any discriminatory elements trying to influence or get elected to the Parliament.

Conclusion

The Scottish Parliament is an interesting legislative body for a number of reasons. It is fairly new, and has been designed to address many of the weaknesses identified in the Westminster system. In particular, committees have an amalgamation of powers that in Westminster are both disaggregated across committee types (legislative and inquiry committees) and absent (right of committees to introduce legislation). There is also a strong attempt in the Scottish Parliament to connect with the public, as committee outreach and the public petitions system attest. The Scottish Parliament is also a body whose remit and powers are on the rise as more control over budgets and legislative areas is granted to Scotland under the move to deeper devolution. However, the Scottish Parliament is also very much a creature of Westminster (see especially Mitchell 2010). Not only are many of the procedures very similar (for example question time), but the parties are not new and an entrenched party political culture ensures that whipping is strong and that very little 'new politics' takes place. Compounding party unity is a very close race between Labour and the Scottish National Party for plurality of seats and hence control of the Government. The need to 'win' elections ensures that those in government do as much as they can to justify their time in office. Consequently, even if the Parliament has more proactive powers than Westminster, like Westminster it has ultimately been quite reactive to the agenda the Government presents. The size of the Scottish Parliament also limits capacity for scrutiny and influence. Compared with Westminster, committees in the Scottish Parliament have not only wider powers but wider remits (and so more to do), and they suffer more problems with turnover and so loss of expertise. Without addressing the issue of low numbers, it is difficult to see how the Scottish Parliament can realise its theoretical potential. Overload is apparently going to be solved by sub-committees. Over-staffing of committees was an issue in the formative years of the Scottish Parliament. It looks as though it might be again.

Notes

Special thanks to Francesca McGrath, Senior Researcher (Culture and Constitution), SPICe at the Scottish Parliament for comments and suggestions.

1 The Scottish Parliament has been asked to decide on varying parliamentary terms, most likely to five years, to avoid overlaps with Westminster. For example, after the 2011 Scottish Parliament elections, the next set of elections would be in 2015, which would clash with likely Westminster House of Commons elections. Moving to a five-year period (like that proposed for Westminster) would keep the two elections in separate years.

2 For fuller details, including amendments, see Schedule 5 of the 1998 Scotland Act via http://www.legislation.gov.uk/ukpga/1998/46/schedule/5 (accessed 13 February 2011).

3 The *Somerville* v *Scottish Ministers* (2009) case exposed anomalies between the Scotland Act 1998 and the Human Rights Act 1998 requiring emergency legislation to standardise time limits for bringing legal actions against Scottish ministers. For more details see Hough (2009).

4 The relevant subject committee considers a proposal's general principles during stage one of a bill's consideration and passes its view (positive or negative) to the whole

chamber. Provided there is parliamentary acceptance (based on the committee's report) of the bill's principles, the bill will be referred back to the lead committee for detailed 'line-by-line' consideration. It is at this stage that the committee will consider amending the bill. During the first and second stages, committees may take evidence and request information from ministers (it is expected that ministers will respond either in person or in writing). Finally, the amended bill, if passed out of the committee, is then referred to the whole chamber. At this third stage the chamber may pass the bill or refer it back to the committee for further 'stage two' consideration (Carman and Shephard 2009, p. 22).

5   When the SNP came to power in 2007 they changed Scottish 'Executive' to Scottish 'Government'. The Scotland Act 2012 amended the Scotland Act 1998 so that the Scottish Executive was renamed the Scottish Government.

6   Data collected by Steven MacGregor at the University of Aberdeen as part of unpublished doctoral research.

7   Given the provisions of the 1998 Scotland Act, initial expectations were that the number of MSPs would reduce from 129 to around 106 to ensure that constituency boundaries for the post-devolution reduction in MPs matched those of constituency MSPs. To keep the ratio of list MSPs to constituency MSPs the same, part of the reduction was also expected to be from the lists. However, in the face of subsequent experience on the ground, this was changed in subsequent legislation, as it was recognised that the Parliament would face significant operational difficulties if it reduced its numbers.

   The Scottish Parliament building was not completed until Autumn 2004 and so the first full year of comparable data for visitor numbers in the new Scottish Parliament building is 2005–06.

9   As an indication of how much the Scottish Parliament cares about outreach and of being representative of the regions in Scotland, as well as for what this says about the level of openness, data is even disaggregated and listed regionally, with figures showing clear evidence of attempts at regional balance.

References

Cairney, Paul (2009) The Scottish Parliament and parties, *Scotland Devolution Monitoring Report*, September, pp. 49–50, http://www.ucl.ac.uk/constitution-unit/research/research-archive/scotland09.pdf (accessed 13 February 2011).

Cairney, Paul and Keating, Michael (2004) Sewel motions in the Scottish Parliament, *Scottish Affairs*, Spring, 47, pp. 115–34.

Carman, Christopher (2009) Engaging the public in the Scottish Parliament's petitions process, Ipsos MORI, http://www.scottish.parliament.uk/S3/committees/petitions/inquiries/petitionsProcess/Engagingthepublicinthepetitionsprocess.pdf.pdf (accessed 21 February 2011).

Carman, Christopher (2010) The process is the reality: Perceptions of procedural fairness and participatory democracy, *Political Studies*, 58 (4), pp. 731–51.

Carman, Chris and Shephard, Mark (2009) Committees in the Scottish Parliament, in *The Scottish Parliament 1999–2009: The First Decade* (Edinburgh: Hansard Society Scotland).

Commission on Scottish Devolution (2009) *Serving Scotland Better: Scotland and the United Kingdom in the 21st Century*, Final Report, June, http://www.commissiononscottishdevolution.org.uk/uploads/2009-06-12-csd-final-report-2009fbookmarked.pdf (accessed 13 February 2011).

Hassan, Gerry and Warhurst, Chris (2002) Future Scotland: The making of the new social democracy, in Gerry Hassan and Chris Warhurst (eds), *Tomorrow's Scotland* (London: Lawrence & Wishart).

HM Government (2010) *Strengthening Scotland's Future*, CM 7973, November.

Hough, Richard (2009) SPICe briefing: Convention Rights Proceedings (Amendment) (Scotland) Bill, *The Scottish Parliament*, 15 June, Briefing 09/44.

Keating, Michael (2010) Government and parliament, in *The Government of Scotland: Public Policy Making after Devolution*, 2nd edn (Edinburgh: Edinburgh University Press).

McGarvey, Neil and Cairney, Paul (2008) *Scottish Politics: An Introduction* (Basingstoke: Palgrave Macmillan).

McLaverty, Peter and Morris, Sue (2007), The Scottish Parliament: A new era for participatory democracy?, in Thomas Zittel and Dieter Fuchs (eds), *Participatory Democracy and Political Participation: Can Participatory Engineering Bring Citizens Back In?* (New York: Routledge).

Mitchell, James (2010) The narcissism of small differences: Scotland and Westminster, *Parliamentary Affairs*, 63 (1), pp. 98–116.

Morgan, Alasdair (2011) Introductory statement to 'Holyrood Highlights Special: A look back on Session 3', http://www.scottish.parliament.uk/ (accessed 5 April 2011).

Peterkin, Tom (2009) Labour rivals hit out at 'work-shy' First Minister, *Scotland on Sunday*, 19 April, http://scotlandonsunday.scotsman.com/scotland/Labour-rivals-hit-out-at.5183893.jp (accessed 14 February 2011).

Scottish Government (2011) Sewel convention – legislative consent motions, http://www.scotland.gov.uk/About/Sewel (accessed 15 February 2011).

Scottish Parliament (2000) *Scottish Parliament Statistics 1999–2000*, http://www.scottish.parliament.uk/corporate/anrep-accts/sps/sps-00/spar00-stat.pdf (accessed 20 February 2011).

Scottish Parliament (2006) *Scottish Parliament Statistics 2005–2006*, http://www.scottish.parliament.uk/corporate/anrep-accts/sps/sps-06/SP-Stats2005-06.pdf (accessed 20 February 2011).

Scottish Parliament (2009) *Standing Orders of the Scottish Parliament*, 3rd edn (4th revision, June), http://www.scottish.parliament.uk/business/so/sto-c.htm (accessed 20 February 2011).

Scottish Parliament (2010) *Scottish Parliament Statistics 2009–2010*, http://www.scottish.parliament.uk/corporate/anrep-accts/sps/SP_Stats_200910.pdf (accessed 20 February 2011).

Scottish Parliament (2011) *Legislative Consent Memorandums and Motions*, http://www.scottish.parliament.uk/business/legConMem/LCM-Stats.htm (accessed 5 April 2011).

Scottish Parliament Public Petitions Committee (2010) *Annual Report*, SP Paper 448, http://www.scottish.parliament.uk/s3/committees/petitions/reports-10/pur10-01.htm (accessed 20 February 2011).

Scottish Parliament Standards, Procedures and Public Appointments Committee (2010) The recommendations of the Commission on Scottish Devolution regarding Scottish Parliament procedures, 5th Report, SP Paper 490.

Shephard, Mark (2010) Comparing the power of committees: The theory and practice of Westminster and Holyrood, Draft paper for Ninth Workshop of Parliamentary Scholars and Parliamentarians, Wroxton College, Wroxton, Oxfordshire, 24–25 July.

Shephard, Mark and Cairney, Paul (2004) Consensual or dominant relationships with Parliament? A comparison of administrations and ministers in Scotland, *Public Administration*, 82 (4), pp. 851–5.

Shephard, Mark and Cairney, Paul (2005) The impact of the Scottish Parliament in amending executive legislation, *Political Studies*, 53 (2), pp. 303–19.

Shephard, Mark, McGarvey, Neil and Cavanagh, Mick (2001) New Scottish Parliament, New Scottish parliamentarians?, *Journal of Legislative Studies*, 78 (2), pp. 79–104.

Strom, Kaare (1998) Parliamentary committees in European democracies, in Lawrence D. Longley and Roger H. Davidson (eds), *The New Roles of Parliamentary Committees* (London: Frank Cass).

18 Conclusion

Legislatures – does size matter?

Michael Rush

> No Man is an island, entire unto itself; every man is a piece of the continent, a part of the main.
>
> (John Donne[1])

What John Donne said of a man is also true of legislatures: they do not exist in total isolation – all have things in common as well as significant differences. Of the 36 legislatures covered in this volume, 27 are situated on islands or groups of islands, with identifiable histories and cultures. Of these 10 are in the Commonwealth Caribbean and 12 are in the Pacific, the others being Bermuda, Malta, Guernsey, Jersey and the Isle of Man. However, four others could be described as 'virtual' islands: Liechtenstein, Gibraltar, Lesotho and Swaziland. Liechtenstein is a small territory bounded by Switzerland to the south and west and Austria to the north and east, and Gibraltar, even smaller, lies at the southern extremity of the Iberian peninsula. Lesotho and Swaziland are much larger in area but are enclaves in the Republic of South Africa. Guyana and Belize are part of mainland Central and South America respectively, Hong Kong part of mainland China, while the remaining two legislatures in Scotland and Nunavut are sub-national legislatures within larger sovereign entities, but all have distinctive histories and cultures, marking them off from those larger entities.[2] In short, all have the potential to be distinctive legislatures, but how much is this because of their histories and cultures and how much because they are *small* legislatures?

However, not only are legislatures part of a particular political system and society, but they are part of a wider world, and this is reflected in their origins and development and their operation. As Nicholas Baldwin illustrates in Chapter 1, legislatures vary greatly in size from those with fewer than a score of members to those with a membership numbered in the hundreds, even the thousands in the case of the National People's Congress of the People's Republic of China (PRC), while some are bicameral, others unicameral. They also vary in shape: some have a rectangular configuration, with opposing political groupings facing one another; others have adopted a semi-circular form, with groupings seated ideologically from left to right; yet others sit in a circular formation; and some sit in what may be termed proscenium theatre style, with leadership figures on the stage and the rest of the members in the auditorium. How far such settings affect and reflect behaviour and practices of the legislature varies. Other things matter too – most notably the relationship between the executive and the legislature and between the legislature and the population at large. The executive–legislative relationship is most commonly characterised by a constitutional fusion of executive and legislative power, as exemplified by parliamentary systems, or by a constitutional separation of powers, as in American-style presidential systems, but there are other ways of organising the executive–legislative relationship which fall outside the two most common forms. The relationship between the legislature and the population is most commonly exercised through some form of election, with individual members of the legislature representing specified sections of the population, usually, though not always, geographically. Members are commonly grouped into political parties, but again not always, so it is likely that parties will play a significant role in the operation of most legislatures and, indeed, in the relationship between the executive and the legislature. Political parties and party systems therefore matter and so also do electoral systems, particularly whether they are majoritarian or proportional.

But does size of the legislature matter? The short answer is yes, the longer answer more complex.

Defining small legislatures

Simply defining a small legislature by the size of its membership is complicated by bicameralism: two-fifths (40.4 per cent) of the legislatures listed by the Inter-Parliamentary Union (IPU) are bicameral,[3] and in almost all cases the chambers concerned operate separately. This affects each chamber's relationship with the executive, especially in parliamentary systems, and their ability to sustain committee systems and to maintain majority and minority groups, especially in the form of government and opposition supporters. The impact of size is therefore better understood if it is assessed on the basis of chambers rather than the combined membership in bicameral legislatures.

It is clear from the IPU data shown in Figure 18.1 that legislative chambers with fewer than 100 members constitute a significant minority among world legislatures – 44.3 per cent. Indeed, those with fewer than 200 members make up nearly three-quarters. Thus large chambers like the UK House of Commons, the United States House of Representatives and the German Bundestag are the exception to the general rule, and most legislative chambers are relatively small. Moreover, if the data for the case studies is broken down further, a substantial proportion have chambers with fewer than 20 members, as Figure 18.2 shows. Figure 18.2 also shows that upper chambers tend to have fewer members than lower chambers in the bicameral legislatures covered in this study.

Not surprisingly, there is a broad correspondence between the size of the legislature and the size of the population of the state or territory concerned. The

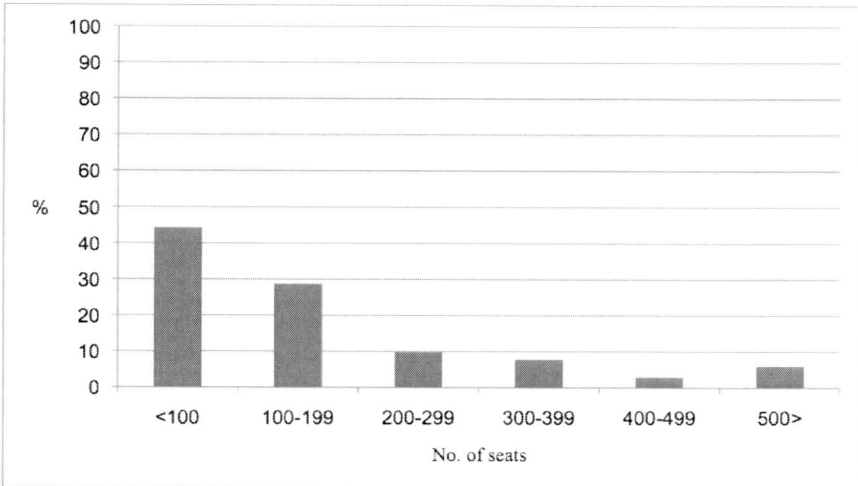

Figure 18.1 The size of legislative chambers

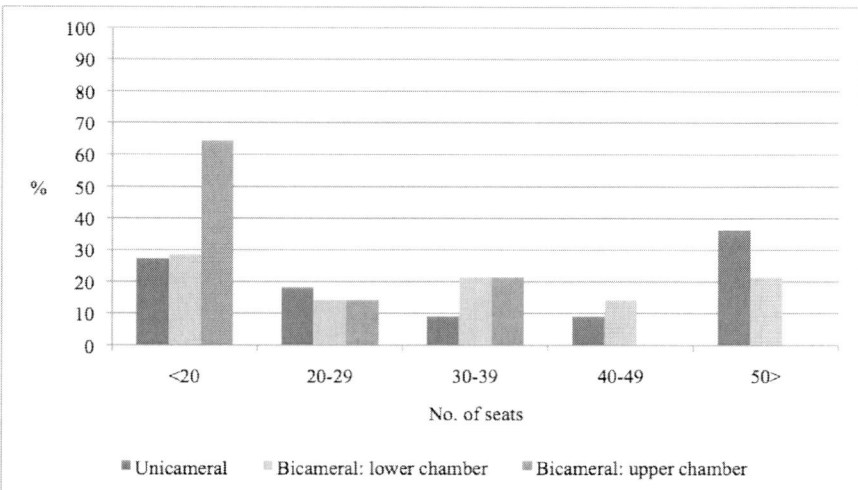

Figure 18.2 Number of seats – unicameral and bicameral (lower and upper) chambers of legislatures studied in this volume

population represented by the 36 legislatures covered in this study ranges from 1,300 in the Pacific Island of Niue to the more than 7 million population of Hong Kong. Nonetheless, 83.3 per cent of the legislatures represent a population of less than a million, and the median is 106,500.

Small legislatures can be divided into three types, those in:

- sovereign entities, i.e. legislatures in independent states;
- semi-sovereign entities, i.e. legislatures in almost entirely self-governing areas or territories, but subject to significant external constraints;[4] and
- sub-national entities, i.e. legislatures in federal, quasi-federal or devolved systems of government.

The application of these categories to the 36 legislatures studied in this volume is shown in Table 18.1.

Legislatures in sovereign entities and in sub-national entities are, of course, the most common, whereas those falling into the second category of semi-sovereign entities are limited in number but are a noteworthy and important variation. Legislatures in all three categories vary considerably in size, but the second and third categories inevitably tend to be smaller, particularly those in the semi-sovereign category, since they are mostly found in small former colonial territories with particular historical antecedents and legal status. Sub-national legislatures are most common in federal systems but also exist in quasi-federal systems, such as Spain, or devolved systems, as in three of the four parts of the UK. Sub-national legislatures also vary considerably in size, with many having a membership of fewer than a hundred, but others have more members than some national legislatures. Furthermore, it is not unusual for sub-national legislatures to represent a population of more than a million. Four of the six Australian states, for example, have lower houses with fewer than 100 members,[5] but all but Tasmania have populations in excess of a million. Similarly, eight of Canada's 10 provinces have legislatures with membership of under a hundred, but six have populations of more than a million.[6] The United States, however, provides the greatest contrast: all but one of the 50 states – Nebraska – have bicameral legislatures;[7] 58 per cent have lower houses with more than a hundred members, including New Hampshire with a massive 400, and populations range from California's 37 million to Vermont's 600,000, but California's Assembly has only 80 members compared with the 150 members of the Vermont House of Representatives.

Sub-national legislatures vary considerably not only in size, but in their relationship with the national political system. Their powers and responsibilities are either determined by the national constitution, as in federal systems, or set out

Table 18.1 Three types of small legislatures

Type	Examples
Sovereign entities	Commonwealth Caribbean countries (12), Pacific islands (12), Lesotho, Malta, Swaziland and Liechtenstein.
Semi-sovereign entities	Bermuda and Gibraltar (British overseas territories) (2), Guernsey, Jersey and the Isle of Man (British Crown dependencies) (3).
Sub-national legislatures	Hong Kong, Nunavut and Scotland.

in primary legislation passed by national legislatures in quasi-federal and devolved systems. In either case, the basic executive–legislative relationship at the sub-national level normally mirrors that of the national level. Thus, parliamentary systems, in which the executive is constitutionally drawn from and responsible to the legislature, normally reproduce parliamentary systems at the sub-national level, and presidential systems, involving a separation of executive and legislative power, normally reproduce similar sub-national systems. For instance, Australia and Canada are parliamentary systems and their respective states and provinces are also parliamentary systems. On the other hand, the United States is the exemplar of the presidential system and it is hardly surprising that the 50 states should replicate the separation of powers, each with a separate governor and state legislature. This does not entirely preclude important variations within such arrangements: the lone adoption by Nebraska of a unicameral state legislature has already been noted; the Australian state of Queensland and several Canadian provinces abolished their upper chambers;[8] Northern Ireland uniquely has a power-sharing executive; and, although the Netherlands has a parliamentary system in that members of the executive are drawn from and responsible to the Dutch Parliament, ministers cease to be members of the legislature once appointed. In short, whether sovereign, semi-sovereign or sub-national, legislatures vary considerably, and small legislatures are no exception.

Origins and development

In 1964, Louis Hartz edited a book entitled *The Founding of New Societies*[9] in which he argued that a number of political systems in the world had developed from what he termed 'fragments' of European societies that were eventually cut off from their 'parent' societies, resulting in each developing their own distinctive political system. Contributory chapters then used the United States, Canada, Australia, South Africa and Latin America as case studies. It would be inaccurate to describe the small legislatures covered in this volume simply as fragments subsequently cut off from their parent societies, but all could be said to have experienced a degree of isolation sufficient to have played an important role in their political development that bears some comparison with Hartz's 'fragments'.

To a significant degree this isolation was geographical. It has already been noted that 27 of the 36 covered in this study are found on islands or groups of islands, another four are 'virtual' islands, but the overwhelming majority have something else in common – a colonial experience, the majority with the UK, others with France, Spain, the Netherlands, Germany, Australia, New Zealand or the United States, in some cases involving more than one of these powers. However, the length and nature of their colonial experience varied considerably. Few involved the extensive European settlement characteristic of Canada, Australia, New Zealand and South Africa, although white domination by European minorities was particularly important in Bermuda and the Commonwealth Caribbean, less so in the Pacific islands. Apart from the sub-national entities of Hong Kong, Nunavut and Scotland, all are sovereign or semi-sovereign entities, those with a colonial past mostly having achieved independence in the second half of the twentieth century. Two, Bermuda and Gibraltar, are British overseas territories, having internal self-government but leaving external affairs and defence in the hands of the UK.[10]

A comparison between Bermuda and the Commonwealth Caribbean, on the one hand, and the Pacific islands, on the other, illustrates just how varied the colonial experience was. The experience was much longer in Bermuda and the Common-wealth Caribbean than among the Pacific islands, dating back to the sixteenth and seventeenth centuries in most cases in the former, but mostly from the nineteenth century with the latter. For Antigua and Barbuda, the Bahamas, Barbados and Bermuda it was exclusively English and then British, but for the rest of the Commonwealth Caribbean other European powers were involved initially through early settlement (not always successful) and trading rivalry, but later and sometimes through privateering and piracy as wider manifestations of wars in Europe, leading to islands changing hands, sometimes more than once. In some cases the treaties ending these wars restored territories to the former controlling power, so, for example, France regained control of Guadeloupe and Martinique but was forced to cede Dominica, St Kitts and Nevis, St Lucia, and St Vincent and the Grenadines to Britain. Of these, French cultural influence is greatest in Dominica, exemplified by the fact that it joined La Francophonie.[11] Although the first European contacts in many parts of the Commonwealth Caribbean were with Spain, the lasting influence of the Spanish language and culture was in South and Central America, so that in the territories covered here it is strongest in Belize, which the British came to dominate. A major consequence of British domination generally was that first the slave trade and then slavery itself were abolished in these entities, and white minorities were increasingly challenged by black majorities, with important cultural and political implications.

In relative contrast, European contacts with the Pacific islands tended to be later, certainly in any colonial sense. A number of European powers were involved – Britain, Spain, France and, perhaps more strikingly compared with many other parts of the world, Germany. Bismarck, Chancellor of the post-1870 united Germany, had embarked on acquiring colonial possessions reluctantly, and much of German expansion occurred under his successors, strongly supported by Kaiser Wilhelm II. Part of this expansion was in the Pacific, involving the Marshall Islands, Micronesia, Nauru, Palau, Samoa and the Solomon Islands. After the outbreak of the First World War, all were occupied by forces from Britain, Australia and New Zealand and, in the case of the Marshall Islands, Micronesia and Palau, Japan. Japan also occupied most of the Pacific islands during the Second World War, but following its defeat several reverted to Britain, Australia or New Zealand, but the Marshall Islands, Micronesia, Palau and part of Samoa came under American control through United Nations mandates. The colonial experience of the Pacific islands was therefore shorter and more varied and, importantly, unlike Bermuda and most of the Commonwealth Caribbean, involved surviving indigenous populations. The Pacific islands also produce two unusual cases – Tonga, which, although a British-protected state between 1900 and 1970, retained its indigenous monarchy and had only the loosest of colonial relationships with Britain; and Vanuatu, which was subject to joint Franco-British rule through condominium status between 1900 and 1980.

Hong Kong's colonial experience was different again: ceded to Britain in 1842 after the First Opium War, it was part of European efforts to open up China yet further to trade, but its position was complicated by further territory being leased to Britain in 1899 for a period of 99 years. As the end of the lease period approached, the People's Republic of China demanded the return of Hong Kong and, in 1997, British rule ended and Hong Kong became a special administrative region of the People's Republic.[12]

In addition, although it is not accurate to describe the relationships between England and subsequently the UK and Scotland, the Isle of Man, Guernsey and Jersey as colonial, they are long-standing. Until the union of the crowns of England and Scotland in the person of King James I of England and VI of Scotland in 1603, Scotland was a sovereign entity with its own Parliament, and legislative union did not take place until 1707. The modern Scottish Parliament dates from 1999, the product of the devolved arrangements set in place by the Labour government elected in 1997. Scotland therefore remains part of the UK unless or until it chooses to become independent, so that the Scottish Parliament is a sub-national legislature. The Isle of Man, Guernsey and Jersey[13] are not part of the UK[14] but are Crown dependencies and are not represented in the UK Parliament. The Isle of Man's link with the English Crown dates back to the fourteenth century, but the Tynwald preceded this link, and its origins, as Jonathan King points out in Chapter 14, can be traced back to the tenth century. Guernsey and Jersey's association with the Crown dates back to 1066, when William, Duke of Normandy became William I of England. Their legislatures date from the sixteenth century. All three continued to develop separately, so that their political systems are distinctive, reflecting the history and culture of the islands.

Nunavut, like Scotland but very different from it, is a sub-national entity, but unlike most parts of Canada not a province, with its powers and responsibilities set out in the Nunavut Act, passed by the Canadian Parliament in 1993. Indeed, constitutionally it is more like a devolved legislature in the UK, but with greater legislative responsibilities. Like Scotland, Nunavut has a strong and distinctive culture, but it is a culture which produces a very different legislature.

Liechtenstein, Lesotho and Swaziland offer yet another variation: all are sovereign entities which have managed to resist absorption by larger and more powerful neighbours. In Europe, San Marino, Monaco and Andorra constitute similar entities. Liechtenstein, like many smaller states of central Europe, survived from feudal times until it became a principality in the Holy Roman Empire in 1719, avoiding absorption by Austria and Germany but forced to accept a customs and monetary union with Switzerland in 1919 in the aftermath of the First World War. It remained neutral during the Second World War and so continued to survive, having developed its own political institutions but adapting them to changing circumstances. In the same way, Lesotho and Swaziland avoided absorption by the Union of South Africa when it was set up in 1909, although Britain anticipated their likely absorption in due course. However, partly because the leaders of the indigenous peoples of Lesotho and Swaziland did not want to join the Union and partly because Britain became increasingly reluctant to encourage absorption once apartheid was adopted by South Africa, they remained separate. A similar situation prevailed in the Bechuanaland Protectorate to the north of South Africa and it too did not become part of the Union of South Africa, but became independent as Botswana in 1966.

The origins and development of all the territorial entities covered in this book played an important part in their political development, not least in the political institutions they adopted. Not surprisingly, those that underwent colonial experiences with Britain almost all developed parliamentary systems, as is indeed the case with most other parts of the British Empire. A few, however, have abandoned their parliamentary systems – Guyana, for instance, has switched to a semi-presidential system. Similarly, it is hardly surprising that some of the Pacific islands that came under American influence adopted presidential systems – Micronesia and Palau, for example, while the Marshall Islands have a semi-presidential system. None of this, however, is a consequence of having political institutions that include a small legislature; that is largely a consequence of having a small population and, in many cases, of being geographically small. What difference, then, does having a small legislature make?

The pertinence of small

Electoral systems and party systems

Electoral systems are not neutral: they have an important but semi-functional relationship with party systems. In particular, two-party systems are more commonly associated with majoritarian or plurality electoral systems and multi-party systems more commonly with proportional electoral systems.[15] In this context two-party means systems dominated by two parties, one of which is normally in government and the other forms the main opposition, not the absence of other parties with representation in the legislature. The relationship is by no means absolute, however: some polities with majoritarian systems have multi-party systems and some with proportional systems have two-party systems; it is a tendency, not an iron law.

Indeed, far from being a simple function of electoral systems, party systems are also the product of the political culture and the socio-economic cleavages of the societies in which they operate. Apropos of this, it is noteworthy that as many as nine of the political systems covered in this study – Guernsey, Jersey, the Isle of Man, Micronesia, Nauru, Nunavut, Palau, Tonga and Tuvalu – either have no parties or are dominated by non-party individuals,[16] a feature rarely found in larger legislatures. No less noteworthy is that, of those with parties, almost all those with two-party systems have majoritarian electoral systems. This is particularly the case with the Commonwealth Caribbean and Bermuda. That said, most of the Pacific islands use majoritarian electoral systems, but only two – the Cook Islands and the

Marshall Islands – have two-party systems, and Liechtenstein and Malta use proportional representation but have two-party systems.

Arguably of greater importance is the disproportionality associated with majoritarian electoral systems, which tends to distort the relationship between the votes cast and the number of representatives elected, whereas proportional systems seek and tend to reflect that relationship. Occasionally, the 'wrong' party wins, that is the party winning the most seats has fewer votes than its nearest rival, as happened in the UK in 1951, when the Conservatives won more seats than Labour but fewer votes, and again in February 1974, when the roles were reversed.[17] More commonly, majoritarian systems tend to increase the size of the winning party's majority in the legislature, enhancing that party's capacity to control the legislature. Majoritarian systems can also result in a substantial turnover of seats on the basis of relatively small electoral swings or shifts in voting patterns, and these can be magnified in small legislatures. This has occurred, for example, in a number of Commonwealth Caribbean states.

In general, the contrast between the Commonwealth Caribbean and the Pacific islands is notable. In both cases the political systems adopted were mostly inherited from the colonial power,[18] but in the case of the Commonwealth Caribbean and Bermuda the colonial experience was much longer and therefore more extensive, so that key elements of the institutional inheritance were more deeply embedded than was the case with the Pacific islands. The same point can be made in respect of Gibraltar, Malta and Scotland.

This emphasises the importance of distinguishing between the effects of being a small legislature and those emanating from past experience. The argument advanced by Louis Hartz is no less applicable to small polities than to large ones – a consequence of historical experience and cultural differences rather than size. However, the impact of the electoral system is arguably greater in small legislatures, particularly where majoritarian systems are used, in affecting the type of party system that develops and, in turn, the relationship between the executive and the legislature.

The relationship between the executive and the legislature

Executive–legislative relationships inevitably vary considerably, as noted in Chapter 1, regardless of size, but the size of the legislature can be an important factor in determining the nature and operation of that relationship.

One of the most striking effects of a small legislature is that in parliamentary systems the executive constitutes a much higher proportion of the legislative membership than in larger legislatures, as Figure 18.3 shows. It compares the parliamentary systems included in the legislatures studied in this volume with selected parliamentary systems with larger legislative memberships. In bicameral systems the majority of executive office-holders are drawn from the lower chamber, but it is common in small bicameral legislatures to appoint more ministers from the upper chamber than in larger legislatures.

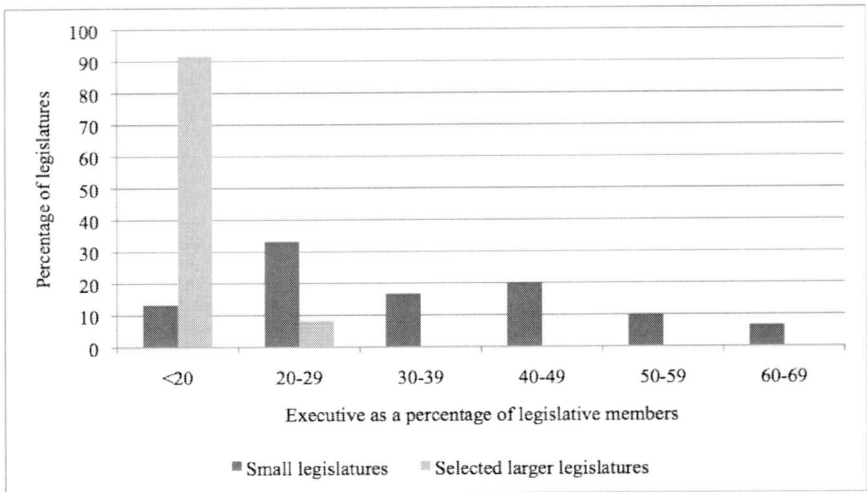

Figure 18.3 The executive as a proportion of the legislative membership in parliamentary systems

Having a high proportion of the legislative membership holding executive office has an important impact on executive–legislative relations in parliamentary systems, especially regarding executive control of the legislature and legislative scrutiny of the executive. The higher the proportion of executive office-holders in the legislature, the smaller the proportion and number of backbenchers, not only on the government side of the legislature but on the opposition side as well, since the opposition needs frontbench spokespersons to 'shadow' members of the executive. As Haresh Budhrani notes in Chapter 11, Gibraltar is the extreme example of this in having no backbenchers – all members of the legislature are either ministers or opposition frontbenchers.[19] Moreover, party cohesion tends to be high in parliamentary systems, but with small numbers of backbenchers the pressure to support the party is even greater and the scope for backbench dissent is inevitably limited.

Small numbers of backbenchers also tend to limit the ability of small legislative chambers to sustain comprehensive committee systems. Most larger chambers operate a committee system well into double figures; most small chambers, including those in this study, operate fewer than 10 permanent committees, although many of them appoint ad hoc committees, especially to deal with individual pieces of legislation or particular issues as they arise. One notable feature is that almost all have a public accounts committee or similar body, although many are of relatively recent origin.

Even in presidential systems, such as Micronesia and Palau in the Pacific, and semi-presidential regimes, such as Guyana in the West Indies and Kiribati and the Marshall Islands in the Pacific, characterised by a full or partial separation of powers, the size of the legislature has an effect on executive–legislative relations. As already noted, polities using majoritarian electoral systems can experience sharp changes in legislative representation and control. In presidential and semi-presidential systems this can undermine or limit the executive's ability to secure and maintain majority support in the legislature, directly affecting its legislative programme. Similarly, the capacity of such systems to sustain a wide range of committees, crucial to legislative scrutiny of the executive, can also be limited.

However, what perhaps most distinguishes the executive–legislative relationship in small legislatures is that their very size tends to foster an intimacy greater than is possible in larger representative bodies. This is illustrated by the example of the Senate in Bermuda, which sits round a table and operates less formally than legislatures normally do, with senators remaining seated while speaking.[20] Even more is such informality illustrated by the Nunavut Assembly, although its basis lies in a strong and distinctive culture.[21] Even in a small legislature with well-established parties, informality often operates through the party caucuses, particularly the governing party caucus. More generally, the emphasis on government by consensus, as in the Isle of Man, Guernsey and Jersey, also appears to be more common in small rather than large legislatures. It may be that the absence of parties in a number of small legislatures is partly a consequence of a greater emphasis on consensus politics. Related to this may also be the fact that many small legislatures meet only on a limited number of days per year and that their members are essentially part-time rather than full-time politicians.

Assessing small legislatures

The size of a legislature matters: it matters in terms of the relationship between the party system and the electoral system and between the executive and the legislature, but it also matters in terms of political culture. Many small legislatures are sub-national legislatures and to a significant degree reflect the political culture of the larger entity of which they are part. This is particularly true of sub-national legislatures in federal systems but, sub-national or not, much depends on the political culture they have in their own right. Thus, the sub-national legislatures covered in this book – the Nunavut Assembly and Scotland – have sufficiently distinctive political cultures to distinguish them from the Canadian Parliament and the Westminster Parliament respectively. Both are recent creations that have consciously sought to operate in a way that differs from that of their parent bodies, but the operation of both is affected by their being small legislatures.

The other small legislatures covered are either totally or substantially independent of their parent bodies and bear comparison with Hartz's societal fragments. However, their historical antecedents differ. Most have a colonial past and are the institutional inheritors of that past, but bring to it their own cultural variations and thus create their own political cultures. Occasionally, political entities decide to break with their colonial inheritance, as the 13 American colonies did in forming the United States, based on a separation of powers, and as Nigeria did in abandoning a Westminster-style parliamentary system and adopting a presidential system, following a period of military rule. Of the political entities covered in this volume, only Guyana has followed such a path. However, even where the inherited institutional framework has been maintained, variations inevitably develop, such as, for example, the practice in Dominica, St Kitts and Nevis, and St Vincent and the Grenadines of having nominated senators who sit with MPs, or Malta's practice of, when necessary, having four added members in the legislature to ensure that the party winning most *votes* has a majority of seats.[22]

In contrast to the 'inheritors', Guernsey, Jersey, the Isle of Man and Liechtenstein have been independent entities for so long that each has developed its own distinctive set of institutions and practices. Even though Guernsey and Jersey have developed similar institutions and practices over a similar period, these institutions and practices are not the same, while the other Channel Islands offer further variations and the Isle of Man is quite different. Similarly, Liechtenstein can usefully be compared historically with San Marino, Monaco and Andorra, but each has a distinctive political culture and set of institutions.

Lesotho and Swaziland also have similar histories, but the latter is arguably close to 'failed state' status and, as Susan Booysen relates,[23] their legislatures have difficulty in operating effectively in such an environment. In this regard, they are far from unique, but, as a special administrative region of the People's Republic of China, Hong Kong is comparable only to Macao. It has a functioning legislature and could be said to have some democratic elements, but its wider environment is not democratic in the Western sense. Yet it, like the other legislatures in this study, exhibits many of the features common to small legislatures. In short, whatever differences there may be in historical antecedents and political cultures, being small makes a difference.

Notes

1   John Donne (1949), Devotions upon emergent occasions, XVII, in John Hayward (ed.), *John Donne: Complete Poetry and Selected Prose*, p. 538 (London: Nonesuch Press).

2   Indeed, even Nunavut could be described as a 'virtual island' given that there are no rail or road links between it and the rest of Canada, quite apart from its cultural distinctiveness.

3   www.ipu.org/parline-e/ParliamentStructures.asp.

4   This does *not* include members of the European Union, who, although subject to the terms of the EU treaties and directives, remain essentially independent states.

5   Queensland and South Australia have unicameral legislatures, whereas those of the other four states are bicameral.

6   All provinces in Canada have unicameral legislatures.

7   Nebraska had a bicameral legislature from its inception as a state in 1867 until the amending of the state constitution in 1934.

8   Queensland in 1922 and, in the Canadian case, Manitoba in 1876, New Brunswick in 1891, Prince Edward Island in 1893, Nova Scotia in 1928 and, most recently, Quebec in 1968. All other Canadian provinces were unicameral from their inception.

9   Louis Hartz (1964) *The Founding of New Societies: Studies in the History of the United States, Latin America, South Africa, Canada, and Australia* (New York: Harcourt, Brace & World).

10 British overseas territories, of which there are 14, are mostly remnants of the British Empire. Most are small islands or groups of islands, the others being the British Antarctic Territory, South Georgia and the South Sandwich Islands, the British Indian Ocean Territory (the Chagos Islands, the indigenous population of which was removed between

1966 and 1971, with the island of Diego Garcia leased to the United States for use as a military base) and the sovereign military base of Akrotiri and Dhekelia on the island of Cyprus.

11 Organisation international de la Francophonie was established in 1970 – see www.francophonie.org. Some 90 per cent of the Dominican population speak Antillean Creole, a French-based language.

12 The Portuguese colony of Macau was similarly returned to China in 1999 and created a special administrative region.

13 The other Channel Islands – Alderney and Sark, Herm, Jethou and Lihou – are separate jurisdictions within the Bailiwick of Guernsey, and the island of Brecqhou is part of Sark. See Ministry of Justice (n.d.) *Background Briefing of the Crown Dependencies: Jersey, Guernsey and the Isle of Man* (London: Ministry of Justice).

14 Nor are they part of the EU, although they have a special relationship with it.

15 See Douglas Rae (1967) *The Political Consequences of Electoral Laws* (New Haven, CT: Yale University Press) and David Farrell (2011) *Electoral Systems: A Comparative Introduction*, 2nd edn (Houndmills, Basingstoke: Palgrave Macmillan).

16 In addition, Niue has loose party groupings rather than parties, and parties are banned in Swaziland.

17 In 1951, however, the Conservatives had an overall majority in the House of Commons, but in February 1974 Labour failed to win a majority and formed a minority government.

18 In this context, the role of the United Sates as a UN trustee in administering the Marshall Islands, Micronesia and Palau is characterised as that of 'colonial power'.

19 Budhrani, Chapter 11, p. 105.

20 Brown, Chapter 10, p. 100.

21 White, Chapter 16, pp. 148–157.

22 This was invoked after the 1987, 1996 and 2008 elections.

23 Booysen, Chapters 5 and 9.

Appendix
Comparative information

Nation, state or territory: Bermuda

Type of system (presidential/parliamentary/etc.): Parliamentary.
Party system (single/two/multi/none): Three-party.
Legislative format (bicameral/unicameral): Bicameral.
Chamber
– *Lower:* House of Assembly.
– *Upper:* Senate.
Number of members
– *Lower:* 36 (all directly elected).
– *Upper:* 11 (3 appointed by Governor-General; 5 appointed by governing party;
  3 appointed by the Opposition).
Electoral system used (majority/proportional/mixed/other)
– *Lower:* Majority – first past the post.
– *Upper:* n/a.
Term (years)
– *Lower:* 5.
– *Upper:* 5.
Full-time/part-time (re backbench members): Information not available.
Average number of sitting days/months: Information not available.
Committee system: A Standing Order Committee exists, and joint committees can
  be established to investigate into and report on issues.
Size (square kilometres): 54.
Population: 68,679.

Nation, state or territory: Channel Islands: Guernsey

Type of system (presidential/parliamentary/etc.): Parliamentary. Parliamentary
  democracy under a constitutional monarchy.
Party system (single/two/multi/none): None.
Legislative format (bicameral/unicameral): Unicameral.
Chamber: States of Deliberation.
Number of members: 50 (45 directly elected plus 2 representatives from Alderney
  and 3 non-voting ex officio members).

Electoral system used (majority/proportional/mixed/other): Elections for the 45 deputies from the Island of Guernsey are conducted on a majority basis. There are 7 electoral districts, each electing 6 or 7 deputies. The candidates in elections securing the highest number of votes corresponding to the number of vacancies are those declared elected. Electors are permitted to cast up to as many votes as there are vacancies. The other 2 members of the States of Deliberation are the Alderney representatives. They are two members of the States of Alderney who have been elected to the States of Alderney through universal suffrage in the island of Alderney, but then are elected to the States of Deliberation only by the voting members of the States of Alderney. In recent years, there has been an informal and non-binding plebiscite in Alderney enabling the electors of Alderney to indicate whom they wish to see elected to represent the island in Guernsey's States of Deliberation, and the members of the States of Alderney have followed the wishes of the people indicated in that manner.

Term (years): 4.

Full-time/part-time (re backbench members): The term 'backbench member' is arguably inappropriate for the States of Deliberation. This is because every member of the States acts both as legislator and as a member of the government/administration. Not every member gets elected by fellow members on to one of the bodies that are described as government departments, but it is commonly the case that all 47 members are elected on to at least one of the subordinate groups to which functions are delegated by the full 47-member parliament. (At present, just two of the 47 members are not on any of the committees.) However, even though the term may not be regarded as appropriate, the straightforward point is that there has recently been a review of payments made to politicians and the independent panel reviewing pay and allowances concluded that *all* members of the States of Deliberation, possibly with the exception of the person who is elected as the Chief Minister, should be regarded as part-time rather than full-time.

Average number of sitting days/months: The States of Deliberation generally meet monthly, except during August. This usually means that 11 meetings are convened in each calendar year, although from time to time, possibly because of something big to discuss, a special meeting will be needed. Meetings are generally convened for a Wednesday, with scope to adjourn into the Thursday and the Friday. Very exceptionally, meetings are convened on a Tuesday to enable a fourth consecutive day to be used. Further, if the business for a meeting is not concluded within the days set aside, there is scope to adjourn further to subsequent days, usually to the fortnight after the day that meeting started. (This was required in January 2012, when the month's debate filled five days.) There were 25 days of sittings in 2011, 27 days of sitting in 2010 and 33 days of sitting in 2009. In 2008, not a 'complete' year because of a general election in the spring, a slightly different approach to the timetabling of meetings resulted. From this it can be deduced that there are 28 days of sittings on average each calendar year (although it could be 30 if one covered the entire four-year term).

Committee system: The States of Deliberation use a committee system. As indicated, some of the committees are what would in other places be ministerial posts, i.e.

they are conducting day-to-day government business, rather than being parliamentary committees. Parliamentary committees also exist, namely a Scrutiny Committee, a Public Accounts Committee, a Legislation Select Committee and a States Assembly and Constitution Committee; the first two are scrutiny committees, the third one is a legislative committee and the fourth one is about internal procedures, i.e. rules, etc. of the parliament.

Size (square kilometres): 78.

Population: 65,068.

Nation, state or territory: Channel Islands: Jersey

Type of system (presidential/parliamentary/etc.): Parliamentary. Parliamentary democracy under a constitutional monarchy.

Party system (single/two/multi/none): None – all elected members are independent members elected on a non-party basis.

Legislative format (bicameral/unicameral): Unicameral.

Chamber: States of Jersey.

Number of members: 58 (12 members directly elected for terms of six years; 12 members (1 from each parish) for terms of three years; 29 directly elected for terms of three years; 5 ex officio members).

Electoral system used (majority/proportional/mixed/other): Majority – first past the post.

Term (years): 6 for 12 members; 3 for 41 members.

Full-time/part-time (re backbench members): The majority undertake their duties on a full-time basis but there is no requirement to do this and some retain outside part-time employment.

Average number of sitting days/months: The Assembly sits from mid-January to mid-July (with a three- or four-week break at Easter) and then from mid-September to mid-December. During these sessions the average number of sittings over the last 10 years has been 54 days a year.

Committee system: There is a Public Accounts Committee (PAC), five scrutiny panels that scrutinise policy and legislation of ministers, and a Chairmen's Committee that comprises the PAC and five scrutiny chairmen and which co-ordinates the scrutiny function. In addition there is a Privileges and Procedures Committee which oversees States procedures and facilities and is responsible for conduct issues.

Size (square kilometres): 116.

Population: 94,161.

Nation, state or territory: Commonwealth Caribbean: Antigua and Barbuda

Type of system (presidential/parliamentary/etc.): Parliamentary.

Party system (single/two/multi/none): Two.

Legislative format (bicameral/unicameral): Bicameral.

Chamber
– *Lower:* House of Representatives.
– *Upper:* Senate.
Number of members
– *Lower:* 19 (17 directly elected plus the Attorney General and the Speaker).
– *Upper:* 17 (17 appointed by the Governor-General on the advice of the Prime Minister and Leader of the Opposition).
Electoral system used (majority/proportional/mixed/other)
– *Lower:* Majority – first past the post.
– *Upper:* n/a.
Term (years)
– *Lower:* 5.
– *Upper:* 5.
Full-time/part-time (re backbench members)
– *Lower:* Part-time.
– *Upper:* Part-time.
Average number of sitting days/months: Information not available.
Committee system: Information not available.
Size (square kilometres): 441 (Antigua 280 and Barbuda 161).
Population: 87,884.

Nation, state or territory: Commonwealth Caribbean: The Bahamas

Type of system (presidential/parliamentary/etc.): Parliamentary.
Party system (single/two/multi/none): Two.
Legislative format (bicameral/unicameral): Bicameral.
Chamber
– *Lower:* House of Assembly.
– *Upper:* Senate.
Number of members
– *Lower:* 41 (all directly elected).
– *Upper:* 16 (all appointed by Governor-General).
Electoral system used (majority/proportional/mixed/other)
– *Lower:* Majority – first past the post.
– *Upper:* n/a.
Term (years)
– *Lower:* 5.
– *Upper:* 5.
Full-time/part-time (re backbench members)
– *Lower:* Part-time.
– *Upper:* Part-time.
Average number of sitting days/months: Information not available.
Committee system: Information not available.
Size (square kilometres): 13,880.
Population: 313,312.

Nation, state or territory: Commonwealth Caribbean: Barbados

Type of system (presidential/parliamentary/etc.): Parliamentary.
Party system (single/two/multi/none): Two.
Legislative format (bicameral/unicameral): Bicameral.
Chamber
– *Lower:* House of Assembly.
– *Upper:* Senate.
Number of members
– *Lower:* 30 (all directly elected).
– *Upper:* 21 (all appointed by Governor-General).
Electoral system used (majority/proportional/mixed/other)
– *Lower:* Majority – first past the post.
– *Upper:* n/a.
Term (years)
– *Lower:* 5.
– *Upper:* 5.
Full-time/part-time (re backbench members)
– *Lower:* Part-time.
– *Upper:* Part-time.
Average number of sitting days/months: 28 days in 2010; an average of 35 days each year between 2000 and 2010.
Committee system
– *Lower:* A total of four committees.
– *Upper:* None.
Size (square kilometres): 430.
Population: 286,705.

Nation, state or territory: Commonwealth Caribbean: Belize

Type of system (presidential/parliamentary/etc.): Parliamentary.
Party system (single/two/multi/none): Two.
Legislative format (bicameral/unicameral): Bicameral.
Chamber
– *Lower:* House of Representatives.
– *Upper:* Senate.
Number of members
– *Lower:* 32 (31 directly elected plus the Speaker).
– *Upper:* 13 (6 members appointed on the advice of the Prime Minister; 3 appointed on the advice of the Leader of the Opposition; 1 appointed on the advice of the Belize Council of Churches and the Evangelical Association of Churches; 1 appointed on the advice of the Belize Chamber of Commerce and Industry and the Belize Business Bureau; 1 appointed on the advice of the National Trade Union Congress of Belize and the Civil Society Steering Committee. Other: the Speaker may be designated from outside the Senate and becomes a member of the Senate by virtue of holding the office of Speaker).

Electoral system used (majority/proportional/mixed/other)
– *Lower:* Majority – first past the post.
– *Upper:* n/a.
Term (years)
– *Lower:* 5.
– *Upper:* 5.
Full-time/part-time (re backbench members)
– *Lower:* Part-time.
– *Upper:* Part-time.
Average number of sitting days/months: Information not available.
Committee system: Standing and select committees.
Size (square kilometres): 22,966.
Population: 321,115.

Nation, state or territory: Commonwealth Caribbean: Dominica

Type of system (presidential/parliamentary/etc.): Parliamentary.
Party system (single/two/multi/none): Two.
Legislative format (bicameral/unicameral): Unicameral.
Chamber: House of Assembly.
Number of members: 32 (21 directly elected; 9 appointed by the head of state; and the Attorney General and Speaker).
Electoral system used (majority/proportional/mixed/other): Majority – first past the post.
Term (years): 5.
Full-time/part-time (re backbench members): Part-time.
Average number of sitting days/months: Between 2002 and 2008 the House of Assembly sat on between 9 and 16 sitting days – an average of 11.42 sitting days – spread over between three and six months of the year. For example, in 2007 the Assembly sat for a total of 10 days in five months of the year: one day in January, one day in April, six days in July, one day in November and one day in December.
Committee system: Select committees include: Public Accounts Committee; Standing Orders Committee; Privileges Committee; Parliamentary Proceedings Broadcasting Committee.
Size (square kilometres): 751.
Population: 72,969.

Nation, state or territory: Commonwealth Caribbean: Grenada

Type of system (presidential/parliamentary/etc.): Parliamentary.
Party system (single/two/multi/none): Two.
Legislative format (bicameral/unicameral): Bicameral.
  Chamber

– *Lower:* House of Representatives.
– *Upper:* Senate.
Number of members
– *Lower:* 15 (all directly elected).
– *Upper:* 13 (all appointed by the Governor-General).
Electoral system used (majority/proportional/mixed/other)
– *Lower:* Majority – first past the post.
– *Upper:* n/a.
Term (years)
– *Lower:* 5.
– *Upper:* 5.
Full-time/part-time (re backbench members)
– *Lower:* Part-time.
– *Upper:* Part-time.
Average number of sitting days/months: Information not available.
Committee system: Information not available.
Size (square kilometres): 344.
Population: 108,419.

Nation, state or territory: Commonwealth Caribbean: Guyana

Type of system (presidential/parliamentary/etc.): Presidential.
Party system (single/two/multi/none): Two.
Legislative format (bicameral/unicameral): Unicameral.
Chamber: National Assembly.
Number of members: 70 (maximum of 72) (65 directly elected and 5 (or as many as 7) others – these include 3 non-elected ministers, 1 non-elected parliamentary secretary and the Speaker. However, a maximum of 4 non-elected ministers and 2 non-elected parliamentary secretaries may sit in the National Assembly. If the Speaker is not an elected member, he or she becomes a member of the National Assembly by virtue of holding the office of Speaker).
Electoral system used (majority/proportional/mixed/other): Proportional.
Term (years): 5.
Full-time/part-time (re backbench members): Part-time.
Average number of sitting days/months: Information not available.
Committee system: Standing, business, sectoral, sessional select and special select committees all exist.
Size (square kilometres): 214,969.
Population: 744,768.

Nation, state or territory: Commonwealth Caribbean: Jamaica

Type of system (presidential/parliamentary/etc.): Parliamentary.
Party system (single/two/multi/none): Two.
Legislative format (bicameral/unicameral): Bicameral.

Chamber
– *Lower:* House of Representatives.
– *Upper:* Senate.
Number of members
– *Lower:* 60 (all directly elected).
– *Upper:* 21 (all appointed by the Governor-General).
Electoral system used (majority/proportional/mixed/other)
– *Lower:* Majority – first past the post.
– *Upper:* n/a.
Term (years)
– *Lower:* 5.
– *Upper:* 5.
Full-time/part-time (re backbench members)
– *Lower:* Part-time.
– *Upper:* Part-time.
Average number of sitting days/months: 50 in 2010.
Committee system: Yes.
Size (square kilometres): 10,991.
Population: 2,868,380.

Nation, state or territory: Commonwealth Caribbean: St Kitts and Nevis

Type of system (presidential/parliamentary/etc.): Parliamentary.
Party system (single/two/multi/none): Two.
Legislative format (bicameral/unicameral): Unicameral.
Chamber: National Assembly.
Number of members: 15 (11 directly elected; 3 appointed by the Governor-General on the advice of the Prime Minister and Leader of the Opposition; and the Attorney General (if not an elected member). The Speaker may or may not be an elected member).
Electoral system used (majority/proportional/mixed/other): Majority – first past the post.
Term (years): 5.
Full-time/part-time (re backbench members): Part-time.
Average number of sitting days/months: Information not available.
Committee system: Yes.
Size (square kilometres): 261 (St Kitts 168 and Nevis 93).
Population: 50,314.

Nation, state or territory: Commonwealth Caribbean: St Lucia

Type of system (presidential/parliamentary/etc.): Parliamentary.
Party system (single/two/multi/none): Two.
Legislative format (bicameral/unicameral): Bicameral.

Chamber
– *Lower:* House of Assembly.
– *Upper:* Senate.
Number of members
– *Lower:* 18 (17 directly elected and the Speaker).
– *Upper:* 11 (all appointed by the Governor-General – 6 on the advice of the Prime Minister, 3 on the advice of the Leader of the Opposition, and 2 by the Governor-General).
Electoral system used (majority/proportional/mixed/other)
– *Lower:* Majority – first past the post.
– *Upper:* n/a.
Term (years)
– *Lower:* 5.
– *Upper:* 5.
Full-time/part-time (re backbench members)
– *Lower:* Part-time.
– *Upper:* Part-time.
Average number of sitting days/months: Information not available.
Committee system: Yes.
Size (square kilometres): 616.
Population: 161,557.

Nation, state or territory: Commonwealth Caribbean: St Vincent and the Grenadines

Type of system (presidential/parliamentary/etc.): Parliamentary.
Party system (single/two/multi/none): Two.
Legislative format (bicameral/unicameral): Unicameral.
Chamber: House of Assembly.
Number of members: 23 (15 directly elected; 6 appointed by the Governor-General; and the Attorney General and Speaker).
Electoral system used (majority/proportional/mixed/other): Majority – first past the post.
Term (years): 5.
Full-time/part-time (re backbench members): Part-time.
Average number of sitting days/months: 17 days in 2010; an average of 16 days each year between 2000 and 2010.
Committee system: Yes.
Size (square kilometres): 389 (St Vincent 344 and the Grenadines 45).
Population: 103,869.

Nation, state or territory: Commonwealth Caribbean: Trinidad and Tobago

Type of system (presidential/parliamentary/etc.): Parliamentary.
Party system (single/two/multi/none): Multi-party.
Legislative format (bicameral/unicameral): Bicameral.
Chamber
– *Lower:* House of Representatives.
– *Upper:* Senate.
Number of members
– *Lower:* 42 (41 directly elected and the Speaker).
– *Upper:* 31 (all appointed by the head of state).
Electoral system used (majority/proportional/mixed/other)
– *Lower:* Majority – first past the post.
– *Upper:* n/a.
Term (years)
– *Lower:* 5.
– *Upper:* 5.
Full-time/part-time (re backbench members)
– *Lower:* Part-time.
– *Upper:* Part-time.
Average number of sitting days/months
– *Lower:* In the nine years between 2002 and 2011 the House sat on an average of between 44 and 45 days each year.
– *Upper:* In the nine years between 2002 and 2011 the Senate sat on an average of between 41 and 42 days each year.
Committee system: Committees fall into three broad categories: (1) those of a general nature concerned mainly with the organisation and powers of the House; (2) those assisting the House in its legislative and policy-making functions; (3) those which act as 'watchdogs' over the executive. There is also the provision for special select committees and joint select committees of both houses. See: http://www.ttparliament.org/committee_business.
Size (square kilometres): 5,128.
Population: 1,227,505.

Nation, state or territory: Gibraltar

Type of system (presidential/parliamentary/etc.): Parliamentary.
Party system (single/two/multi/none): Multi.
Legislative format (bicameral/unicameral): Unicameral.
Chamber: Parliament.
Number of members: 18 (17 directly elected and the Speaker).
Electoral system used (majority/proportional/mixed/other): Majority.
Term (years): 4.
Full-time/part-time (re backbench members): No backbenchers.

Average number of sitting days/months: From January 2012 the Parliament sat on an average of two full days each month. This settled into an average of three full days each month, save for the budget session in June. It was anticipated that the Parliament would sit on or around the third Thursday of each month except April and August.

Committee system: Committees are very rarely used. During the committee stage in the enactment of legislation, the whole House resolves itself into a committee. The only standing committee is a Committee on Members' Interests. The last time there was a select committee was in 1981 to look into landlord and tenant matters as a prelude to legislation, which was enacted in 1983.

Size (square kilometres): 6.5.

Population: 28,956.

Nation, state or territory: Hong Kong

Type of system (presidential/parliamentary/etc.): Special Administrative Region of China.

Party system (single/two/multi/none): Multi-party system.

Legislative format (bicameral/unicameral): Unicameral.

Chamber: Legislative Council.

Number of members: 60 (30 directly elected; 30 indirectly elected by functional constituencies).

Electoral system used (majority/proportional/mixed/other): Half of the seats of the Hong Kong Legislative Council are returned by universal suffrage by the proportional representational system (using the largest remainder method and the Hare quota) in five geographical constituencies. The other half are elected by a limited franchise in 28 functional constituencies whose election methods are not uniform as there is no law governing this. Nevertheless, most of the functional constituencies adopt the first-past-the-post method, with several exceptions that use the preferential elimination system.

Term (years): 4.

Full-time/part-time (re backbench members): Some members have other jobs or occupations, whereas others do not. They can be part-time; there are no restrictions on this.

Average number of sitting days/months: The Hong Kong Legislative Council as a whole meets every Wednesday between October and July (approximately 40–44 days). (The committees meet on their own schedules.)

Committee system: The Hong Kong Legislative Council uses a committee system which is a mix of different types of committees including the House Committee and subcommittees, standing committees, bills committees, panels, select committees, investigation committees and the Committee on Rules of Procedure.

Size (square kilometres): 1,104.

Population: 7,122,508.

Nation, state or territory: Isle of Man

Type of system (presidential/parliamentary/etc.): Parliamentary. Parliamentary democracy under a constitutional monarchy. Head of state is the Queen, Lord of Man, represented by the Lieutenant Governor. Head of government is the Chief Minister, appointed by the Lieutenant Governor on the nomination of Tynwald.

Party system (single/two/multi/none): Non-party political tradition.

Legislative format (bicameral/unicameral): Bicameral.

Chamber: Tynwald.

– *Lower:* House of Keys.

– *Upper:* Legislative Council.

Number of members

– *Lower:* 24 (all directly elected).

– *Upper:* 11 (President of the Tynwald, Bishop of Sodor and Man, the Attorney General and 8 indirectly elected – in two overlapping groups of 4 – by the House of Keys).

Electoral system used (majority/proportional/mixed/other)

– *Lower:* Majority – first past the post.

– *Upper:* Indirectly elected by the House of Keys; absolute majority of Keys members needed.

Term (years)

– *Lower:* 5.

– *Upper:* 5.

Full-time/part-time (re backbench members)

– *Lower:* Full-time.

– *Upper:* Full-time.

Average number of sitting days/months

– *Lower:* 35 days over 10 months.

– *Upper:* 35 days over 10 months.

Committee system

Legislative committees: These are not part of the routine legislative process but are established from time to time for particularly controversial bills.

Scrutiny committees: Four permanent standing committees with scrutiny functions exist; further scrutiny by temporary ad hoc committees known as 'select committees' can also take place.

Internal/housekeeping committees also exist.

Size (square kilometres): 572.

Population: 84,655.

Nation, state or territory: Lesotho

Type of system (presidential/parliamentary/etc.): Parliamentary constitutional monarchy with the King as head of state.

Party system (single/two/multi/none): Multi.

Legislative format (bicameral/unicameral): Bicameral.

Chamber

– *Lower:* National Assembly.

– *Upper:* Senate.

Number of members

– *Lower:* 120 (all directly elected).

– *Upper:* 33 (11 appointed by the King on the advice of the Council of State, and 22 principal chiefs).

Electoral system used (majority/proportional/mixed/other)

– *Lower:* Mixed member proportional (MMP) system (80 members elected on first past the post and 40 on proportional representation).

– *Upper:* n/a.

Term (years)

– *Lower:* 5.

– *Upper:* 5.

Full-time/part-time (re backbench members)

– *Lower:* Full-time – but are allowed to hold other jobs simultaneously.

– *Upper:* Full-time – but are allowed to hold other jobs simultaneously.

Average number of sitting days/months: Members sit in parliament for about 73 days only. On those 73 days they start work at 2.30 and finish at 6 p.m. They have 90 days of winter break, 60 days of Christmas break, 14 days of Easter break and 14 days of Independence break.

Committee system: Parliamentary committees in Lesotho remain in embryonic form. It was only in June 2008 that work was done to develop strategies for committees in the houses of parliament. For example, there is the National Assembly's Finance and Economic Development Committee, which scrutinises the government budget and assists in writing the report that is debated and voted on in the chamber. Committees meet only when there is an agenda, such as bills to consider or matters of oversight to do. There is no stipulated schedule of committees. Civil control of security forces can be exercised by the state through legislation by parliament and its committee.

Size (square kilometres): 30,355.

Population: 1,924,886.

Nation, state or territory: Liechtenstein

Type of system (presidential/parliamentary/etc.): Parliamentary. Parliamentary democracy under a constitutional monarchy.

Party system (single/two/multi/none): There are currently three parties represented in the parliament. Over many decades there were only two parties, each of them holding about 50 per cent of the seats. At present, one party holds 13 seats, another party 11 seats, and a third party holds 1 seat. Historically, the two dominating parties usually build a coalition government, and since 1936 there have been only two phases with one party governing: 1997–2001 and 2001–05.

Legislative format (bicameral/unicameral): Unicameral.

Chamber: Landtag – Diet.

Number of members: 25 (all directly elected).

Electoral system used (majority/proportional/mixed/other): Proportional. Proportional electoral system with two constituencies and a threshold of 8 per cent of all valid votes nationwide (not only in one of the two constituencies); only parties with 8 per cent or more of all valid votes can gain seats in the parliament.

Term (years): 4.

Full-time/part-time (re backbench members): All members of the parliament are non-professionals, including the president of the parliament.

Average number of sitting days/months: The average number of sitting days during the last four years has been 20 days per year. It usually begins with 1 day in February and continues with between 2 and 4 days per month from March to June and from September to December. A whole legislature of 4 years therefore amounts to about 80 sitting days.

Committee system: Most debates take place in the plenary assembly. As a routine, there are only three permanent committees (*Kommission*), namely on foreign policy, finances, and the control of the public administration. Other committees can be established (for example to prepare a legal draft or for special duties), but this is done only rarely. Another option is the establishment of a parliamentary investigation commission to analyse an issue or problem in depth. The affirmative votes of 7 of the 25 members can establish such a special commission.

Size (square kilometres): 160.

Population: 35,236.

Nation, state or territory: Malta

Type of system (presidential/parliamentary/etc.): Parliamentary.

Party system (single/two/multi/none): Since 1966, only two parties have obtained seats in the Maltese parliament. Pre-1966 there were also other parties. Alternattiva Demokratika (Green Party) contests elections but has never elected a member to parliament.

Legislative format (bicameral/unicameral): Unicameral.

Chamber: House of Representatives.

Number of members: 65 and 'bonus seats' (65 directly elected and co-opted members ('bonus seats') to ensure a majority).

Electoral system used (majority/proportional/mixed/other): Proportional representation – single transferable vote (STV) – in electoral districts.

Term (years): 5.

Full-time/part-time (re backbench members): Part-time.

Average number of sitting days/months: Plenary normally sits three days a week (Monday, Tuesday and Wednesday) throughout the year, with recesses at Christmas and Easter and in the summer. In most recent years the summer recess has tended to last two months.

Committee system: Standing committees cover a number of subjects, typically: legislative (committee stage); scrutiny – Public Accounts Committee; internal

– House Business Committee; Social Affairs Committee; Foreign and European Affairs Committee (scrutiny of EU instruments); and a number of ad hoc select committees.

Size (square kilometres): 316.

Population: 408,333.

Nation, state or territory: Nunavut (Canada)

Type of system (presidential/parliamentary/etc.): Parliamentary. Parliamentary democracy under a constitutional monarchy.

Party system (single/two/multi/none): None.

Legislative format (bicameral/unicameral): Unicameral.

Chamber: Legislative Assembly.

Number of members: 19 (all directly elected).

Electoral system used (majority/proportional/mixed/other): Single-member plurality.

Term (years): 4–5; no fixed schedule.

Full-time/part-time (re backbench members): Full-time.

Average number of sitting days/months: Over its first 12 years (1999–2011) the average was 38 days per year; there are typically three 2- to 3-week sessions a year, in February–March, May–June and October–November. There are also several weeks a year devoted entirely to committee meetings.

Committee system: All kinds of committees are used (though, since the numbers are so small, individual committees are often multi-functional): legislative review; financial and administrative scrutiny; policy review; internal housekeeping.

Size (square kilometres): 2,093,190.

Population: 31,906.

Nation, state or territory: Pacific islands: Cook Islands

Type of system (presidential/parliamentary/etc.): Parliamentary. Parliamentary democracy under a constitutional monarchy.

Party system (single/two/multi/none): Two-party.

Legislative format (bicameral/unicameral): Unicameral (modified).

Chamber: Parliament.

Plus: House of Ariki.

Number of members

– *Parliament:* 24 (all directly elected).

– *House:* 14 (traditional leaders appointed by the Governor-General).

Electoral system used (majority/proportional/mixed/other)

– *Parliament:* Single-member plurality system.

– *House:* n/a – appointed.

Term (years)

– *Parliament:* 5.

– *House:* n/a.
Full-time/part-time (re backbench members)
– *Parliament:* Part-time.
– *House:* Part-time.
Average number of sitting days/months: Parliament meets at such places and at such times as the Queen's representative from time to time appoints, provided that Parliament meets no later than 90 days after the holding of a general election and at least once in every year thereafter.
Committee system: Nine subject selected committees. Three standing committees (legislative/scrutiny).
Size (square kilometres): 236.
Population: 11,124.

Nation, state or territory: Pacific islands: Kiribati

Type of system (presidential/parliamentary/etc.): Semi-presidential.
Party system (single/two/multi/none): Multi-party system (with loose groupings rather than disciplined blocs).
Legislative format (bicameral/unicameral): Unicameral.
Chamber: House of Assembly (Maneaba Ni Maungatabu).
Number of members: 46 (44 directly elected, 1 appointed by the Banaban community and 1 ex officio member (the Attorney General)).
Electoral system used (majority/proportional/mixed/other): Two-ballot majority system.
Term (years): 4.
Full-time/part-time (re backbench members): Part-time.
Average number of sitting days/months: Three periods of approximately six weeks each year.
Committee system: Three standing committees. Select committees are appointed on motions approved by the Maneaba.
Size (square kilometres): 811.
Population: 100,743.

Nation, state or territory: Pacific islands: Marshall Islands

Type of system (presidential/parliamentary/etc.): Parliamentary.
Party system (single/two/multi/none): Two-party.
Legislative format (bicameral/unicameral): Unicameral (modified).
Chamber: Parliament (Nitijela).
Plus: Council of Iroij: 12 traditional leaders.
Number of members: 33 (all directly elected).
Electoral system used (majority/proportional/mixed/other): Single-member plurality system.
Term (years): 4.
Full-time/part-time (re backbench members): Part-time.

Average number of sitting days/months: The Nitijela meets in regular session on the first Monday in January in each year and remains in session for 50 sitting days. Special sessions may also be called.
Committee system: 7 standing committees.
Size (square kilometres): 181.
Population: 67,182.

Nation, state or territory: Pacific islands: Federated States of Micronesia

Type of system (presidential/parliamentary/etc.): Presidential.
Party system (single/two/multi/none): No political parties.
Legislative format (bicameral/unicameral): Unicameral.
Chamber: Congress.
Number of members: 14 (all directly elected).
Electoral system used (majority/proportional/mixed/other): Single-member plurality system.
Term (years): 2 years for 10 members and 4 years for 4 members.
Full-time/part-time (re backbench members): Part-time.
Average number of sitting days/months: The second regular session of the 17th Congress extended from 12 September to 1 October 2011, and the third regular session of Congress extended from 16 January to 4 February 2012.
Committee system: 7 standing committees.
Size (square kilometres): 702.
Population: 106,836.

Nation, state or territory: Pacific islands: Nauru

Type of system (presidential/parliamentary/etc.): Parliamentary.
Party system (single/two/multi/none): None.
Legislative format (bicameral/unicameral): Unicameral.
Chamber: Parliament.
Number of members: 18 (all directly elected).
Electoral system used (majority/proportional/mixed/other): A system of preferential voting known as the Borda Count (known locally as the 'Dowdall System').
Term (years): 3.
Full-time/part-time (re backbench members): Part-time.
Average number of sitting days/months: No regular schedule of sittings; generally sits at least one day in every month, usually more frequently.
Committee system: Currently 9 standing committees and 3 select committees; also Committee of the Full House.
Size (square kilometres): 21.
Population: 9,322.

Nation, state or territory: Pacific islands: Niue

Type of system (presidential/parliamentary/etc.): Parliamentary.
Party system (single/two/multi/none): Multi-party (loose Assembly groupings).
Legislative format (bicameral/unicameral): Unicameral.
Chamber: Legislative Assembly.
Number of members: 20 (6 directly elected from a common electoral role and 14 directly elected village representatives).
Electoral system used (majority/proportional/mixed/other): Single-member plurality.
Term (years): 3.
Full-time/part-time (re backbench members): Part-time.
Average number of sitting days/months: The Niue Assembly meets at such places and at such times as the Speaker, acting on request of the Premier, from time to time determines. If more than 6 weeks have elapsed since the time of the last meeting, any 4 or more members of the Assembly may request the Speaker to appoint a place and time.
Committee system: The Assembly may appoint select committees and refer matters to them for consideration and report.
Size (square kilometres): 260.
Population: 1,311.

Nation, state or territory: Pacific islands: Palau

Type of system (presidential/parliamentary/etc.): Presidential.
Party system (single/two/multi/none): None.
Legislative format (bicameral/unicameral): Bicameral.
Chamber (Olbiil Era Kelulau).
– *Lower:* House of Delegates.
– *Upper:* Senate.
Number of members
– *Lower:* 16 (all directly elected).
– *Upper:* 13 (all directly elected).
Electoral system used (majority/proportional/mixed/other)
– *Lower:* Single-member plurality – block vote.
– *Upper:* Single-member plurality – block vote.
Term (years)
– *Lower:* 4.
– *Upper:* 4.
Full-time/part-time (re backbench members)
– *Lower:* Part-time.
– *Upper:* Part-time.
Average number of sitting days/months: Each house of the Olbiil Era Kelulau convenes its meeting on the second Tuesday in January following the regular general election and meets regularly during the four years. Each house may be

convened at any time by the presiding officer, or at the written request of the majority of the members, or by the President.

Committee system: Currently 8 standing committees.

Size (square kilometres): 459.

Population: 20,956.

Nation, state or territory: Pacific islands: Samoa

Type of system (presidential/parliamentary/etc.): Parliamentary.

Party system (single/two/multi/none): Multi-party.

Legislative format (bicameral/unicameral): Unicameral.

Chamber: Legislative Assembly.

Number of members: 49 (all directly elected). 49 seats are reserved for ethnic Samoans; 2 seats are open to members of other communities.

Electoral system used (majority/proportional/mixed/other): Single-member plurality.

Term (years): 5.

Full-time/part-time (re backbench members): Part-time.

Average number of sitting days/months: The Legislative Assembly meets at such times and at such places as the head of state appoints from time to time, provided that the Assembly meets not later than 45 days after the holding of a general election and at least once in every year thereafter. For example: October 2010, two sittings (4th, 15th); February 2012, one sitting (15th).

Committee system: There are 15 standing committees appointed at the commencement of each parliamentary term. Select committees are appointed to consider special issues as required from time to time.

Size (square kilometres): 2,831.

Population: 193,161.

Nation, state or territory: Pacific islands: Solomon Islands

Type of system (presidential/parliamentary/etc.): Parliamentary.

Party system (single/two/multi/none): Multi-party.

Legislative format (bicameral/unicameral): Unicameral.

Chamber: National Parliament.

Number of members: 50 (all directly elected).

Electoral system used (majority/proportional/mixed/other): Single-member plurality.

Term (years): 4.

Full-time/part-time (re backbench members): Part-time.

Average number of sitting days/months: Parliament usually meets on average three times a year, and the meetings usually last for 3–4 weeks. Parliament sits only on weekdays.

Committee system: Five standing select committees (different areas of responsibility). Special select committees are appointed under an order specially made.

Size (square kilometres): 28,896.
Population: 571,890.

Nation, state or territory: Pacific islands: Tonga

Type of system (presidential/parliamentary/etc.): Monarchy.
Party system (single/two/multi/none): Multi-party (pressure groups rather than electoral vehicles).
Legislative format (bicameral/unicameral): Unicameral.
Chamber: Legislative Assembly (Fale Alea Tonga).
Number of members: 28 (17 directly elected, 9 indirectly elected (nobles) and 2 ex officio Cabinet members).
Electoral system used (majority/proportional/mixed/other): Majority–single member plurity system.
Term (years): 4.
Full-time/part-time (re backbench members): Part-time.
Average number of sitting days/months: The Legislative Assembly meets at least once in every 12 calendar months (but it is lawful to summon it at any time).
Committee system: Standing committees are appointed by the Assembly for the life of the Assembly. Select committees are appointed by the Assembly from time to time to examine specific issues for a limited period of time.
Size (square kilometres): 747.
Population: 105,916.

Nation, state or territory: Pacific islands: Tuvalu

Type of system (presidential/parliamentary/etc.): Parliamentary.
Party system (single/two/multi/none): None.
Legislative format (bicameral/unicameral): Unicameral.
Chamber: Parliament.
Number of members: 15 (all directly elected).
Electoral system used (majority/proportional/mixed/other): Majority–single-member plurality.
Term (years): 4.
Full-time/part-time (re backbench members): Part-time.
Average number of sitting days/months: Parliament meets at such places in Tuvalu and at such times as the head of state, acting in accordance with the advice of the Cabinet, appoints. Sessions of Parliament are held in such a way that no period of 12 months intervenes between the end of one session and the beginning of the next. There are normally at least two sessions each year.
Committee system: There are 4 standing committees, including the Public Accounts Committee. A select committee may be set up to consider any matter referred to it.
Size (square kilometres): 26.
Population: 10,544.

Nation, state or territory: Pacific islands: Vanuatu

Type of system (presidential/parliamentary/etc.): Parliamentary.

Party system (single/two/multi/none): Multi-party.

Legislative format (bicameral/unicameral): Unicameral (modified).

Chamber: Parliament.

Plus: National Council of Chiefs (no set number).

Number of members: 52 (all directly elected).

Electoral system used (majority/proportional/mixed/other): Mixed – including an element of proportional representation.

Term (years): 4.

Full-time/part-time (re backbench members): Part-time.

Average number of sitting days/months: Parliament meets in two ordinary sessions during each calendar year. The first ordinary session convenes in the middle of the month of March, the second in the middle of the month of August. Neither Parliament nor any of its committees meet during the periods 20 December to 20 January or 20 June to 20 July.

Committee system: The ninth Vanuatu legislature had 6 committees.

Size (square kilometres): 12,189.

Population: 224,564.

Nation, state or territory: Scotland (Great Britain)

Type of system (presidential/parliamentary/etc.): Parliamentary. Parliamentary democracy under a constitutional monarchy.

Party system (single/two/multi/none): Multi-party system (four main parties – Scottish Nationalist (SNP), Labour, Liberal Democrat and Conservative – plus Greens, etc.).

Legislative format (bicameral/unicameral): Unicameral.

Chamber: Parliament.

Number of members: 129 (73 directly elected from individual geographical constituencies; 56 elected from eight 'additional member' regions).

Electoral system used (majority/proportional/mixed/other): Mixed member proportional (MMP) system (sometimes referred to as the 'additional member system'): 73 seats through a majority (first past the post), 56 seats through the proportional/d'Hondt method (7 seats per region, with seats reflecting party balance in a region, controlling for constituency allocation, 8 regions in total).

Term (years): 4.

Full-time/part-time (re backbench members): Full-time (care has been taken to steer clear of dual mandates).

Average number of sitting days/months: During 2011–12 there were 121 days that the Parliament did not sit (but was not dissolved). These coincide with the school holidays (July and August, and 3 weeks for Christmas and 2 weeks for Easter). Therefore there was a total of 83 sitting days if weekends are subtracted (although fewer if bank holidays are subtracted).

Committee system: Committees are prominent and combine legislative and scrutiny functions in one committee, including the ability to introduce bills.

Size (square kilometres): 78,772.

Population: 5,222,100.

Nation, state or territory: Swaziland

Type of system (presidential/parliamentary/etc.): Constitutional monarchy, noted as practising authoritarian monarchism, building aspects of traditionalism into representation. Supreme legislative authority rests with the King-in-parliament.

Party system (single/two/multi/none): Swaziland is officially a non-party state. Political parties have been banned since 1973. Notwithstanding the introduction of Section 25 in the 2005 Constitution, which guarantees freedom of assembly and association, the government has not provided any mechanism for the administration or registration of political parties. Party political activity has also been proscribed under the Suppression of Terrorism Act of 2008.

Legislative format (bicameral/unicameral): Bicameral.

Chamber (Libandla)

– *Lower:* House of Assembly.

– *Upper:* Senate.

Number of members

– *Lower:* 66 (55 directly elected, 10 appointed by the head of state, and the Speaker).

– *Upper:* 30 (10 elected by the House of Assembly, 20 appointed by the head of state).

Electoral system used (majority/proportional/mixed/other)

– *Lower:* The existence of an absolute monarch combines with the provisions that prevent political parties from existing legally (and participating in elections) to give the context for the electoral system. The tinkhundla system is a system of political, military and administrative mobilisation that divides the country into constituencies defined by traditional chiefdoms. Primary elections are held at chiefdom level. The top three candidates proceed into the secondary elections. The second-round winner is declared the elected MP. Elections are conducted by secret ballot. Candidates are nominated in individual capacity; only persons known within the chiefdom through participation in its cultural events and traditional loyalists are likely to be nominated. The election process is conducted by an elections and boundaries committee established by the King.

– *Upper:* n/a.

Term (years)

– *Lower:* 5.

– *Upper:* 5.

Full-time/part-time (re backbench members)

– *Lower:* Full-time.

– *Upper:* Part-time.

However, no restrictions are placed on members of the legislature from also being employed in the private sector or being self-employed. They are, however, required to attend all sessions of parliament.

Average number of sitting days/months: Parliament has three annual sessions – to consider and approve the Budget and Appropriation Bill, legislative bills, and Cabinet reports on various portfolio activities.

Committee system: The constitution provides for sessional committees (for the discharge of functions of parliament) and standing committees (to oversee the activities of the ministries of government). There are 20 standing committees, not all active. Active ones include the Public Finance Committee, the Public Accounts Portfolio Committee and the Public Finance Portfolio Committee.

Size (square kilometres): 17,364.

Population: 1,370,424.

Sources

Chapters in this volume.

Parline database of the Inter-Parliamentary Union (see http://www.IPU.org/parline-e).

World Factbook (see https://www.cia.gov/library/publications/the-world-factbook).

Index